Reasoning
and
Rhetoric
in Religion

Reasoning and Rhetoric in Religion

Nancey C. Murphy

Trinity Press International
Valley Forge, Pennsylvania

Quotations of scripture, unless otherwise noted, are from the New Revised Standard Version (Nashville: Holman Bible Publishers, 1989).

In chapter 1, the material from *The Complete Monty Python's Flying Circus: All the Words,* vol. 2 (New York: Pantheon Books, 1989), is used courtesy of Monty Python's Flying Circus.

In chapter 7, the sermon, "Be Careful for Nothing," is from *Twenty Centuries of Great Preaching,* ed. Clyde E. Fant and William M. Pinson, Jr. 1971, Word, Inc., Dallas Texas. Used with permission. The sermon "Beginnings," by Marguerite Shuster is from *God, Creation, and Revelation: A Neo-Evangelical Theology* by Paul K. Jewett, © 1991 by William B. Eerdmans Publishing Co., Grand Rapids, MI. Used by permission.

Material quoted in exercises for chapter 12 from Charles Wood, *Vision and Discernment: An Orientation in Theological Study* (Atlanta: Scholars Press, 1985), 37–54, is used with permission of Scholars Press.

Trinity Press International
P.O. Box 851
Valley Forge, PA 19482

Library of Congress Cataloging-in-Publication Data

Murphy, Nancey C.
    Reasoning and rhetoric in religion / Nancey Murphy.
        p.   cm.
    Includes bibliographical references and index.
    ISBN 1-56338-098-6 :
    1. Theology—Methodology. 2. Reasoning. 3. Rhetoric—Religious aspects—Christianity. I. Title.
BR118.M876   1994
230'.01—dc20   94-36455
                                                                     CIP

Printed in the United States of America

94   95   96   97   98   6   5   4   3   2   1

to
Dave Beck
Swasti Bhattacharyya
Mark Lazenby
Michael Patzia
Pamela Williams Paez

Table of Contents

Part One. Basic Reasoning

This chapter defines an argument and introduces its two most basic parts: the claim (conclusion) and the grounds upon which it is based. So an argument in its most basic form can be represented as:

The warrant is a general statement or rule that licenses the inference from grounds such as *G* to claims such as *C*. When a warrant is called into question, the considerations brought to bear to support it are called the backing. With these additions, the basic form of an argument can be represented as follows:

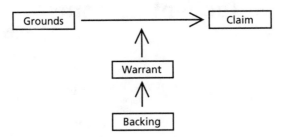

This chapter deals with the strength and reliability of arguments. Qualifiers such as 'possibly' and 'necessarily' reflect the strength. Rebuttals acknowledge the conditions under which the argument may fail. The full schematization of an argument is:

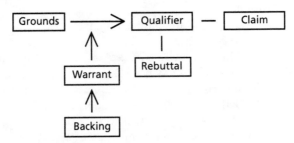

Hypothetical reasoning refers to the amplification of our knowledge by forming hypotheses, which are justified by the fact that they are needed to explain things that we already know. This form of reasoning is used in theology as well as in science.

This chapter places reasoning *(logos)* within the broader context of communication theory.

This chapter relates the preceding material on reasoning and communication to the writing task. The familiar devices of scholarly writing are considered in the light of making and defending a persuasive argument.

Part Two. Reasoning in Religion

This chapter draws on the resources of both practical reasoning and rhetoric to help understand the assorted communication devices used in sermons. The different uses made of these resources throughout the history of homiletics are highlighted by examining the writings of figures from the fifth, nineteenth, and twentieth centuries.

This chapter introduces both theological and philosophical ethics, summarizing some of the changes in each over the centuries, primarily by analyzing typical examples.

 In everyday moral reasoning we make claims about the right or wrong of particular actions using philosophical or theological warrants. One of the main tasks of the ethics scholar is to provide backing for such warrants.

This chapter covers the standard tools of historiography, explaining them in terms of the argument forms learned in part 1. It also raises questions from the philosophy of history concerning the nature of historical claims.

This chapter covers the basic methods used in biblical studies, describing and illustrating typical arguments.

In history and biblical studies there is a great deal of agreement about methods; consequently, one can speak of typical arguments in these disciplines. In theology this is not the case. So this chapter explores theological reasoning by analyzing arguments of some of its most important contributors.

Part Three. The Rationality of Religion

This chapter uses the understanding developed above of the reasoning that makes up the various theological disciplines, along with the epistemology of W. V. O. Quine, to develop a new model for thinking about the interconnections within the theological curriculum.

This chapter provides an overview of philosophy of religion by distinguishing it from philosophical theology and by examining the way changing views of the nature of philosophy have affected approaches to one of its major projects: arguments for the existence of God.

This chapter surveys the history of apologetics and takes up one of the most pressing current problems: whether and how one can make truth claims for a particular religion when one is aware of the plurality of such systems. The chapter introduces several answers to this question.

Preface and Acknowledgments

What *is* this book? First, it is a survey of the methodologies (or methods of reasoning) of the several disciplines making up the theological curriculum. A characteristic of the modern period (beginning c. 1650 in philosophy) has been its keen interest in methodology: to be rational is to follow correct methods in reasoning. This book examines the reasoning used in ethics, historical studies, biblical studies, systematic theology, sermons, philosophy of religion, and apologetics. Because reflection on the methods of an intellectual discipline is a philosophical task, this book is a treatise in philosophy. More specifically, since it reflects on the methods of disciplines pertaining to the Christian religion, it is a treatise in philosophy of religion.

A survey of apologetics (the defense of Christianity) would show that this discipline varies from age to age depending upon context. If the modern period has been one preoccupied with questions of rationality, then for those who have been shaped by modern concerns, apologetics will appropriately be preoccupied with questions of the rationality of Christian thought. If rationality, furthermore, is understood primarily as following correct methods of reasoning, then showing that the methodologies of the theological disciplines employ correct forms of reasoning ought to be an important aspect of apologetics. So this book is also an apologetic treatise. As such, it represents a position that nonetheless goes counter to much contemporary thinking about the status of religious belief. Many have argued that religion—a matter of 'faith' or 'values'—is so radically different from intellectual disciplines such as science that it is neither possible nor appropriate to judge its claims by standards of reasoning. The *appropriateness* must be argued elsewhere; the *possibility* will be demonstrated herein.

But what are the "correct forms of reasoning"? How does one evaluate the arguments and patterns of argument that constitute a discipline's methods? The evaluation of formal arguments is the specialty of logicians, but some recent authors have pointed out that analysis and evaluation of informal reasoning requires a different set of concepts and forms than those developed by formal logicians. I have found Stephen Toulmin's work in this area to be the most enlightening. His approach to informal ("practical," "critical") reasoning is *described* in the first three chapters of this book, and is then *used* throughout.

If Christianity in the abstract is to be reasonable, then the concrete individuals who embody it must exercise the skills of reasoning in their writing, reading, and speaking. Thus, to the question, what is this book? there is yet another answer: this is a practical reasoning text—it is designed to teach not only the theory but also the skills of good reasoning. For this purpose, exercises at the end of each chapter provide opportunity for practice, for reasoning skills are only learned in the doing. An answer key is available from Trinity Press International.

The text also includes a chapter on rhetoric—the broader communicative context within which reasoning must be understood—and a chapter on writing academic papers—the context in which Christian reasoners, especially student reasoners, most often have opportunity to apply their reasoning skills.

As a practical reasoning text, this book's originality lies primarily in the application of Toulmin's work to the field of theology and religion. However, I have added a chapter on hypothetical reasoning—a form of reasoning not directly accommodated in Toulmin's scheme. Philosophers of science are to be credited with recognizing the value of hypothetical reasoning, but I claim it is equally important in religious and theological thought.

As a survey of methods in the theological curriculum, this book aims to be quite unoriginal. I have tried to summarize the consensus on methods in disciplines where one exists (for example, in some aspects of historiography and biblical criticism); where consensus is lacking (for example, in theological ethics and systematic theology), I have aimed at a representative survey. While chapter headings presuppose an unoriginal division of labor among the theological disciplines, more recent views are mentioned in a chapter on theological curriculum, and my own proposal is developed therein.

The book's uniqueness, overall, lies in the way it brings together the concerns of practical reasoning, methodology, and apologetics. As critical reasoning text and survey of current theory of knowledge, the book works from small to large scale: from individual arguments and their parts, through methodology, to an account of how the knowledge comprising an entire tradition of inquiry is structured and evaluated. As essay in philosophy of religion and apologetics, the book moves from individual arguments advanced by biblical scholars, theologians, and others, through the methodologies of the theological disciplines, to an overview of the interrelations of these disciplines within the theological curriculum, and ultimately within the vast network of beliefs that comprise the Christian tradition. In so doing it provides the necessary resources for a cumulative argument for the rationality of that tradition.

The multiple aims of this book suggest that it may well have a varied reading audience. I hope that it will be of use to readers ranging from college students to seminary professors. Yet one has to write for a particular audience, and the one I have chosen is seminary students. I begin at what I hope will be an unintimidating level, and move gradually to introduce the reader to more sophisticated levels of philosophical thought.

My indebtedness to Stephen Toulmin has already been mentioned. I thank him for his encouragement and for permission to adopt and adapt his ideas on the 'fine-structure' of arguments.[1] I am indebted to W. V. O. Quine and especially to Alasdair MacIntyre for the understanding of how arguments fit into a "web of beliefs," and ultimately into a tradition of inquiry—the 'coarse-structure' of rational thought.

Several years ago I had the opportunity to teach a course called Rhetoric and Philosophy at the Dominican School of Philosophy and Theology in Berkeley, California. In the medieval curriculum such a course, covering logic and rhetoric, would have served as an introduction to theological studies. The need to develop a course suitable for our own day and age was the source of the idea for this book. I thank Larry Burke, O.P., then dean of the Dominican School, for the invitation to teach there.

I also express gratitude to colleagues and friends who have read and commented on all or parts of the manuscript, or contributed in other ways: Mary Ann Bowman, James Bradley, Mitties DeChamplain, Michael Goldberg, Donald Hagner, Richard Muller, Dennis Patterson, Wayne Pipkin, Marguerite Shuster, Marianne Meye Thompson, Claude Welch, and last but by no means least, my colleague and husband, advisor and critic, James William McClendon, Jr.

Dave Sielaff in the word processing center at Fuller Theological Seminary produced the typescript and the vast number of detailed diagrams. Laura Barrett at Trinity Press International was invariably courteous and efficient. My thanks to both of them.

Finally, thanks to my students at the Dominican School and especially at Fuller Theological Seminary, whose interest, challenging questions, and encouragement have made these subjects a joy to teach, and this text a work of love. I dedicate it to all of them, but with special mention of a few who contributed in special ways.

---

[1]Toulmin's basic approach to informal reasoning is worked out in *The Uses of Argument* (Cambridge: Cambridge University Press, 1958). See also his critical reasoning text (co-authored with Richard Rieke and Allan Janik), titled *An Introduction to Reasoning* (New York: Macmillan, 1978). I have also been much influenced by Toulmin's account of the character of and historical motivations for modern thought in *Cosmopolis: The Hidden Agenda of Modernity* (New York: The Free Press, 1990).

PART ONE

Basic Reasoning

CHAPTER ONE

Claims and Grounds

1. Arguments

Our primary concern in this book will be with *arguments*—how to formulate sound ones and how to evaluate those tendered by others. As a Monty Python skit illustrates, it is not always clear what is meant by the word 'argument.'[1] The skit involves two characters: Mr. Vibrating, sitting at a desk, and a man.

(Knock, knock)

Mr. Vibrating: Come in.

Man: (The man enters the room.) Is this the right room for an argument?

Mr. Vibrating: I've told you *once*.

Man: No you haven't.

Mr. Vibrating: Yes I have.

Man: When?

Mr. Vibrating: Just now!

Man: No you didn't.

Mr. Vibrating: Yes I did!

Man: Didn't!

Mr. Vibrating: I'm telling you I did. . . .

Man: Look, this isn't an argument.

Mr. Vibrating: Yes it is.

Man: No it isn't, it's just a contradiction.

Mr. Vibrating: No it isn't.

Man: Yes it is.

Mr. Vibrating: It is not.

---

[1]A convention used by philosophers will be adopted here, namely to indicate that a word or sentence is being spoken of (rather than being used) by enclosing it in single quotation marks. Single quotation marks will also be used for 'scare quotes.'

Man: It is. You just contradicted me.

Mr. Vibrating: No I didn't! . . .

Man: Oh look, this is futile.

Mr. Vibrating: No it isn't.

Man: I came here for a good argument.

Mr. Vibrating: No you didn't, you came here for an *argument*.

Man: Well an argument's not the same as contradiction.

Mr. Vibrating: It can be.

Man: No it can't. An argument is a connected series of statements to establish a definite proposition.

Mr. Vibrating: No it isn't.

Man: Yes it is. It isn't just contradiction.

Mr. Vibrating: Look, if I argue with you I must take up a contrary position.

Man: But it isn't just saying "No it isn't."

Mr. Vibrating: Yes it is.

Man: No it isn't! An argument is an intellectual process and contradiction is just the automatic gainsaying of anything the other person says.

Mr. Vibrating: No it isn't. . . .

Man: I've had enough of this!

Mr. Vibrating: No you haven't!

Man: Oh shut up! (He exits)[2]

The *Random House Dictionary of the English Language* offers a wide assortment of definitions for 'argument,' among which are the following:
1. An oral disagreement; verbal opposition; contention, altercation.
2. A discussion involving differing points of view; debate.
3. A process of reasoning; series of reasons.
4. A statement, reason, or fact for or against a point.
5. An address or composition intended to convince or persuade; persuasive discourse.

While Mr. Vibrating was obviously engaged in an argument in the sense of definition 1, the Man was expecting an argument in the sense of definitions 3 and 4; we are interested in the latter sense as well. An argument is a process of reasoning or a series of reasons used to support a point. The 'point' being supported we shall here call a *claim*. In practical reasoning, an argument is intended to convince or persuade (definition 5), but we

---

[2] *The Complete Monty Python's Flying Circus: All the Words* (New York: Pantheon Books, 1989), 2:86–89.

must add the qualification that it is intended to persuade *by means of* the reasons provided—not, for instance, by means of threat, bribery, or sheer obfuscation.[3] A debate or discussion involving different points of view (definition 2) may or may not involve arguments in the sense intended here; an oral disagreement or altercation (definition 1) generally does *not* involve argument in this sense, since it seems to bring out the worst of people's reasoning abilities.

While religion and theology are famous for inciting arguments in the sense of definition 1, we intend to explore the ways arguments (in the sense of ordered reasoning) are employed in the various theological disciplines.

This is an appropriate point at which to make another terminological distinction—between 'theology' and 'religion.' As used here, 'religion' will refer to a broad cultural phenomenon that generally involves worship, moral practices, and beliefs. Theology is an academic discipline that (among other things) reflects in a sustained way on the worship, morals, and beliefs of a religious community. Thus we can distinguish liturgical theology, moral theology (or theological ethics), and doctrinal theology. Liturgics will not concern us here, but in part 2 we will examine typical forms of reasoning in theological ethics and doctrinal theology (hereafter referred to simply as theology).

The distinction between theology and religious belief was simple enough to draw in the preceding paragraph but it is often more difficult to draw in practice, since theologians and ordinary believers often talk about the same things: for example, the nature of God, or the forgiveness of sins.

Despite the difficulties, I believe this is an important distinction to keep in mind for at least two reasons. First, the purpose of religion is much different from the purpose of theology. In the case of Christianity, the purpose of religion as a whole is worship and service of God; the purpose of theology is shaped by its character as an academic discipline. While most Christians hope that their beliefs, such as about God or salvation, are held rationally, this is not the first criterion one thinks of in evaluating the Christian religion. Theology, however, aims at rational reflection on the phenomena and beliefs of the religion and therefore rational criteria are of the highest importance. Among the criteria for rational reflection are the demands of good reasoning. So this book could more accurately be titled *Reasoning in Theology,* but that isn't as catchy.

A second reason for remembering the distinction between theology and religion is that these are self-involving subjects—subjects wherein the claims we make have a deep impact on our lives. This fact sometimes makes clear thinking more difficult, but it helps to bear in mind that criticism of a *theological* argument is not necessarily an attack on the religious *beliefs* of the person who made the argument.

---

[3]I shall use the term 'practical reasoning' to distinguish our concerns in this book from formal reasoning or formal logic, as is found in the writings of logicians and mathematicians. However, the term is sometimes used more narrowly to refer to reasoning about moral issues.

2. Claims and Grounds

The position or point for which one supplies reasons in an argument is called the *claim*. Claims can be *about* anything, but they all share the form of an assertion—that is, they all must say something about something. Thus 'the divinity of Christ' cannot be a claim because it does not by itself make an assertion. 'Christ is divine' does make an assertion and could, therefore, take its place as a claim in an argument.

The second of the two most basic parts of an argument is the *grounds* that are put forward to support the claim. Grounds for arguments can vary widely; definition 4 above suggests 'facts' and 'reasons' as near synonyms; we could add still others, such as 'data' and 'supporting evidence.'

The most basic form of an argument can be represented as follows:

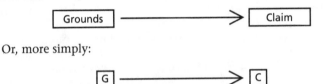

Or, more simply:

Note the *arrow* pointing *from* the grounds *to* the claim. This symbol is highly significant. It suggests that an argument must *go* somewhere. It is not the mere assertion of a group of statements, but an invitation to the reader or listener to move from one position (acceptance of the grounds) to another (acceptance of the claim).

Here it is instructive to return to definition 5. The purpose of an argument is to persuade. When located in the context of practical reasoning, an argument works by showing that if an audience believes the statements that are adduced as grounds, then they ought also to accept (or at least give serious consideration to) the claim. So, in its most basic form an argument presents grounds intended to support a claim. In more psychological terms, we can say that in making an argument one adduces grounds (presumably already accepted by the audience) in order to persuade them to accept a (further) claim. In later chapters we will consider some of the ways arguments can go wrong, but it is clear already that an argument deployed to convince an audience of a claim it already accepts and an argument based on grounds the audience does not accept are equally unhappy occurrences.

It is important to bear in mind that we are developing here a set of interrelated technical terms. We have already distinguished between the use of the word 'argument' in the context of reasoning and its use in, say, family therapy. Likewise, the word 'claim' has many uses outside of our technical sphere. Here it refers to a specific part of an argument. It is a claim because it functions this way in an argument—because it is supported by grounds. In other contexts 'claim' is used differently. For example, advertisers often make claims about their products that are not supported in any way. But such 'claims' are not claims in our technical sense. Similarly, grounds are not grounds in and of themselves. They only become grounds because of the way they are used—as a part of an argument to support a claim. In short, the parts of an argument are *functionally interdefined*—that is, according to their *use* and *relative* to one another.

Because claims and grounds can only be distinguished by their role in an argument, they cannot be recognized simply by looking at the assertions themselves. For example, the assertion 'Christ was raised from the dead' might function as the *claim* in an argument such as:

> Christ appeared to a number of the disciples after his death.
> Therefore he was raised from the dead.

But the same assertion might equally serve as *grounds* for a different argument; for example:

> Christ was raised from the dead, so we can expect to be raised
> up as well.

Therefore we need clues—called here *rhetorical marks*—to distinguish what the author is arguing for (the claim) from what the claim is based upon (the grounds). For example, look at the first sentence of this paragraph. 'Because' signals to the reader that the following clause provides the grounds for the argument; therefore the second clause must be the claim. We have the following argument in schematic form:

This same argument could be written using a number of different rhetorical marks. For example:

> *Since* claims and grounds can only be distinguished by their
> role in an argument, they cannot be recognized simply by look-
> ing at the assertions themselves.

Or,

> *Due to the fact that* claims . . . they cannot be recognized . . .

Or,

> *On account of the fact that* . . .

The words and phrases substituted above are all clues for recognizing that what follows serves as the grounds for an argument, and there are others besides.

Alternatively, we could write:

> Claims and grounds can only be distinguished by their role in
> an argument; *therefore* they cannot be recognized simply by
> looking at the assertions themselves.

Or,

> Claims and grounds . . . ; *thus,* they cannot be recognized . . .

Or,

> Claims and grounds . . . ; *consequently*, they cannot be recognized . . .

Or,

> Claims and grounds . . . ; *so* they cannot be recognized . . .

Again, there are other marks as well.

In some cases the meaning of the sentence(s) makes clear which is the claim and which the grounds, so no marks are needed. For example, in

> Christ was raised from the dead; we can expect to be raised up as well.

it is still obvious that the claim has to do with our resurrection. However, this is not the case with our earlier example,

> Claims and grounds can only be distinguished by their role in an argument; they cannot be recognized simply by looking at the assertions themselves.

which could plausibly be read as '*Because* claims and grounds can only be distinguished by their role in an argument, they cannot be recognized simply by looking at the assertions themselves.' It could also be read as a parallel construction—the two clauses saying pretty much the same thing in different language—in which case it would be no *argument* at all. So here the rhetorical marks are essential.

The reader now might well be wondering: If the argument is reversible—if one can plausibly argue from either clause to the other—why did the argument as it occurred above go the way it did rather than the other way around? The answer is found in the context. It had already been stated in the previous paragraph that claims become claims (and grounds, grounds) by virtue of their use (or role) in an argument. It could therefore be assumed that the reader accepted this statement, and so it could be used as support for the further claim that claims (and grounds) cannot be recognized simply by looking.

Notice that the words used as markers to distinguish claims and grounds have other uses as well. For example, I might say, "I had run out of money, *so* I went to the bank," or "*Because* I had run out of money, I went to the bank." Here I'm not trying to argue for the claim that I went to the bank; I'm simply telling you that I did, and telling you why.

3. Complex Arguments

If the claim of one argument can be the grounds for another, it should be possible to 'chain' the two arguments (or even several arguments) together;

this is in fact what we often do, as Paul has done in this example:

> For if the dead are not raised, it follows that Christ was not raised; and if Christ was not raised, your faith has nothing to it and you are still in your old state of sin. (1 Cor. 15:16-17 REB)

This argument could be diagrammed as follows:

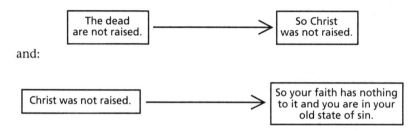

and:

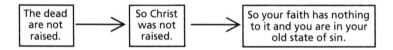

Alternatively, we can combine them into a chain argument:

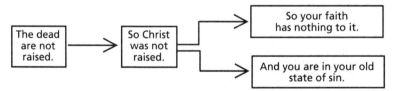

Notice that the final conclusion of this argument is really two different claims: that the Corinthians' faith has nothing to it, and that they are still in their state of sin. So more accurately we might diagram the argument:

It is more common to find arguments with multiple grounds adduced to support one claim than to find arguments like the one above with two (or more) claims supported by the same line of reasoning. Consider an earlier argument in Paul's letter to the Corinthians:

> First and foremost, I handed on to you the tradition I had received: that Christ died for our sins, in accordance with the scriptures; that he was buried; that he was raised to life on the third day, in accordance with the scriptures; and that he appeared to Cephas, and afterwards to the Twelve. Then he appeared to over five hundred of our brothers at once, most of whom are still alive, though some have died. Then he appeared to James, and afterwards to all the apostles. Last of all he appeared to me too. (1 Cor. 15:3–8 REB)

In this passage Paul argues for Christ's resurrection using a cluster of different grounds. First, he *implies* that it ought to be accepted on the basis of the fact that it is a part of the tradition. Then he recounts a series of appearances, ending with his own experience. One could diagram the argument as follows:

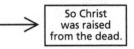

| It is part of the tradition that Christ was raised on the third day, and he appeared to Cephas and to the Twelve, then to over 500, to James, to all the apostles, and to me. | → | So Christ was raised from the dead. |

However, it is more instructive to separate out the different kinds of grounds that are provided for the conclusion, as follows:

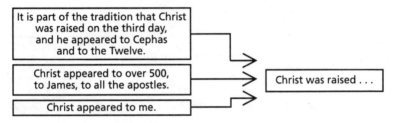

It will become clear in the next chapter why it is important to separate grounds according to the type of evidence they provide: here tradition, eyewitness accounts of others, and one's own eyewitness account.

EXERCISE ONE

1. Which of the following are assertions?
   a. The word of God.
   b. Adultery is a sin.
   c. Jesus' resurrection from the dead.
   d. The Gospel of Mark was written before the Gospel of Matthew.
   e. Jesus was crucified on Pentecost.

2. Are the following assertions claims or grounds?
   a. Christians have a duty to obey the lawful government.
   b. Jesus' resurrection is the key to Christian theology.

3. Decide whether or not each of the following is an argument. If it is, identify the claim by writing the number that precedes the appropriate sentence or clause.
   a. (1) John committed adultery against his wife, (2) because he divorced her and married another.
   b. (1) John divorced his wife (2) because she committed adultery.
   c. (1) Many Christians fell away during the early centuries of the church (2) because of persecution.
   d. (1) Since Christ endured bodily suffering, (2) you also must arm yourselves with the same disposition (1 Pet. 4:1 REB).
   e. (1) Christians sometimes have a duty to resist the state (2) since their

first loyalty belongs to Christ.

f. (1) Because attendance is declining, (2) many mainline churches are taking a new interest in evangelism.

g. (1) Susan's sermon was excellent. (2) It had a clear thesis and memorable illustrations, and (3) it was based on sound exegesis.

h. (1) Therefore God raised him to the heights and bestowed on him the name above all names, (2) that at the name of Jesus every knee should bow—in heaven, on earth, and in the depths—and every tongue acclaim, (3) "Jesus Christ is Lord," to the glory of God the Father. (4) So you too, my friends, must be obedient, as always (Phil. 2:9–12a REB).

i. (1) Always be ready to make your defense when anyone challenges you to justify the hope which is in you. (2) But do so with courtesy and respect, keeping your conscience clear, (3) so that when you are abused, those who malign your Christian conduct may be put to shame (1 Pet. 3:15b-16 REB).

Note: if you decided that all of these are arguments, go back to the end of section 2.

4. Make diagrams of the following arguments. You may want to simplify them as in the following example:

> It is now commonplace, and rightly so, to admit that we can never get a 'pure,' 'basic' experience: it is already laden with interpretation according to inherited belief systems. Nor can we get at a world beyond our interpreted experience to test it. So of course we cannot simply find the truth of things by checking off our experience against a world objectively considered.[4]

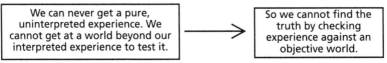

a. Because we are by our nature physical beings, linked by our bodily metabolism both with one another and with the rest of the material world, our resurrection will involve nothing less than the transformation of the whole material order.[5]

b. Women should be consulted about such things as housing and domestic architecture because, under present circumstances, they have still to wrestle a good deal with houses and kitchen sinks and can bring special knowledge to the problem.[6]

c. You have no defense, then, whoever you may be, when you sit in judgment—for in judging others you condemn yourself, since you, the judge, are equally guilty. (Rom. 2:1 REB)

---

[4]Vernon White, *The Fall of a Sparrow* (Exeter, England: Paternoster Press, 1985), 19.

[5]E. L. Mascall, *Christian Theology and Natural Science* (London: Longmans, Green & Co., 1956), 17.

[6]Dorothy Sayers, *Are Women Human?* (Grand Rapids: Eerdmans, 1971), 30.

d. It can hardly be denied that recent history has provided a powerful motive for skepticism about technical, utilitarian reason. For instance, James Cone observes that "For black and red peoples in North America, the spirit of the Enlightenment was socially and politically demonic, becoming a pseudo-intellectual basis for their enslavement or extermination."[7]

e. "We do not observe that God even intervenes with an occasional miracle as He was believed to do in the days of the Bible. It would not tempt a responsible religious commentator on events to attribute the calm sea and fog on the English Channel that facilitated the evacuation of Dunkirk to a divine miracle as the plague that defeated the hosts of Sennacherib before the gates of Jerusalem was interpreted as a miracle." If this point of view is accepted then it is also questionable whether ancient theologians were justified in thinking in terms of miracles.[8]

5. The following argument (or arguments) can be understood and diagrammed in a number of different ways. Decide what is the best way to understand the passage and then diagram it. (You may put the numbers in the boxes rather than the entire sentences.)

(1) We theologians and statesmen from 1815 to 1865, hold that the Bible says nothing to condemn slavery as sinful, (2) and some of us maintain that the Bible in fact commands slavery. (3) Rooted in Noah's prophetic cursing of Ham-Canaan's descendants, (4) slavery has been and (5) should be practiced by God's people. (6) Abraham, champion of faith, had many slaves. (7) God told the Israelites to buy slaves and gave specific instructions pertaining to their service. (8) Jesus never spoke against slavery, (9) but used the slave image as a model for Christian conduct. (10) Paul and Peter instructed masters and slaves in how to conduct themselves as Christians, (11) and Paul obeyed the fugitive slave law in sending the runaway slave Onesimus back to Philemon, his master. (12) Nowhere does the Bible condemn slavery. (13) Either believe the Bible and support slavery, or oppose slavery and throw out the Bible as God's authoritative word.[9]

---

[7]Richard Grigg, *Theology as a Way of Thinking* (Atlanta: Scholars Press, 1990), 31.
[8]Frank Dilley, "Does the 'God Who Acts' Really Act?" in *God's Activity in the World,* ed. O. Thomas (Chico, Calif.: Scholars Press, 1983), 54.
[9]J. H. Hopkins, *A Scriptural, Ecclesiastical, and Historical View of Slavery . . . ;* quoted by Willard Swartley in *Slavery, Sabbath, War and Women* (Scottdale, Pa.: Herald Press, 1983), 32–33.

Chapter Two

Warrants and Backing

A national sensationalist tabloid once published the theory that the wife of a famous entertainer was the descendant of aliens. A key piece of evidence supporting the theory was that the lady had slightly lower than average blood pressure. Now lower than average blood pressure is indeed empirical data, but there is no reason to connect it with alien ancestry. Real science requires that there be some *rational* connection between explanatory theory and empirical data.

Del Ratzsch, *Philosophy of Science*

1. Warrants

In this section we examine a third component of arguments. To see why the account in the previous chapter is incomplete, consider the following:

> Since their first loyalty belongs to Christ, Christians sometimes have a duty to resist the state.

> Since there are 27 books in the New Testament, Christians sometimes have a duty to resist the state.

Why does the first argument work but not the second? It is certainly not because the grounds in the second are false. The answer is that there is no conceivable *connection* between the number of books in the New Testament and any conclusion about how Christians ought to relate to the state. The grounds provide no support for the claim because they are *irrelevant*.

This shows that in each of the arguments we considered in chapter 1, insofar as the argument works, we must be assuming something to be true about a connection between the argument's claim and its grounds. Consider, for example:

> Since Christ endured bodily suffering, you also must arm yourselves with the same disposition.

This argument works only if we assume something about Christians' attitudes and behavior needing to be modeled on those of Christ. Similarly, in

> Susan's sermon was excellent. It had a clear thesis and memorable illustrations, and it was based on sound exegesis.

the argument depends on our agreeing about certain criteria for good preaching.

We can formulate the connection between grounds and claim and make it an explicit part of the argument; this part is here called the *warrant*. Schematically, the addition looks like this:

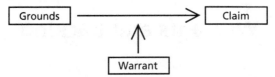

Notice again the arrows. To ask for the warrant is to ask why it is *legitimate* to go from the grounds to the claim; it is a question about the *connection* between these two parts of the argument, or about why the grounds are *relevant* to this claim. So the arrow from the warrant points to (i.e., supports) the *arrow* from the grounds to the claim.

Note also that the warrant will ordinarily be a *general* statement, answering the question why grounds *of this sort* should be used to support a claim *of this sort*. So we could think of the warrant as an inference rule for making arguments of this type.

1.1. Examples

We find an assortment of warrants in everyday reasoning and especially as we examine different disciplines. In fact, much of learning a discipline is becoming familiar with the accepted warrants used in arguments in that field of inquiry. Later chapters will discuss typical warrants in theological disciplines. Let us look at some examples from other fields.

1.1.1. Science, Mathematics, Engineering

Warrants for arguments in these fields are often formulas or laws. In algebra, for example, the formula $x = 3y$ can be used to construct an infinite number of arguments with values of one variable given in the grounds and appropriate values for the other in the claim (conclusion).

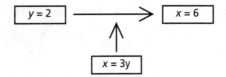

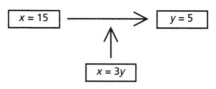

So the formula is a rule for calculating the value of one variable from information about the value of the other.

Formulas play a similar role in science and engineering. For example, the formula $f = ma$ (force equals mass times acceleration) can be used in a variety of arguments, such as the following:

> The acceleration of a body falling toward Earth is approximately 9.8 meters per second, per second. The body weighs 1,000 kilograms. Therefore the force with which it will strike the ground is 9,800 MK/sec².

Schematically, the argument looks like this:

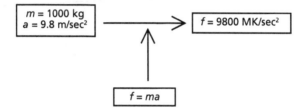

1.1.2. Law

Two important kinds of warrants in legal arguments are *statutes* (laws) and *precedents*. In a criminal court, for example, the jury's estimate of what actually happened will serve as the grounds, and their judgment of guilt or innocence will be the claim. This conclusion will be warranted by applicable laws. Suppose that a jury is satisfied that Jones did in fact shoot Smith. Smith's body was found on the floor just inside the window of Jones's bedroom, the window having been forced open. The jury's verdict is that Jones is not guilty of murder, for in this state there is a statute (no. xxxxx) permitting a property owner to shoot trespassers. Furthermore, there is a precedent (*John Doe v. Joe Blow*) for determining whether or not the victim was trespassing on the basis of whether the body is found on or off the defendant's property.

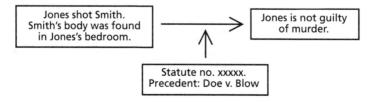

Again we can see that the warrants are general rules for making arguments of this sort. The same law or precedent will be used by other juries trying different defendants.

1.1.3. Ethics

We will look in more detail at ethical arguments in chapter 8, so a brief example will do here. Many arguments in this area are intended to pass judgment on particular acts by bringing to bear general principles of moral conduct. The principle serves as the warrant for the argument:

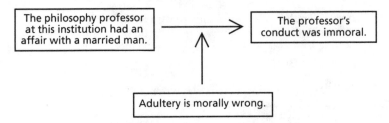

1.1.4. Policy and Prudence

In addition to ethical judgments, we often make judgments about people's conduct in light of established policy or generally accepted notions of prudent action. So, for example, we might also argue:

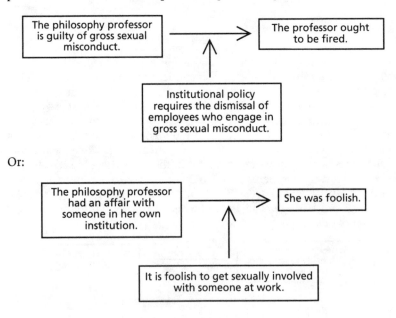

Or:

1.1.5. Medicine

Clinicians make claims about the condition of a patient on the basis of the patient's symptoms (the grounds) and a description of the usual manifestations of the disease (the warrant). For example:

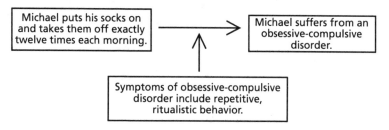

1.1.6. Definitions

In all fields, and in everyday reasoning as well, definitions often serve as important warrants for arguments. For example:

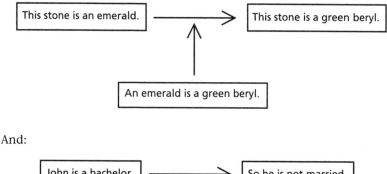

And:

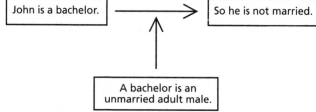

If anyone ever stated this last argument in full it would raise doubts about his or her mental competence. This illustrates a fact about many of our arguments: the warrants are often not stated, but only assumed. The reason is that warrants involve our general, shared knowledge about the topics at issue. If the principles, definitions, formulas are *not* already known and widely accepted, the argument may not be worth making at all.

1.1.7. Observed Regularity

One last category of warrants to be mentioned here is observed regularities. In our everyday reasoning we bring to bear a wealth of generalizations about typical behavior of things we encounter, about causal connections, about signs and symptoms. Here are a few examples:

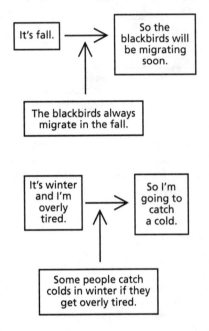

1.2. Rhetorical Marks of Warrants

Remember that when you hear or read an argument it is quite likely that the warrant will *not* be stated. Your interlocutor will expect the warrant to be provided by your own background knowledge. Warrants are generally only stated when they are unusual or questionable.

Usually, the first clue for recognizing a warrant when it is supplied is a difference in generality between the grounds and the warrant. Recall that the warrant makes a statement about things of the sort described in the grounds: about emeralds in general, as opposed to this particular emerald; about trespassers in general, not just this one. Notice, though, that generality is a matter of degree. Compare:

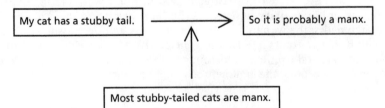

with:

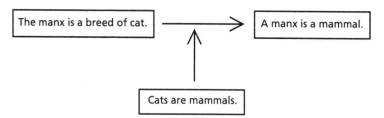

My cat is a member of the manx breed, so statements about the breed are more general than those about my cat. Thus, in the first argument the warrant is about the breed, the grounds refer to my cat. In the second argument the breed becomes the particular, and the warrant is more general still; it makes an assertion about cats in general and the larger class of mammals. The relative generality of these concepts can be represented as follows:

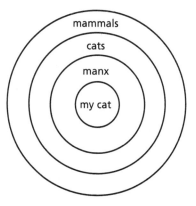

It is often necessary to judge from the meaning of the words whether one assertion is more general than another, but signs to watch for include words that suggest that some sort of generalization is being made: 'whenever,' 'all,' 'any,' 'most.'

The second criterion for recognizing a warrant is that it will often use some words or phrases from both the grounds and the claim. For example, in the argument above, the warrant picks up 'stubby-tailed' from the grounds and connects it with 'manx' in the claim.

Let us look at some of the types of connection that can be involved in the wording of a warrant. To observe warrants in action it is helpful to deprive ourselves of previous knowledge about the things being discussed. To do so we will employ some simple symbolic devices from formal logic.

First, let's allow the capital letters *P* and *Q* to stand for assertions—any old assertion. Consider the following argument form:

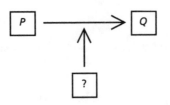

What assertion would warrant such an argument? Here are some possibilities:

> If P, then Q.
> If P, then one can expect that Q.
> From the fact that P, one can infer that Q.
> From the fact that P, one can presume that Q.
> Whenever P, Q.

To check whether these formulas work, let P stand for 'It's raining' and Q for 'The streets are slippery.' Our potential warrants become:

> If it's raining, the streets are slippery.
> If it's raining, then one can expect that the streets are slippery.
> From the fact that it's raining, one can infer that the streets are slippery.
> Whenever it's raining, the streets are slippery.

We also need to look at what is 'inside' an assertion to see how warrants work. So let lowercase letters (e.g., *a, b*) stand for individuals—for persons and things—and let uppercase letters stand for properties, classes, relations. 'Dobbin is a horse' can be represented as *Hd,* where *d* stands for Dobbin, and *H* stands for the predicate 'is a horse.' Likewise, 'Adam is tall' becomes *Ta;* 'Dobbin is faster than Adam' becomes *dFa.* Now look at the following argument:

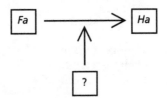

For a warrant here we need an assertion that connects the predicates *F* and *H.* For example:

> All *F*s are *H*s.
> Any *F* will be *H.*
> Anything that is *F* is *H.*
> Many (most, some) *F*s are *H*s.
> From the fact that something is *F,* you can infer it is also *H.*

Now, to try out these forms, let *a* stand for a person, Amy; let *F* stand for 'Fuller Seminary student'; let *H* stand for 'hard-working.' Our possible warrants, then, are:

All (or many or most) Fuller students are hard-working.
Any Fuller student will be hard-working.
From the fact that some[one] is a Fuller student, you can infer
that [she or he] is also hard-working.

Note that there are ways of writing a general statement that can make it appear to be particular: for example, 'A Fuller student will generally be hard-working.' This sentence is not referring to a particular student; it is an odd way of speaking of *any* Fuller student, which is equivalent to speaking of *all* Fuller students.

1.3. Warrants in Complex Arguments

Complex arguments will obviously demand more than one warrant. Here are some possible forms:

A chain argument:

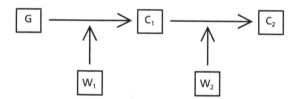

Two independent arguments for the same claim:

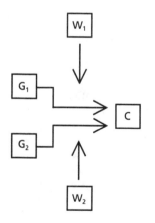

Two claims supported by the same grounds:

Recall our diagram at the end of chapter 1 of Paul's argument for the historicity of Jesus' resurrection. Here we need at least two different warrants: one to legitimate a conclusion based on the apostolic tradition; one to legitimate conclusions based on eyewitness accounts. In addition, we might want to argue differently for the author's own account than for secondhand reports. More on this in chapter 9, "Reasoning in History."

These are just a few of the 'shapes' arguments may take. To see even more complex forms, leaf through the book and look at the diagrams that have been provided.

2. Backing

Return now to the question of what makes a good argument. So far we can say that:

1. The grounds must be true;
2. The grounds must be relevant to the claim; this is equivalent to saying:
2′. There must be a good warrant (stated or assumed). A good warrant:
   a. must indicate an appropriate connection between the grounds and claim;
   b. the warrant must be true, or at least plausible.

This last criterion calls for comment. As noted above, the warrant is often left unstated. In evaluating an argument, therefore, the reader will have to invent a warrant that will provide a suitable connection between the claim and the grounds that have been provided. It is always possible to devise some warrant, but often the warrant that is needed will be neither obviously true nor obviously false—one can only judge whether it is plausible or implausible. Consider the argument:

> Jesus commanded his followers to love one another; therefore popcorn ought to be provided in all the classrooms.

In order to make this argument work one needs to devise a warrant such as: 'Offering popcorn to students is a good way to live out the love commandment.' While this assertion is not generally accepted, it is not obviously false either. This section deals with the problem of disputed warrants. The considerations we bring to bear in defense of a disputed warrant we here call the *backing*. This is the next component of an argument to be included, and the diagram now looks like this:

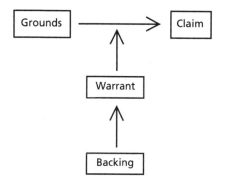

2.1. Types of Backing

We have just seen that there are a number of different types of warrants. Consequently, there are a number of different sorts of information that might legitimately be presented to back a warrant. There are at least five such categories: experience or observation, citation of authority, matters of definition, theoretical considerations, and consistency.

2.1.1. Experience or Observation

Recall that one sort of warrant mentioned above was observed regularity: for example, 'The blackbirds always migrate in the fall.' The obvious way to back such a warrant is by means of reports of observations. One might say, 'I've been a bird-watcher for thirty years and there has never been an exception.'

For the warrant 'It's foolish to get involved sexually with someone at work,' a likely backing would be to cite a few cases one knows about where such involvement led to disaster.

Laws in science are regularly backed by observations; here a scientist who was challenged might bring out her stack of computer printouts analyzing the data from a set of experiments.

2.1.2. Citation of Authority

In the legal argument above we have already given (fake) citations of statute and precedent within the warrant, so no further backing is called for. However, a more illuminating way to lay out a legal argument would be to quote the statute or precedent in the warrant and cite the statute number or precedent in the backing.

In biblical studies and other theological disciplines, scripture citations are often used as backing for an argument. For example, the warrant 'Adultery is wrong' can be backed by citing Exodus 20:14.

To back a warrant regarding matters of policy, one cites the handbook or other authoritative document.

2.1.3. Matters of Definition

When a warrant is a definition of a common word, we can cite a dictionary. However, when using a technical term for which there is no universally agreed usage we sometimes have to *argue* that our rule for the use of the term is the best one. Matters of definition and matters of experience are not entirely independent of one another; we need to define words in such a way that our language 'cuts the world at its joints.' So, for instance, at some time in the past someone had to provide an argument to the effect that it makes more sense (fits the world better) to define a whale as a seagoing mammal than to classify it as a fish.

2.1.4. Theoretical Considerations

Often the general principles that function as warrants in arguments are held because they are logically tied to other general, theoretical principles. For example, Newton's law $f = ma$ is not simply a generalization from observations; it is a part of a system of laws and theories where the *consistency* of one with the others provides strong justification for each.

Some theological propositions have no direct backing in experience or observation, or even from scripture citations. Their justification comes from the network of beliefs in which they play an essential part.

2.1.5. Consistency

Another sort of consistency plays a role in backing warrants. Since warrants are general rules to be used in classes of arguments, we cannot reasonably use the warrant in ninety-nine cases but then reject it in the one-hundredth case because we do not happen to like the claim it supports. For example, some sort of statement about fair and equal treatment warrants numerous ethical arguments. And just because a large part of our ethical thinking depends on it, we cannot arbitrarily reject it in some particular case.

2.2. Backing and the Interconnections among Arguments

In general, when we are asked to provide backing for a warrant we are being called upon to tie the argument we are making, in one way or another, to other parts of our system of knowledge. Consequently, the information and arguments that are required to do an adequate job of defending the warrant will often not fit conveniently into a little box in a diagram. If we cannot agree with our interlocutors about the warrant in question, then it is often time for a long, drawn-out discussion (and scholars spend a great deal of their professional energies on just such discussions). In these cases, the proposed warrant itself becomes a claim, with its own grounds and (additional) warrant.

Consider the following example:

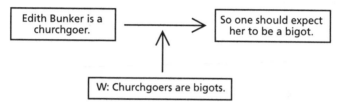

One might get away with backing this warrant by calling to mind a few bigoted churchgoers, but anyone with sophistication in reasoning knows that anecdotal information can be very misleading. So a scientific study is needed, involving a scale to measure prejudice, an adequate sample of churchgoers, and a control group; then we have to see if there is a significant difference between the prejudice scores of the two groups. But to know if the scale is valid, how large the samples have to be, and what counts as a significant difference, we need to invoke some fairly sophisticated theories. The argument, still much abbreviated, would then look like this:

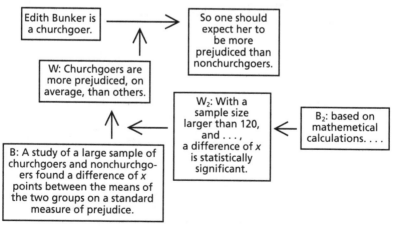

Statistical theory will function as a warrant in innumerable arguments of this sort, and is supported both by mathematical calculations and by the principle of consistency—we cannot reject it here without rejecting all of the other claims it has been used to support.

It has surely become apparent by now that our knowledge forms a complex, interwoven system of arguments. Any argument can be questioned: One can ask about the truth of the grounds, in which case we take a step 'backwards' and provide a more basic sort of evidence, making a chain argument. One can also ask about the warrant, in which case we provide backing that can in turn be questioned as to the truth or relevance of the observations or general principles that support it—and on and on. There is often no 'natural' place to stop; we stop when we reach agreement or run out of ideas about how to continue.

EXERCISE TWO

1. Indicate whether each of the following assertions is particular or general.
   a. Baptists are nonconformists.
   b. The Baptist denomination split during the Civil War.
   c. Anyone who believes in me will be raised up on the last day.
   d. A text that is historically conditioned and produced by a patriarchal society will be patriarchal in character.

2. In each of the following arguments, fill in appropriate claims or grounds.
   a.

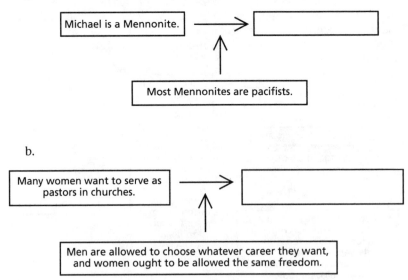

   b.

c.

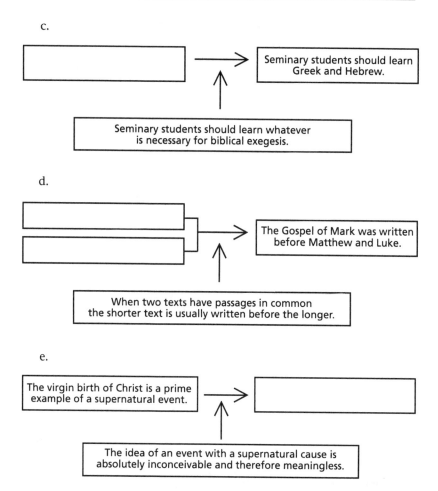

Seminary students should learn Greek and Hebrew.

Seminary students should learn whatever is necessary for biblical exegesis.

d.

The Gospel of Mark was written before Matthew and Luke.

When two texts have passages in common the shorter text is usually written before the longer.

e.

The virgin birth of Christ is a prime example of a supernatural event.

The idea of an event with a supernatural cause is absolutely inconceivable and therefore meaningless.

3. Write a suitable warrant for each of the following arguments.
   a. The form [of John 1:1–18] is in favor of considering it as poetry. The lines are simple, many of them very nearly the same length, interlocking with one another in various forms of parallelism, or in sequences where one sentence begins with the word which concluded the previous one.[1]
   b. Since the biblical texts are historically conditioned and were produced by a patriarchal society, they are patriarchal in character. They must, therefore, be approached with suspicion.[2] (Note that there is a chain argument here, so you need to provide two warrants.)

---

[1]John Howard Yoder, *He Came Preaching Peace* (Scottdale, Pa.: Herald Press, 1985), 70–71.

[2]Alice Laffey, *An Introduction to the Old Testament: A Feminist Perspective* (Philadelphia: Fortress Press, 1988), 2.

   c. The orthodox belief in special revelation denied the reign of causal law in the phenomenal realm of space and time, . . . therefore, this orthodox view of revelation represented a primitive, prescientific form of religion and should be modernized.[3]

   d. This understanding of Hebrew religion is strictly "liberal," since it pictures reality as a consistent world order and religious truth as a human interpretation based on religious experience.[4]

   e. [The Baptists] were genuine nonconformists. They extended Protestant themes to new, more radical conclusions. They called for complete religious liberty. They objected to war. They distributed relief to the poor. They allowed women to preach. They elected pastors from the ranks of working people.[5]

   f. [It] not only teaches us how to think about values; it teaches us how to think. This book should be required reading in schools.[6]

4. Write the number of the statement that contains the warrant in each of the following arguments.

   a. (1) Christian theology must be the recitation in faith of God's mighty acts; (2) therefore it must be composed of confessional and systematic statements of the form: "We believe that God did so and so," and not composed of statements of the form: "The Hebrews believed that God did so and so." For, as biblical scholars have reminded us, (3) a religious confession that is biblical is a direct recital of God's acts, not a recital of someone else's beliefs.

   b. If (1) knowledge of God is based only on his revelatory acts, and (2) before the Exodus events there were only creative interpretations of history by the Israelites, (3) then prior to Exodus-Sinai there was no valid knowledge of God at all.

   c. (1) When we speak of God as acting, we mean that we are confronted with God, addressed, asked, judged, or blessed by God. (2) Therefore, to speak in this manner is not to speak in symbols or images, but to speak analogically. (3) For whenever we speak in this manner of God as acting, we conceive God's action as an analogue to the actions taking place between people.

   d. (1) It is impossible to carry through demythologization consistently, (2) since, if the message of the New Testament is to be retained at all, we are bound to speak of God as acting. (3) In such speech there remains a mythological residue. (4) For it is mythological to speak of God as acting.

5. Assume that each of the following statements is a warrant for an argument. State the one category to which the most likely backing for each warrant would belong (observation, authority, definition, theory, consistency).

---

[3]Langdon Gilkey, "Cosmology, Ontology, and the Travail of Biblical Language," in *God's Activity in the World,* ed. O. Thomas (Chico, Calif.: Scholars Press, 1983), 30.

[4]Gilkey, "Cosmology, Ontology, and the Travail of Biblical Language," 40.

[5]Paul Dekar, "Baptist Peacemakers," in *Seek Peace and Pursue It,* ed. H. Wayne Pipkin (Memphis: Baptist Peace Fellowship of North America, 1989), 77.

[6]A. Bartlett Giamatti, cover of *A Question of Values* by Hunter Lewis (San Francisco: Harper and Row, 1990).

a. Cats are mammals.
b. From the fact that it is raining one can infer that the streets are slippery.
c. People should not run on an icy sidewalk.
d. People must not drive 50 MPH in this neighborhood.
e. Most Mennonites are pacifists.
f. Men are allowed to choose whatever career they want and women ought to be allowed to do the same.
g. When two texts have passages in common the shorter text is usually earlier.
h. The idea of an event with a supernatural cause is absolutely inconceivable and therefore meaningless.
i. An inconceivable idea is meaningless.

CHAPTER THREE

Qualifiers and Rebuttals

1. Qualifiers

Consider the difference between these two arguments from the previous chapter:

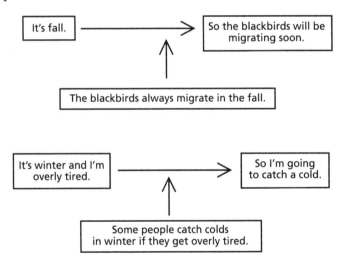

Assuming that the grounds and warrants of both are true, there is a difference in the amount of confidence we have in the truth of each claim. This difference in confidence well reflects a difference in the *strength* of the warrants. The blackbirds always migrate in the fall, but people do not always catch colds when they are tired. The second warrant expresses a weaker connection between the grounds and the claim than does the first. Does this mean that the first argument is better than the second? Not necessarily. Let us review what we know so far about what makes a good argument.

First, the grounds must be *true*. Formal logicians are interested in arguments with false premises, but in ordinary reasoning we ordinarily are not. Also, the grounds must provide *relevant* support for the claim. This means that the argument must have a good warrant. A good warrant must be *true,* and we usually want the warrant to be *strong* as well. However, the world is such that, in many cases, we have to settle for a weak warrant; it is simply a fact of nature that while there is an observed relation between getting tired and catching a cold, it is not as regular an effect as bird migration.

A good argument, then, will reflect its own strength in the way it is stated. 'I'm overly tired so I'm going to catch a cold' is *not* a good argument as it stands—it overstates its claim, going beyond what the knowledge expressed in its grounds and warrant allows. The following, however, is a good argument because it makes a more guarded claim—one more in line with the strength of the warrant.

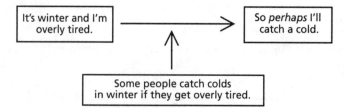

'Perhaps' is used here to qualify the claim—hence we shall call it a *qualifier*. We have a handy array of such terms in English:

necessarily
certainly
undoubtedly
presumably
probably
apparently
possibly
perhaps
there is a chance that
it is conceivable that

And there are others as well. Note that these are listed more or less in order of descending confidence. The qualifier can be given its own location in the argument as follows:

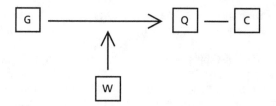

But often we simply incorporate it as needed into the claim.

In different areas of reasoning some qualifiers are more appropriate than others. In pure mathematics, and when making claims on the basis of definitions, we can use the strongest possible qualifiers. The strongest in our repertoire is 'necessarily'; 'certainly' is also appropriate here.

'Presumably' is a handy qualifier in many areas, including science, law, and policy. Its sense is that the claim can be expected to be true unless some factor has not been taken into account. For example, the 1,000-kg object (in the argument in chapter 2) will have an impact of 9,800 MK/sec^2, *unless* it happens to be a gigantic goose-down pillow—in which case air resistance needs to be figured into the equation. In law, ethics, and policy matters we often leave room for extenuating circumstances or the unearthing of new evidence.

Most of our knowledge of human behavior supplies only relatively weak warrants. If the warrant contains words such as 'many,' 'often,' or 'sometimes,' then the qualifier must be correspondingly weak: if *many* or *most* foxes are red, and x is a fox, then x is *probably* red. If only *some* foxes are red, then *possibly* x is red.

Notice the slightly different uses of 'probably' and 'possibly,' on one hand, and 'presumably' on the other. 'Possibly' and 'probably' recognize what we already know—that the warrant expresses a less-than-universal generalization (not all foxes are red). 'Presumably' recognizes that, while the warrant is a strong one, there may be complications we have not taken into account.

1.1. Inductive and Deductive Reasoning

This is a good point at which to introduce some traditional terms used for classifying arguments and to show how they relate to the understanding of reasoning put forward in this volume. It is common to distinguish between two kinds of reasoning: deductive and inductive.

A deductive argument is one such that *if the premises are true the conclusion must be true*. To put it in our language, a deductive argument is one whose warrant is strong enough to *guarantee* the truth of the claim, given the truth of the grounds.

The Greek philosopher Aristotle (384–322 B.C.) contributed a great deal to our understanding of deductive arguments. He was interested in forms of arguments called *syllogisms*. The following are a few examples:

> Socrates is a man.
> All men are mortal.
> _____
> Therefore Socrates is mortal.

(No reasoning text would be complete without this tired old example!)

> All manx are cats.
> All cats are mammals.
> _____
> Therefore, all manx are mammals.

> All philosophers are clever.
> Some logicians are philosophers
> _____
> Therefore some logicians are clever.

We can express the forms of these arguments with symbols. The last example would be:

All A is B.
Some C is A.
Some C is B.

Syllogisms fit neatly into the argument form used in this text. Notice that the more general of the two premises functions as the warrant:

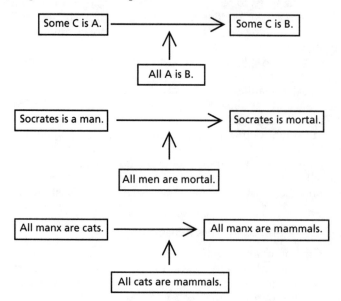

Most recent work in deductive logic depends on the use of symbolic notation in order to investigate valid forms—that is, those forms of argument that are like syllogisms in that the truth of their premises guarantees the truth of their conclusions. Some of these symbolic devices have been suggested in chapter 2:

If P then Q $P \rightarrow Q$
P or: P
—————   —————
Therefore Q $\therefore Q$

For every x, if x is a fox then x is red.
Anabel is a fox.
—————
Therefore, Anabel is red.

becomes:

$(x)(Fx \rightarrow Rx)$
Fa
—————
Ra

The various systems of symbolic notation have reached a high level of sophistication—axiomatized systems (like geometry) that allow for proof of the validity of argument forms.

Why do deductive arguments work? How do they manage to convey certitude regarding their claims? The usual way of answering these questions (since the development of modern logic, at least) is to say that the claim is already contained (implicitly) in the premises. So, for example, the knowledge that *all* men are mortal *includes* the knowledge that the man Socrates is mortal. We may become aware of something new, psychologically speaking, by means of deductive argument, but we never actually expand or increase our knowledge.

This raises another question: If deductive reasoning cannot lead to genuinely new knowledge, where *do* we get new knowledge? Whence come the general statements that are the stock-in-trade of deductive arguments? A common answer to these two interrelated questions is *induction*. If deduction (as it is said) reasons from the general (All men . . .) to the particular (Socrates), then induction is its converse—reasoning from a collection of particulars to a general statement: Fox number 1 is red; fox number 2 is red; fox number 3 is red. . . . Therefore all foxes are red. This is induction at its simplest. And just as there are deductive arguments more complex than a syllogism, so there are inductive arguments more complex than this one. What they all have in common is that their claims enlarge upon, go beyond, the evidence. So inductive reasoning is essential for expanding our knowledge. Its drawback is that it does so at the expense of the comforting certitude of deductive reasoning—we can never be sure that the next fox will not be grey.

Our most valuable intellectual tool for protecting against rash inductive generalizations is statistics. Statisticians have intriguing methods and formulas for calculating the *probability* that a generalization is accurate based on the size of the sample observed and on a few other assumptions. They have formulated precisely the intuitive recognition that (to revert to an example from chapter 2) if I have only observed a few prejudiced church members, I am on very shaky ground concluding that all (or most) churchgoers are bigots. However, if I have tested several hundred churchgoers and an equally large control group who do not attend church, and have found that the churchgoers' mean score on a prejudice scale was much higher than that of the controls, I have good grounds for making the generalization. The shape of such an argument is as follows:

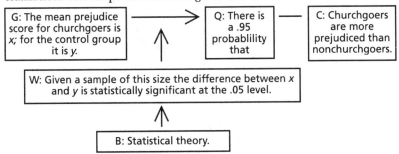

The actual probability (the level of statistical significance) depends on the sizes of the sample and the control group, the difference between the means for each group, and the amount of variation within each group. Inductive reasoning is a powerful tool in science and in everyday reasoning as well; nonetheless, it does not provide an adequate account of how knowledge grows. In our example, the inductive generalization raises more questions than it answers: Why are church people so prejudiced? How can this be if religion teaches love of neighbor?

We will discuss another, more powerful form of scientific reasoning in the next chapter—a form of reasoning suited to answering the "why" questions.[1]

2. Rebuttals

If we are 95 percent sure that churchgoers tend to be more prejudiced, then we are on pretty firm ground in supposing that if Edith goes to church she will also be somewhat more prejudiced than the typical church-avoider. But of course there are exceptions, and a good argument will make this possibility explicit. *Rebuttal* (or potential rebuttal) is the part of the argument that acknowledges where and how the argument may lead to a wrong conclusion. There are two kinds of rebuttals (or we might say, we use the term 'rebuttal' in two ways): One kind of rebuttal simply calls attention to the argument's built-in loopholes. The other seeks to demolish an argument by calling its grounds or warrant into question.

Our argument about churchgoers has a built-in loophole: the fact that the mean score for churchgoers is higher than the mean score for the controls does not entail that all churchgoers are more prejudiced than all of the controls—the two groups may overlap, and there may well be a wide variation within each group. As a matter of fact, additional research has shown that church members who attend frequently and who have deeply internalized their beliefs tend to be much less prejudiced than infrequent attenders, and less prejudiced even than the average nonattender.

So our argument must be modified to take this important class of exceptions into account:

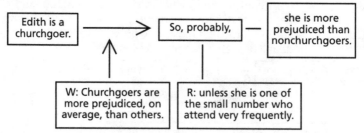

---

[1]For a summary of research on the relation between religiosity and prejudice, see Gordon Allport and J. Michael Ross, "Personal Religious Orientation and Prejudice," *Journal of Personality and Social Psychology* 5, no. 4 (1967): 432–43.

Recall from our discussion of qualifiers above that 'presumably' is an appropriate qualifier for alerting one's audience to the fact that there may be exceptions, extenuating circumstances, factors at work that one can usually ignore but that sometimes interfere with the outcome. It improves the quality of an argument to be explicit about these factors when they represent real possibilities. However, in any argument about things in the real world there is at least a bare possibility that extenuating or exceptional factors may be present. We should not (and could not) list all of the more outlandish ones, for example:

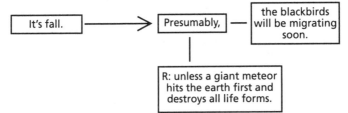

We add rebuttals of the first type to our own arguments to make them better. As with the adding of qualifiers, the recognition of possible rebuttals makes the argument more honest, more precise.

The second sort of rebuttal is one that our opponents provide—these are attempts to defeat the argument by providing evidence that the case in point *is* one of the exceptions, or by providing evidence against the grounds or warrant. To provide this sort of rebuttal is to begin an argument for a different claim altogether. For example:

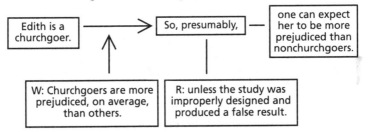

This rebuttal, if taken seriously, would cast doubt on the truth of the warrant and thereby defeat the entire argument. But in order for it to be taken seriously (since someone can always think up some such possibility) the one who puts it forward will have to have some evidence (some grounds) for the claim that the study was improperly designed. If such an argument is provided then the original argument is indeed defeated—we are back to square one. Of course, the proposer of the original argument may be able to rebut (defeat) the rebuttal and reestablish the original claim.

3. Presumption and the Burden of Proof

In an American criminal court an important principle is the *presumption* of innocence—the accused is presumed innocent until proven beyond a reasonable doubt to be guilty. A correlative principle is that the burden of proof falls on the prosecution—the defense does not have to make a positive case for innocence, but only has to cast doubt on the prosecution's case.

These terms apply to other sorts of arguments as well. We can say that generally accepted facts, generalizations, principles have presumptive truth—we do not have to argue for everything we believe. However, to take up a position counter to generally accepted knowledge does require an argument. Generally accepted beliefs have the presumption of truth on their side; the one who raises a challenge bears the burden of proof.

The possibility of supplying rebuttals for an opponent's argument only to have those rebuttals defeated in turn by further considerations suggests that debates of this sort could go on forever. In practice, however, they usually end after a few rounds. Sometimes the most one side can accomplish is to shift the burden of proof—that is, to show that there is enough evidence against the assumed position that it can no longer be presumed true, but now requires justification. However, this is not an insignificant outcome.

Let us examine a passage that illustrates these points. The following text by John W. Cooper is a summary of the (quite extended) argument to date regarding biblical anthropology: Are humans essentially composed of two kinds or entities, body and soul, or not?

> Traditional Christianity has held fast to an ontological distinction between body and soul mainly because it follows from the doctrine of the intermediate state. Historically both beliefs have been taken by the overwhelming majority to be the teaching of Scripture itself. But in modern times body-soul dualism has come under a series of attacks mounted both by Christians and non-Christians. Philosophers have criticized traditional arguments for the substantiality and immortality of the soul and have proposed nondualist theories of human nature. Scientists have turned up a great deal of evidence demonstrating the dependence of mental and psychological states on the brain, thereby undermining the basis for considering the soul a separate substance. Biblical scholars have subjected anthropological terms and texts to careful analysis and have concluded that the biblical view of human nature is not dualistic at all, but is quite emphatically holistic. Historians of Christianity have confirmed that the roots of traditional anthropology are nourished by the soil of the Hellenistic worldview, not by Scripture as had always been assumed. And finally, many Christians who devote themselves to radical obedience and witnessing the whole gospel for all of life have charged that the body-soul distinction of traditional Christianity is one of the root causes of the many ways in which the faith has been distorted and prevented from effecting the complete salvation of humanity and the whole creation.
>
> All of these charges are voiced from different directions, but they all conclude the same thing—dualism is out, holism or monism is in. As David Myers puts it: "the truth is that we do not *have* bodies, we *are* our bodies. On this

important concept scientific research and biblical scholarship seem to be approaching a consensus."

Altogether this represents a truly formidable cumulative case against anthropological dualism. If it stands up, or even if some of the individual charges are accurate, there is very good reason for repentance from dualism and conversion to monism-holism.

But thus far we have heard only from the prosecution. The evidence certainly seems incriminating. But is there a defense? Have philosophy and science falsified dualism? Does a body-soul distinction really lead to the distortion of Christian faith and practice? . . . But the most fundamental issue of all for those who regard biblical teaching as authoritative is whether historical Christianity has really just read anthropological dualism into Scripture where it is not present at all. Christian belief must be normed by biblical teaching. . . . [2]

So, according to Cooper, the original presumption lay with dualism—it was the position assumed by traditional Christianity. But in modern times, he tells us, enough objections were raised to the dualist assumption that it was finally overturned. Now the presumption lies with monism or holism, and the burden of proof has shifted to those who wish to defend dualism. This is what Cooper intends to do, first, by showing that scripture provides grounds for dualism, and then by rebutting all of the standard arguments against it.

Cooper's book is a recent publication, so I believe it is fair to say that the jury is still out on the issue. Whatever happens next in the debate will have to involve an evaluation of Cooper's arguments to see whether his rebuttals (of the rebuttals of traditional dualism) can be in their turn rebutted.

A series such as this, of arguments and counterarguments, reflects the pattern of much scholarship. To know a field is to know where the arguments stand on important issues—which side bears the burden of proof. It is also to know the strength and limits of applicability of the arguments— that is, to be able to recognize appropriate qualifiers and to provide suitable rebuttals. So the ability to employ in one's chosen field of study the tools of argument covered in this chapter is a great part of what differentiates the student from the accomplished scholar.

---

[2]John W. Cooper, *Body, Soul, and Life Everlasting* (Grand Rapids: Eerdmans, 1989), 34–35. The quotation from David Meyers is found in *The Human Puzzle* (San Francisco: Harper and Row, 1978), 88.

EXERCISE THREE

1. Choose the best qualifier for each of the following arguments:
   a. My cat is stubby-tailed; most stubby-tailed cats are manx. So my cat is a manx.
   (*probably, perhaps, undoubtedly*)
   b. Michael puts his socks on and takes them off exactly twelve times each morning. Obsessive-compulsive disorder manifests itself in repetitive, ritualistic behavior. So Michael suffers from obsessive-compulsive disorder.
   (*possibly, presumably, certainly*)
   c. $y = 2$; $x = 3y$. Therefore $x = 6$.
   (*undoubtedly, probably, necessarily*)
   d. This stone is an emerald. Emeralds are green beryls, so this is a green beryl.
   (*probably, certainly, apparently*)
   e. Shirley has red hair and redheads have been known to be hot-tempered, so Shirley is hot-tempered.
   (*presumably, possibly, probably*)
   f. Many women want to serve as pastors, and since men are allowed to choose whatever career they want, women ought to be allowed to be pastors if they wish.
   (*presumably, perhaps, undoubtedly*)
   g. The virgin birth of Christ is a prime example of a supernatural event. The idea of an event with a supernatural cause is absolutely inconceivable and meaningless. Thus the virgin birth is a meaningless idea.
   (*presumably, certainly, probably*)

2. a. Which of the qualifiers listed in the first question are suitable for use in a deductive argument?
   b. Which are suitable for an inductive argument?

3. Provide a rebuttal for each of the following arguments in the form of an exception or extenuating circumstance.
   a. Whoever divorces his wife and marries another commits adultery against her. Jude divorced his wife and remarried, so he is an adulterer.
   b. Many women want to serve as pastors, and since men are allowed to choose whatever career they want, women ought to be allowed to be pastors if they wish.
   c. The Gospel of Mark has many passages in common with Matthew and Luke, but it is shorter than these other two gospels. When two texts have passages in common, the shorter text is usually earlier, so Mark was probably written first.
   d. [It] not only teaches us how to think about values; it teaches us how to think. This book should be required reading in schools.

4. Read the following passages and answer the questions that follow:

> What does a Christian defend? . . . Jude 3 gives the answer to this question: We are to "contend for the faith which was once for all delivered to the saints." It is the truth contained in Scripture, "the faith" that we are to express and defend. . . .
>
> *But is it really necessary to defend Christianity?* If the gospel is the power of God unto salvation, who are we to seek to defend it? After all a lion does not need to be defended; it need only be released.[3]

   a. What is the function of the second paragraph in this argument, that is, what *part* of an argument does it constitute?

> The first challenge [to Christianity] was . . . to persuade the Jews that Jesus, who suffered an ignominious death, was the Messiah predicted by the Old Testament prophets. From the very first, the apostles proclaimed publicly that by raising Jesus from the dead, God had kept his promises to David (Acts 2:32–36 and 13:34). As Jesus explained to the travelers on the road to Emmaus, his sufferings were part of God's plan of glorifying his servant (Lk. 24:26–27). It was therefore necessary for the apostles to meet head on the offense associated with Christ's death on the cross. Paul responded by using the Old Testament idea of a curse resting on one who does not keep the law (compare Deut. 21:23 and 27:26 with Gal. 3:10, 13). In an argument reminiscent of the rabbinic style, he showed that Christ had to bear the curse of lawbreakers by dying on the cross.[4]

   b. If the claim at issue here is that Jesus was the Messiah, what fact, according to this passage, has been offered as a rebuttal?

   c. How can Paul's response be characterized using the terms introduced in this chapter?

> What does it mean to say that "God is"? What or who "is" God? If we want to answer this question legitimately and thoughtfully we cannot for a moment turn our thoughts anywhere else than to God's act in His revelation. So says Barth, and he surely has a point: to be thinking and talking about God at all already assumes a certain kind of God, namely one who has given himself in a revealing action. . . .
>
> These of course are the assertions and assumptions which determine that context of Christian theism in which we are operating. They are not necessary truths of mathematical and logical certainty, nor are they strictly deducible from experience.[5]

   d. What is the presumption with which all theology must begin, according to this passage?

   e. To which component of an argument is the second paragraph relevant?

---

[3]William Dyrness, *Christian Apologetics in a World Community* (Downers Grove, Ill.: InterVarsity Press, 1983), 19.

[4]Dyrness, *Christian Apologetics,* 24.

[5]Vernon White, *The Fall of a Sparrow* (Exeter, England: Paternoster Press, 1985), 22.

The issue itself is novel. In the Middle Ages, no one was expected to *become* a theist because of the authority of this or that account of a miracle. The authenticity of certain miracles came part and parcel with an entire network of beliefs and commitments not yet called into question. One became a theist as a matter of course. Latitudinarian theology, however, requires miracles as marks of revelation. Revelation itself is on the defensive, requiring certification by reason. Miracles become central when revelation becomes problematic.

Hume's essay "Of Miracles" belongs to this dialectical setting. As several commentators have pointed out, Hume makes no attempt to prove that miracles cannot occur. He is responding directly to latitudinarian claims. Latitudinarian theology appeals to miracles to solve a problem. Hume's point is that the solution does not work. He argues that "a miracle can never be proved, so as to be the foundation of a system of religion." The point is epistemological. We could never have *reason to believe* that a miracle has *probably* occurred.[6]

f. Using the concepts introduced in this chapter, how should belief in God during the Middle Ages be described?
g. By the time of the Latitudinarians, what has changed about the argument for the existence of God?
h. What grounds do the Latitudinarians offer for the claim that God has revealed himself?
i. What role does David Hume play in all of this?

[6]Jeffrey Stout, *The Flight from Authority: Religion Morality and the Quest for Autonomy* (Notre Dame, Ind.: University of Notre Dame Press, 1981), 118–19.

CHAPTER FOUR

Hypothetical Reasoning

1. An Analogy

Deductive reasoning might be compared to burying your money in the ground. It is safe and secure, but you never get out of it (the claim) any more than you put in (the grounds and warrant). Induction, then, is like lending at interest. You do get back (in the claim) more than you put in, but there is a risk involved. And the chance of being wrong (the risk) tends to vary with the amount of increase (the interest).

If we pursue this analogy, hypothetical reasoning—the topic of this chapter—is to inductive reasoning as investment is to lending at interest. To see why, let us first review what was said in chapter 3 about induction.

Induction is the process of reasoning by which we form generalizations based on a limited number of instances. For example, from a set of reports about a given number of red foxes we conclude that all foxes are red. We project our knowledge of the observed to the unobserved. But even so, we still have knowledge of nothing but foxes. This kind of reasoning is inadequate to account for our knowledge of the world around us. If scientific reasoning were limited to induction, we would have a collection of natural laws based on observed regularities but we would have no *theoretical* knowledge. And it is the theoretical knowledge that *explains* the regularities. So we have to have a form of reasoning that gives us a different kind of return on our money. This is just what we find with hypothetical reasoning.

Consider this example: you come home from work, find the front door ajar and muddy tracks leading into the kitchen. These are the facts or observations. You form a *hypothesis:* the kids are home. You haven't seen them, but you infer that they are there because their presence provides the best *explanation* of the facts you have observed.

Note the difference between hypothetical reasoning and induction. The latter would allow you to conclude something like the following: I see muddy tracks in the hall; I see muddy tracks in the kitchen. Probably there are muddy tracks in all the other rooms as well. Hypothetical reasoning is not aimed at knowledge of more tracks but at the cause of the tracks—the explanation of how they got there. To return to the analogy with which we began, hypothetical reasoning gives one a different *kind* of return on one's money.

2. Forming Hypotheses

So we can see why this kind of reasoning is called "hypothetical." We extend our knowledge by inventing hypotheses which, if true, would explain the observed facts. When we reason this way we are relying on a warrant that may be expressed as follows:

> *W:* One is entitled to infer the truth of the hypothesis that best explains a set of data (facts, observations).

We have a rough-and-ready sense of what it means to claim that a hypothesis explains a set of observations, but can we make this notion of explanation more precise? One suggestion: A hypothesis can be said to explain a set of observations if statements describing those observations can be inferred *deductively* from the hypothesis (or from the hypothesis along with other premises). As a matter of fact, many philosophers of science call this form of reasoning "hypothetico-deductive" to emphasize the role of deduction in relating an explanation to the facts it is supposed to explain.[1]

However, later philosophers of science recognized that the requirement of a *deductive* argument linking the hypothesis with its facts is too much to ask (and so we drop 'deductive' and refer to this form of reasoning simply as 'hypothetical reasoning'). In the language of this text, we might better say that a hypothesis H explains a set of observations O_1 through O_n if a good argument can be constructed with H as a part of the grounds or warrant and O_1 through O_n as its claim. So, while we cannot deduce the conclusion that the door will (*necessarily* or *certainly*) be left ajar and that there will be tracks in the kitchen from the hypothesis that the kids are home, we can make an argument to the effect that, given previous experiences of their carelessness about closing doors and the fact that the sidewalk is muddy, we have *good reason* to expect that their presence will lead to observations like the ones we have just noted.

So in its simplest form a hypothetical argument goes as follows, where O_1 through O_n represent a set of observations and H stands for our preferred hypothesis:

---

[1]The suggestion is Carl Hempel's. Although the form of reasoning we are discussing here has been recognized for a long time, it was Hempel who gave it the name 'hypothetico-deductive.' See his elegant exposition in *Philosophy of Natural Science* (Englewood Cliffs, N.J.: Prentice-Hall, 1966).

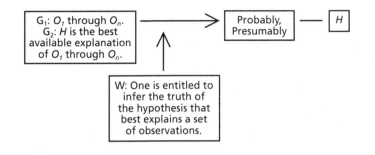

3. Confirming Hypotheses

Note the qualifiers in the schema above. We can never be certain of a conclusion based on hypothetical reasoning, because we can never be sure that there is no better explanation of the data than the one(s) we have considered. In the example above, it may turn out that the open door and muddy tracks were instead left by a prowler. Thus we ought always to bear in mind a potential rebuttal for any hypothetical argument:

> *R:* Unless some better explanation is found.

The number of competing hypotheses we can dream up to explain a set of facts is limited only by the failure of our imaginations. So the qualification that only our *best* explanation is warranted by hypothetical reasoning is an important one. What does it take to claim that one explanation is better than another? It must be shown to be *better confirmed* than its existing rivals. Let us look at a more complex example: the discovery by Ignaz Semmelweis of the cause of childbed fever.[2] The facts to be explained were statistics regarding the death rates for women in two different maternity wards in the Vienna General Hospital in the 1840s. In the First Maternity Division the death rate for 1844 was 8.2%; in 1845 it was 6.8%; and in 1846, 11.4%. For the same years in the Second Maternity Division the rates were 2.3%, 2.0%, and 2.7%.

Semmelweis began by considering various explanations that were current at the time. Some he rejected outright as incompatible with well-established facts; others he subjected to tests. One hypothesis was that overcrowding was the cause of death in the First Division. But this suggestion was rejected on the grounds that the Second Division was even more crowded.

A second suggestion was based on the fact that medical students practiced in the First Division, while midwives delivered the babies in the Second. The hypothesis was that the higher death rate in the First Division was due to injuries resulting from rough examinations by the medical students. Semmelweis rejected this hypothesis for three reasons: (1) injuries

---

[2]Described by Hempel in *Philosophy of Natural Science,* 3–6.

resulting from birth itself are more extensive than those caused by rough examinations; (2) the midwives examined their patients in the Second Division in much the same way; and (3) when examinations given by medical students were reduced in order to test the hypothesis, the number of deaths did not decline.

A third hypothesis was psychological, and was based on the fact that the priest who administered the last rites had to pass through the wards of the First Division but not the Second to reach dying patients. The appearance of the priest was thought to have a terrifying and debilitating effect on the patients. Semmelweis tested this hypothesis by persuading the priest to go by a different route so as not to be seen by the women in the First Division. However, the death rate did not drop.

Finally, an accident gave Semmelweis a clue for yet another hypothesis. A colleague received a wound in the hand from the scalpel of a student who was performing an autopsy and died after an illness closely resembling childbed fever. Semmelweis hypothesized that "cadaveric matter" from the scalpel caused the illness and that the same agent, from the hands of the medical students, caused childbed fever. He tested this hypothesis by requiring medical students to wash with a solution of chlorinated lime between autopsies and examinations of women giving birth. The death rate promptly fell to 1.27%.

This story nicely illustrates the process of testing competing hypotheses. One asks of each hypothesis, *if* it is true, *then* what other observable effects should follow from it? For example, if the hypothesis about the priest is true, then keeping him out of the wards should reduce the mortality rate. The further observations will either confirm or disconfirm the hypothesis.

So, in the process of reasoning, one begins with a set of observations (in our example, O_1 through O_6, representing the statistics from two maternity divisions over three years). One then formulates all the reasonable hypotheses (we mentioned four: H_1: overcrowding; H_2: rough examinations by medical students; H_3: fear of the priest; H_4: cadaveric material).

Next, one sees what further observable consequences follow from each hypothesis if it is true, and then one makes the observations or checks the facts. This often allows for the rejection of all but one hypothesis, which, having been confirmed by the additional evidence, can therefore be said to be the best available hypothesis. It is accepted, then, as *probably* true, pending further evidence or new and better hypotheses.

If more than one hypothesis passes the test of further observations, then there follows the difficult task of attempting to show that one hypothesis has more or stronger confirmation than the other. Much of the work of philosophers of science from the 1930s through the 1970s was dedicated to attempting to find a systematic way to make such assessments.

So in our general schema for a hypothetical argument, the statement that *H* is the best available hypothesis to explain the original set of observations is a *claim* based on a set of prior arguments. These arguments have to show that *H* has positive confirmation, while all of its known competitors are either falsified by further tests or else have less positive support than *H*.

The backing for the warrant in a hypothetical argument is simply *consistency*. We can use it in a particular instance because it serves us well in countless other arguments; to reject it in one case would require giving up a huge proportion of the rest of our body of accepted knowledge.

4. Examples from Theological Disciplines

Hypothetical reasoning has been named and studied by philosophers of science, but it plays an equally important role in most other disciplines. Let us look at two examples: one from biblical studies and one from systematic theology.

4.1. The Documentary Hypothesis

For many years both Jews and Christians believed Moses to be the author of the Pentateuch (the first five books of the Bible), despite the fact that the Pentateuch itself nowhere claims Moses as its author. However, in the sixteenth and seventeenth centuries scholars became increasingly aware of difficulties with this hypothesis:

> Mosaic . . . authorship of the Pentateuch came to be challenged on a number of grounds. (1) As anachronisms, scholars pointed to the account of Moses' death (Deut. 34), to the anachronistic reference to the city of Dan (Gen. 14:14; see Judg. 18:29), to Gen. 36:31, which assumes knowledge of the Hebrew monarchy, to references to Canaanites still in the land (Gen. 12:6; 13:7), to the Philistines (Gen. 21:34; 26:14–18; Ex. 13:17), and so on—all of which suggest a post-Mosaic date. (2) Multiple accounts of the same events were noted: Beersheba is so named on two occasions (Gen. 21:31; 26:33); reference to the naming of Bethel appears in two passages (Gen. 28:9; 35:15); Jacob's name is twice changed to Israel (Gen. 32:28; 35:10); on three occasions a patriarch passes off his wife as his sister (Gen. 12:10–20; 20; 26); and, in a span of nine verses, Moses is called to go up and goes up Mt. Sinai three times (Ex. 24:9–18) without ever coming down; and so forth. (3) Disagreements between narratives were frequently pointed out: the character and order of creation differ between Gen. 1:1–2:4a and 2:4b-25, the flood story contains contrary statements about the number of animals taken into the ark (compare Gen. 6:19–20 with 7:2,8–9), and so on. (4) Differences in the laws have been noted: Ex. 20:24 allows for altars to be built at every place God appoints, but Deut. 12:14 forbids altars except at a single and centralized sanctuary. Ex. 21:2–11 stipulates that female slaves are not to be released after six years, while Deut. 15:12 stipulates that they are to be. . . . (5) Some texts specify that God was known and worshiped by the name Yahweh from earliest times (see Gen. 4:26), while elsewhere it is claimed that this name was only revealed at the time of Moses (see Ex. 6:2–3). (6) Various differences in style and in the concept of God (compare Gen. 1:1–2:4a with 2:4b–25) have been noted as suggesting diversity of authorship.[3]

[3]John H. Hayes, *An Introduction to Old Testament Study* (Nashville: Abingdon, 1979), 158–59.

The hypothesis formulated to explain these observations is called the documentary hypothesis. At its simplest it states that these five books in their present form are the end product of the joining together and inter-weaving of four originally independent documents:

> The earliest of these documents, probably tenth century B.C., was the J docu-ment, emanating from southern Judean circles. E, a more or less parallel north-ern tradition, was dated some two centuries later. The legislative kernel of our present book of Deuteronomy, chapters 12–16, was the third, D, document. It had been the basis of an attempted radical religious reformation in Judah under King Josiah in the year 621 B.C. The fourth document was P, a priestly document of post-exilic date, probably fifth century B.C. D was the fixed chro-nological point in what is known as the Graf-Wellhausen hypothesis after two nineteenth-century German scholars who were largely responsible for its final formulation.[4]

The majority of scholars have accepted something like this hypothesis, some adding additional sources, some disagreeing about the probable dates of the composition of the original documents, some claiming that the original sources were oral rather than written traditions. However, the Mosaic hypothesis continues to be defended by some authors who attempt to explain its apparent disconfirmation by means of additional (auxiliary) hypotheses. For example:

> There are, of course, difficulties in the position that Moses himself wrote the Pentateuch. But these seem to be almost trifling when compared with the tremendous difficulties that emerge upon any alternate theory of composi-tion. There are, however, certain factors which have not received sufficient consideration.
>
> (i) For one thing, it is perfectly possible that in the compilation of the Pentateuch Moses may have made excerpts from previously existing written documents. If he did so, this fact may account for some of the alleged difficul-ties that appear. For example, it might *in certain cases* explain the use of the divine names in Genesis.
>
> (ii) On the other hand we must remember that the Bible, when considered in its human aspect, is an Oriental book. Now, parallels from antiquity show that the Oriental mind did not always present his material in the so-called logical order of the Occidental. The fact that the Pentateuch is, considered from the human side, a product of the Orient, may to some extent account for its form.[5]

Here we have a situation where there is a set of facts or observations about the texts of the Pentateuch, which the documentary hypothesis was formulated to explain—to suggest a reasonable means by which the texts could have come to exhibit these particular features. A variety of later refinements has been suggested. And while the Mosaic hypothesis is still seen as viable by some, its supporters recognize that additions have to be

[4]Robert Davidson, *Biblical Criticism*, vol. 3 of *The Pelican Guide to Modern Theology*, ed. R. P. C. Hanson (Harmondsworth, England: Penguin Books, 1970), 72–73. See Exercise 10, part 1, for a fuller account of the characteristics of the four documents.
[5]E. J. Young, *An Introduction to the Old Testament* (Grand Rapids: Eerdmans, 1949), 153.

made to account for the facts that led to the formulation of the documentary hypothesis.

What is not mentioned in the passages I have quoted is the reasoning that led scholars to believe that the relevant facts about the texts *follow from* the documentary hypothesis. We cannot go into all of these arguments here, but consider just one case, the duplications in the stories. The hypothesis here states that two narratives developed somewhat independently in the northern and southern kingdoms. It is assumed that if the editor who wove the two accounts together had great respect for the texts, he or she would not have felt free to discard passages that recorded identical or similar events. So, for example, if both accounts record the changing of Jacob's name, both accounts will have to be worked into the new narrative. Thus, from the hypothesis of two similar sources, by means of warrants describing how a faithful editor could be expected to do the work, we infer that duplications are to be expected in the text.

A complete account of the development of the documentary hypothesis would also include a survey of the way in which the theory has been confirmed by drawing further consequences from it and checking whether they fit the texts or not. In addition, archaeological data are important for confirming the hypothesized dates for the writing of the original sources.

4.2. The Resurrection of Jesus

In the following passage, Wolfhart Pannenberg argues that the most credible hypothesis to explain the accounts in scripture of Jesus' appearances after his crucifixion is that he did indeed rise from the dead.

> Since David Friedrich Strauss, repeated attempts have been made to explain the experiences of the resurrection appearances on the part of Jesus' disciples in terms of mental and historical presuppositions on the side of the disciples with the exclusion of the reality of the resurrection. These explanations have failed to date.
>
> To maintain, first, that the appearances were produced by the enthusiastically excited imagination of the disciples does not hold, at least for the first and most fundamental appearances. The Easter appearances are not to be explained from the Easter faith of the disciples; rather, conversely, the Easter faith of the disciples is to be explained from the appearances. All the attempted constructions as to how the faith of the disciples could have survived the crisis of Jesus' death remain problematic precisely in psychological terms, even when one takes into account the firm expectation of the imminent end of the world with which Jesus presumably died and in which his disciples lived. . . .
>
> Although the attempts at a purely psychological explanation of the Easter appearances as imaginations of the disciples thus fail, because, on the one hand positive points of contact for the application of the psychiatric concept of vision are lacking and, on the other, serious difficulties that argue against this are present in the tradition, the historian still remains obligated to reconstruct the historical correlation of the events that has led to the emergence of primitive Christianity. Certainly the possibilities that he can consider in this will depend upon the understanding of reality that he brings with him to the task. If the historian approaches his work with the conviction that "the dead do not rise," then it has already been decided that Jesus also has not risen (cf.

I Cor. 15:16). If, on the other hand, an element of truth is to be granted to the apocalyptic expectation with regard to the hope of resurrection, then the historian must also consider this possibility for the reconstruction of the course of events as long as no special circumstances in the tradition suggest another explanation. We have seen that the latter is not the case. Therefore, the possibility exists in reconstructing the course of events of speaking not only of visions of Jesus' disciples but also of appearances of the resurrected Jesus. In doing so, one speaks, then, just as the disciples themselves, in metaphorical language. However, that need not hinder us, just as it did not hinder them, from understanding the course of events with the help of what is designated by such language when other possibilities for explanation remain unsatisfactory.

Thus the resurrection of Jesus would be designated as a historical event in this sense: If the emergence of primitive Christianity, which, apart from other traditions, is also traced back by Paul to appearances of the resurrected Jesus, can be understood in spite of all critical examination of the tradition only if one examines it in the light of the eschatological hope for a resurrection from the dead, then that which is so designated is a historical event, even if we do not know anything more particular about it.[6]

In this passage Pannenberg is evaluating two hypotheses regarding the scriptural accounts of Jesus' appearances after his death. One widely accepted explanation is that the accounts merely record visions that the disciples experienced as a result of excitement—their "Easter faith." The more traditional hypothesis is, of course, that Jesus actually rose from the dead and appeared to the disciples. Pannenberg favors the latter hypothesis because, apart from the resurrection, there appears to be no way to account for the disciples' Easter faith. Only the resurrection, he says, can explain both the appearances and the excitement.

5. Argument from Analogy

Before concluding this chapter it is appropriate to mention another common form of reasoning used in science and elsewhere, and show how it can be understood using the model of reasoning presented in this text. In analogical reasoning we state or imply that two things, events, situations are similar and, furthermore, that one of these has a property (P). On the basis of these grounds we claim that the other will also have P.

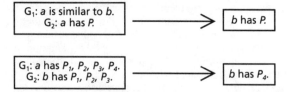

Or:

The assumed warrant in each case is something like the following:

W: Things that are similar in some respects may be expected to be similar in other respects.

[6]Wolfhart Pannenberg, *Jesus—God and Man*, trans. Lewis L. Wilkins and Duane Priebe (Philadelphia: Westminster, 1968), 95–98.

The backing for this warrant is experience in other cases.

As in the case of hypothetical reasoning, it is clear that analogical reasoning can only be *probable;* one never knows in advance how far the similarities will extend. So the way to rebut an argument from analogy is to provide a reason for thinking that one has in fact reached the limits of the similarity.

5.1. Models

Analogical reasoning is often used in science. When an analogy is used systematically to discover new properties of a thing being investigated we speak of the extended analogy as a *model*. Consider the following example:

> One of the classic models in the history of science is the so-called planetary model of atomic structure. This was the view that the atom could be conceived of rather as a miniature solar system, with a nucleus that was extremely heavy compared with the "planets" swinging around it (which correspond to the electrons). . . . Now it turned out that this way of thinking about the structure of the atom was able to account for a great many of the phenomena that were known to physics at the time it was most popular. Notice that nobody was suggesting that all the properties of the solar system were shared by the atom. For example, there was no suggestion that the planetary electrons had satellites. A nice feature of models, and of analogies in general, is that they often suggest further similarities which, on investigation, turn out not only to hold but also to explain some puzzling phenomenon. In this particular case, an experiment, known as the Stern-Gerlach experiment, produced results quite impossible to explain on any known model of the atom, including the simple planetary model. Then somebody thought of the fact that in the solar system, the planets not only revolve around the sun, but they also rotate about their own axes. Suppose that one was to postulate the same in the atom, that is, suppose that each electron had some spin as well as a rate of revolution about the central nucleus. This would clearly give the system dynamic properties different from one in which the electrons had no significant spin; for example, they would have a store of energy over and above the kinetic energy due to the rotation in orbit. Hence, the results of interactions between streams of bombarding particles—or strong magnetic fields—and atoms would be different. It turned out that this difference was just about right to explain the results of the Stern-Gerlach experiment.[7]

Note that in this case the model served as the source of a hypothesis (electron spin) that explained some observations. So hypothetical and analogical reasoning sometimes work together to produce some remarkable discoveries.

5.2. An Example from Biblical Studies

An interesting example of the use of models in biblical studies is the work of Bruce Malina, who employs sociological models developed by cultural

---

[7]Michael Scriven, *Reasoning* (New York: McGraw-Hill, 1976), 214.

anthropologists to better understand the Bible. These models describe typical symbolic systems found in Mediterranean cultures that shape speech and behavior. These symbolic systems are assumed to be similar to those of Jesus' day. For example, in a chapter describing cultures based on a system of honor and shame he states the following:

> Honor is always presumed to exist within one's own family of blood, i.e., among all those one has as blood relatives. A person can always trust his blood relatives. Outside that circle, all people are presumed to be dishonorable, guilty, if you will, unless proved otherwise. It is with all these others that one must play the game, engage in the contest, put one's own honor and one's family's honor on the line. Thus no one outside the family of blood can be trusted until and unless that trust can be validated and verified. So men of the same village or town who are not blood relatives relate to each other with an implied deep distrust which in practice prevents any effective form of cooperation. Strangers to the village, that is, people of the same cultural group but not resident in the same place, are looked upon as potential enemies, while foreigners, that is, those of other cultural groups just passing through, are considered certain enemies. Consequently, any interaction or conversation between two unrelated men or two unrelated women (the sexes usually don't mix) are engagements in which both sides probe for the least hint of the other's intentions or activities. Such interactions are not concerned with sociability, but rather are expressions of opposition and distance.[8]

This passage gives us the model we need to answer Malina's question why the interaction between Jesus and the Syrophoenician woman (in Mark 7:25ff.) takes the turn it does. The relevant passage is as follows:

> From there he set out and went away to the region of Tyre. He entered a house and did not want anyone to know he was there. Yet he could not escape notice, but a woman whose little daughter had an unclean spirit immediately heard about him, and she came and bowed down at his feet. Now the woman was a Gentile, of Syrophoenician origin. She begged him to cast the demon out of her daughter. He said to her, "Let the children be fed first, for it is not fair to take the children's food and throw it to the dogs." But she answered him, "Sir, even the dogs under the table eat the children's crumbs." Then he said to her, "For saying that, you may go—the demon has left your daughter." So she went home, found the child lying on the bed, and the demon gone. (Mark 7:24–30)

From the *analogy* with the behavior of other Mediterranean peoples we can draw a number of conclusions about this passage: Since the woman is not only from outside Jesus' family but also a foreigner, her approach to Jesus would at first be seen as a challenge, and she would be presumed to be untrustworthy. While bowing at Jesus' feet is a mark of respect adding to Jesus' honor, it apparently was not enough to satisfy him of her intentions. When Jesus' challenge to her (his implication that her people are dogs) was met not with anger but with submission Jesus had additional reason to conclude that her intentions were honorable. Her trustworthiness had been verified and he then treated her as an insider.

---

[8]Bruce Malina, *The New Testament World: Insights from Cultural Anthropology* (Atlanta: John Knox Press, 1981), 33.

So here the actions and words of Jesus and of the woman can serve as grounds. Claims can be made about the significance and motives of the words and actions. We can represent the arguments in either of two ways, as the following examples illustrate:

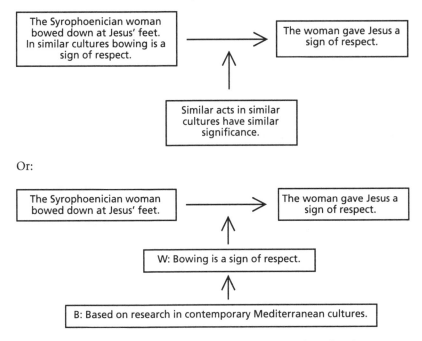

Or:

The question that might have come to mind in reading the above interpretation is: To what extent is Jesus a man of his culture? To what extent can we expect similarities to hold between his behavior and that of his contemporaries? This is a version of the question that must always be kept in mind when using analogical arguments: Do we have reason to believe that the similarities have come to an end at this point? One reason that might be cited in rebuttal of this interpretation is the evidence that a great deal of Jesus' teaching and behavior contradicts the cultural norms of his day. One example is the very fact that he was willing to engage in public conversation with a woman. Does Jesus reject the system of honor described by Malina, or does he merely redraw the boundaries of family?

6. Conclusion

The history of Western epistemology (theory of knowledge) might be described as the quest for a method of reasoning that assures certain knowledge. But philosophers have now come to the conclusion that there is no way to reason that both extends our knowledge and certifies the results. Deductive reasoning certifies our conclusions but offers no genuine extension of knowledge. Induction extends our knowledge from observed instances to the unobserved, but in this case we must forego certitude.

In this chapter we have looked at two other common sorts of reasoning that are valuable for extending knowledge: hypothetical and analogical reasoning. But again the results are never more than probable. Both forms of reasoning are backed by their success in other instances, but there are also instances in which they have led us astray.

It appears to be an inevitable part of the human condition to be wanting certain knowledge of everything, but to have to live with our fallibility. And there is, perhaps, no area of life wherein our fallibility is more of a worry to us than in the domain of theology and biblical studies.

EXERCISE FOUR

Read the following passages and answer the questions:

1. (1) By our actions we cause contingent events by bringing about conditions necessary for them which would otherwise be subject to chance. (2) But if human persons can intervene in the course of nature in this way, why cannot God do so as well? (3) Divine action in the world need therefore not take the form of miraculous intervention in violation of the natural order, any more than human action need do so.[9]

    a. What kind of reasoning is found in this passage?
    b. What role in the argument does 1 play?
    c. Rewrite 2 to make it suitable as one of the grounds for his argument.
    d. In which sentence is Brummer's claim found?
    e. There is a third ground implied in 3. Write it out.
    f. What is the warrant for this argument?

2. Perhaps the most famous exponent of the empirical argument for theism is Cambridge philosopher F. R. Tennant. . . . Tennant denied any possibility of religious knowledge except through the senses. . . . Nor can we base our faith on revelation alone. . . . We must be able to test all religious belief in some public way. . . .

    Tennant begins with the experience of everyday life, what he calls *presumptive knowledge*. From these raw data, he believes, ethics and religion can be abstracted; every perception has the promise of thought when it is clarified and explained. This process of clarification leads us from presumptive knowledge to larger and larger laws and hypotheses which account for the data of our experience. Tennant called this process "epigenesis."

    . . . According to Tennant, epigenesis is the only way to ground or support statements about God or the world. Thus we are driven by faith—the ineradicable effort of the will to carry verification to its conclusion—to suggest hypotheses that go beyond the data of our experience in order to account ultimately for that experience. . . .

    How can we establish the existence of God? Tennant bases his argument here on the "conspiration of innumerable causes to produce, by their united and reciprocal action, and to maintain, a general order of nature." This order,

[9]Vincent Brummer, *What Are We Doing When We Pray?* (London: SCM Press, 1984); quoted by A. R. Peacocke in *Theology for a Scientific Age* (Oxford: Basil Blackwell, 1990), 150.

which he calls "cosmic teleology," cannot be explained by chance. "The multitude of interwoven adaptations by which the world is constituted a theatre of life, intelligence, and morality, cannot reasonably be regarded as an outcome of mechanism, or of blind formative power, or of ought but purposive intelligence. . . ."

In his semi-popular book *The Nature of Belief,* Tennant adds another element worth noting: he argues that faith can be pragmatically verified. Just as the truth of a scientific hypothesis is verified by appeal to external facts, so faith is verified by its fruitfulness in practical life.[10]

    a. What term is used in this chapter for what Tennant calls "epigenesis"?

    b. What is the source of the facts Tennant claims are the only grounds for theistic arguments?

    c. Upon what, in particular, does Tennant base his argument for the existence of God?

    d. Diagram Tennant's argument for the existence of God.

    e. What hypotheses are being rejected by Tennant?

    f. What kind of facts provide additional confirmation for the hypothesis of God's existence?

3.   Different codes of conduct are appropriate to the successive stages of this process. Whenever men have employed some degree of moral criticism in reading the Scriptures of the Old Testament, some have been perplexed to read (for example) that God commanded Jehu to entrap and slaughter "all the prophets of Baal, all his worshippers, and all his priests" (II Kings 10:18–28). Our grandfathers dealt with this perplexity by explaining that God indeed is unchanging, but man's understanding of Him grows from stage to stage; the divine commands in the Old Testament which shock our consciences were all that men could understand of His will for them. To us it seems more adequate to say that God is indeed unchanging, and always wills the truest welfare of all His children; but at a certain stage of their development it is good for them to do and to suffer what at a later stage would no longer be good for them. Therefore, being then as always Holy Love, He may have chosen for the worshippers of Baal that they should be slain and for Jehu that he should slay them, even by treachery, because only by such means would Israel be turned from a religion that for them, at any rate, was worse than none, and only so could Jehu express and fortify such faith in the God of Righteousness as his gross nature was capable of holding.[11]

    a. What is the fact to be explained here?

    b. What hypothesis does Temple explicitly reject?

    c. What is Temple's own hypothesis?

    d. There is a simpler explanation of the facts in question that is not discussed explicitly, but both positions (Temple's and his predecessors') are clearly formulated to evade this consequence. What is it?

[10]William Dyrness, *Christian Apologetics in a World Community* (Downers Grove, Ill.: InterVarsity Press, 1983), 54–56.

[11]William Temple, *Nature, Man and God* (London: Macmillan, 1956), 187–88.

4. The majority of modern scholars think that Mark was the first gospel, that Matthew and Luke used Mark or something like it, and that since Matthew and Luke were not known to each other, the non-Markan passages in Matthew and Luke which have approximately the same wording come from a lost source. This source is designated Q, perhaps from the German word *Quelle*, "source." . . . The material assigned to Q is distributed differently in Matthew and Luke, but it falls in about the same order, Luke usually preserving both content and order slightly better. There are some minor disagreements about the exact extent of Q, especially in passages where the verbal agreement between Matthew and Luke is less precise or where Q seems to overlap with Mark, but scholars can usually account for the former problem in terms of the evangelists' editorial changes and the latter phenomenon by proposing that they shared common oral tradition. Thus, the problems are not insurmountable to those who hold the hypothesis; in fact, the agreement and similarity in language between Matthew and Luke in most passages is so clear that scholars are led to the conclusion that the source as it came to Matthew and Luke was written, not oral, and written in the Greek language, not Aramaic. In terms of quantity, Q material makes up about one-third of Matthew and about one-fourth of Luke.

There is no absolutely certain way to date Q, other than to say that it was put in writing before Matthew and Luke used it. Yet, because of its apocalyptic orientation, and the almost unanimous belief that it ultimately emanates from a type of early Jewish apocalyptic Christianity found in Palestine or southern Syria, most judge it to have been written within the first two generations after the death of Jesus. There is also no way to determine any individual who put Q into writing. In short, whatever is said about Q and the type of Christian community it represents must be said on the basis of internal analysis of the material.[12]

a. What is the main hypothesis being discussed here?
b. What are the facts or observations to be explained?
c. Diagram the main hypothetical argument discussed in the passage.
d. In the argument *from H to O* (that is, the argument to show that *H* explains *O*), what warrant is assumed? (Note, this question may seem difficult because the answer will appear too simple to be worth stating.)
e. What independent confirmation for *H* does this passage describe (if any)?
f. What possible disconfirming evidence is mentioned?
g. Diagram the argument for the further hypothesis (*H₂*) that Q was written, not oral, and that it was written in Greek rather than Aramaic.
h. What warrants are assumed in the argument *from H₂ to* the observation it explains?

---

[12]Norman Perrin and Dennis C. Duling, *The New Testament: An Introduction*, 2d ed. (New York: Harcourt, Brace Jovanovich, 1982), 100.

CHAPTER FIVE

Rhetoric and Communication

1. Introduction

The title of this book, *Reasoning and Rhetoric in Religion,* employs two rhetorical devices. The use of words beginning with the same sound is called *alliteration.* The ambiguous use of 'rhetoric' is an instance of *syllepsis,* which is defined as "the use of a word understood differently in relation to two or more other words."[1] The intention in using these devices is, in both cases, to catch the reader's (or bookstore browser's) attention. Alliteration does so, one presumes, because we, as much as children, enjoy playful sounds. Perhaps, also, because the concurrence of three words beginning with the same letter is unusual. We have twenty-six letters in our alphabet; the probability of getting three such words in a row merely by chance is once in 676 combinations ($1/26^2$).[2]

The deliberate ambiguity, however, is probably more effective in attracting attention. We use the word 'rhetoric' in two senses. One is to refer to the study or theory of persuasive communication. In its other sense it is a pejorative word used to refer to communication that trades on emotional appeal (and perhaps deception) in the absence of serious reasoning. So when 'rhetoric' is paired with 'reasoning' it is likely to be read in the first way. But when paired with 'religion' it has emotional appeal, since many a reader would like to see an exposé of the abuses of language perpetrated by pulpiteers. Sorry—this chapter is about communication theory.

The fact that the title of a book serves a wider purpose than that of a mere label for what is inside—that it is intended to appeal to the reader's

[1]Edward P. J. Corbett, *Classical Rhetoric for the Modern Student,* 3d ed. (New York: Oxford University Press, 1990), 448.

[2]Actually, this statement is false. It assumes that first letters are evenly distributed among the possibilities provided by our alphabet. A look at the dictionary shows that some letters (such as *s* and *p*) occur much more often at the beginning of words than others (*q* and *z*).

Catching authors who lie with statistics is a widely recognized part of practical reasoning. However, since theologians have not yet become adept at this, we omit consideration of it here.

interests and emotions—nicely illustrates why a book on reasoning does well to include at least one chapter on rhetoric. Reasoning is but one aspect of communication. Other goals and methods of communication interact with the goal of rational persuasion by means of sound argument. So in this chapter we survey some of the history of rhetoric and see, as we go along, the ways reasoning fits into the broader task of communication, and also how rhetorical devices figure into the making of arguments.

2. The Rhetorical Theory of Classical Greece

Corax, of the city of Syracuse, is credited as the founder of the art or science of rhetoric; he wrote the first rhetoric text in the fifth century B.C. Corax's instruction was aimed at helping citizens of a newly established democracy plead their claims in court. An important contribution to later theories was a formula for the parts of a judicial oration: proem (introduction), narration (statement of the facts of the case), arguments (for one's own case and against the opponent), and peroration (conclusion). This plan for the structure of a legal discourse has since been applied to persuasive speech and writing of all kinds. Already we see a sense in which reasoning (arguments) can be described as but a part of the more general task of communication.

2.1. Aristotle

The philosopher Aristotle has been one of the most important contributors to the field of rhetoric. Aristotle defined rhetoric as "the faculty of discovering in every case the available means of persuasion."[3] There are three such means, called *logos, ethos,* and *pathos.*

2.1.1. Logos

'Logos' refers to the appeal to reason, and so would encompass all that we have covered so far in this volume. Aristotle may have been the first to devise a theory of reasoning, and while his account of reasoning is different from that presented here, we are all much indebted to his work. Aristotle sought to formulate a theory of deductive or demonstrative reasoning—that in which the truth of the premises (grounds and warrant) insures the truth of the conclusion.[4] However, an important aspect of his rhetorical theory was based on the recognition that most of the matters about which people argue are not the sort where demonstrative proof is possible; we must deal in probabilities. Since only strict proofs are rationally *compelling*[5] we need to

---

[3]See *The Rhetoric of Aristotle: A Translation* (Cambridge: Cambridge University Press, 1909), 5. Quoted in J. Golden, G. F. Berquist, and W. E. Coleman, *The Rhetoric of Western Thought,* 4th ed. (Dubuque, Iowa: Kendall/Hunt, 1978), 31.

[4]See "Inductive and Deductive Reasoning," in chapter 3, sec. 1.1.

[5]And some would say that even here there is no rational compulsion; one can always conclude that the argument shows instead that one of the premises must be false since taken together they lead to a false conclusion. We call an argument of this sort a *reductio ad absurdum.* See "Arguments" (chap. 7, sec. 3.1) for a definition and "Anselm's Ontological Argument" (chap. 13, sec. 2.1.1) for an example.

take into consideration, in practical reasoning, nonlogical factors that contribute to our case. And so it makes sense to consider issues such as the arrangement or order of presentation of our arguments as well as their strength, grounding, and so forth.

Aristotle's theory of demonstrative reasoning describes the syllogism in its several forms and distinguishes valid inferences from invalid or fallacious forms. For example:

All As are Bs
x is an A
_____
Therefore, x is a B. (valid)

All As are Bs
x is a B
_____
Therefore, x is an A. (invalid)

Students hunting for arguments in the texts they read might have noticed that most arguments of this sort omit one of the premises, most often the general statement or warrant. Recognizing this, Aristotle provides us with the term 'enthymeme' to refer to the nearest thing we find to a syllogism in practical reasoning. An enthymeme differs from a syllogism, first, in that its general statement warrants only a probable conclusion and, second, in that the most obvious of the two premises is usually unstated. For example:

John must be a communist because he advocates civil rights for minority groups.

The missing premise here is the warrant: Those who advocate civil rights for minority groups are communists.

Notice that we can make a full-fledged syllogism out of this argument by specifying that *all* who advocate civil rights for minority groups are communists. What we gain in logical rigor, though, we lose in credibility of the warrant. While it *may* be true that *some* who advocate civil rights for minority groups are communists, few will believe that the universal generalization holds. So in making or reconstructing an argument, there is often a tradeoff between the strength of the argument as a whole and the truth of its warrant. Our recommendation is to aim for truthful premises and acknowledge the consequent weakness with an appropriate qualifier.

Note also that we can reconstruct the above enthymeme as an *invalid* argument by supplying the following warrant:

All communists advocate civil rights for minorities.[6]

[6]This fallacy, by the way, is called the fallacy of affirming the consequent. Most reasoning texts include a section on fallacies and require students to learn them by name. This text omits such an exercise, first, because in practical reasoning (as opposed to formal logic) there is no sharp distinction between a valid and an invalid argument; most are, as Aristotle notes, merely probable, and can more usefully be classed as better or worse, weaker or stronger. Second, having worked through the preceding chapters, students already have the basic knowledge they need for assessing the worth of arguments.

Charity, however, recommends construing an author's argument in the best form possible.

Aristotle's discussion of the sources of premises for enthymemes provides additional insight into the nature and sources of warrants. One category of such premises he labels "probability," the other "signs." Probabilities are general statements that are generally true and contain a causal element; for example, 'Children tend to love their parents.' A sign is an indication or concomitant of something else; for example, 'Where there is smoke there is fire.' Signs can be either fallible or infallible. Hearing thunder is an infallible sign that there has been lightning; seeing a red sunrise is a fallible sign of windy weather.

The second major form of reasoning discussed in Aristotle's *Rhetoric* is reasoning from examples. It can be said that, in rhetoric, example is to inductive reasoning as enthymeme is to deductive. An orator has not the time, nor an audience the patience, to examine all known instances that support a generalization, so one or several instances must be selected and described. The following excerpt from the Letter to the Hebrews illustrates the rhetorical use of example. The author is actually arguing for (at least) two claims in this passage. One is about the nature of faith; the other is about God's approval of the faithful.

> Now faith is the assurance of things hoped for, the conviction of things not seen. Indeed, by faith our ancestors received approval. . . .
>
> By faith Abel offered to God a more acceptable sacrifice than Cain's. Through this he received approval as righteous, God himself giving approval to his gifts; he died, but through his faith he still speaks. By faith Enoch was taken so that he did not experience death; and "he was not found, because God had taken him." For it was attested before he was taken away that "he had pleased God." . . .
>
> By faith Abraham obeyed when he was called to set out for a place that he was to receive as an inheritance; and he set out, not knowing where he was going. By faith he stayed for a time in the land he had been promised, as in a foreign land, living in tents, as did Isaac and Jacob, who were heirs with him of the same promise. For he looked forward to the city that has foundations, whose architect and builder is God. By faith he received power of procreation, even though he was too old—and Sarah herself was barren—because he considered him faithful who had promised. Therefore from one person, and this one as good as dead, descendants were born, "as many as the stars of heaven and as the innumerable grains of sand by the seashore."
>
> All of these died in faith without having received the promises, but from a distance they saw and greeted them. (Heb. 11:1–2, 4–5, 8–13)

An argument from example is a fairly weak sort of argument, since induction at its best, with a large number of instances handled with statistical sophistication, still yields only probable results. Here the sample of instances is reduced to one or a few, and there is always the threat of a rebutting counterexample. When conflicting examples have been adduced, the issue must be decided on the basis of the relative impressiveness and pertinence of the conflicting examples, the availability of other arguments for one side or the other, and upon Aristotle's two remaining means of persuasion, to which we now turn.

2.1.2. Ethos

According to Aristotle, ethical appeal is exerted when the speech convinces the audience that the speaker is a person of good sense, high moral character, and benevolence. The reasons for attention to ethos are easy to imagine. We will not be convinced by the words of speakers whom we suppose either to be easily deceived themselves or whom we suspect of wanting to deceive us, either because of lack of concern for the truth or because they bear us ill will.

A common place to find statements intended for ethical appeal is the introduction. Paradoxically, speakers often begin with self-deprecating remarks, on the assumption that a person of sound judgment and good character is not boastful or self-deceived.

We can now see the rationale for suggestions made elsewhere in this text that a good argument will not overstate its claim. Whenever it is obvious to an audience that too much is being claimed (for example, by means of an unsupportable universal generalization in the warrant or by means of an overly strong qualifier), it will cast doubt either on the speaker's good sense or integrity.

How do speakers convince their audiences that they are people of good sense, high moral character, and benevolence? Edward Corbett offers the following suggestions:

> If a discourse is to exhibit a person's good sense, it must show that the speaker or writer has an adequate, if not a professionally erudite, grasp of the subject being talked about, that the speaker or writer knows and observes the principles of valid reasoning, is capable of viewing a situation in the proper perspective, has read widely, and has good taste and discriminating judgment. If a discourse is to reflect a person's moral character, it must display an abhorrence of unscrupulous tactics and specious reasoning, a respect for the commonly acknowledged virtues, and an adamant integrity. If the discourse is to manifest a person's good will, it must display a person's sincere interest in the welfare of the audience and a readiness to sacrifice any self-aggrandizement that conflicts with the benefit of others.[7]

It is difficult to think of anyone who is more adept at ethical appeal than Paul, as in the following passage from 1 Thessalonians:

> You yourselves know, brothers and sisters, that our coming to you was not in vain, but though we had already suffered and been shamefully mistreated at Philippi, as you know, we had courage in our God to declare to you the gospel of God in spite of great opposition. For our appeal does not spring from deceit or impure motives or trickery, but just as we have been approved by God to be entrusted with the message of the gospel, even so we speak, not to please mortals, but to please God who tests our hearts. As you know and as God is our witness, we never came with words of flattery or with a pretext for greed; nor did we seek praise from mortals, whether from you or from others, though we might have made demands as apostles of Christ. But we were gentle among you, like a nurse tenderly caring for her own children. So deeply do we care for you that we are determined to share with you not only the gospel of God

---

[7]Corbett, *Classical Rhetoric*, 81.

but also our own selves, because you have become very dear to us. (1 Thess. 2:1–8)

Here Paul is very explicit about not using unscrupulous tactics: no deceit, trickery, flattery. The virtue Paul emphasizes is courage, understood as the willingness to suffer in the course of doing what is right. His integrity is indicated by his claim to pure motives: to please God, not mortals.

Paul's sincere interest in the welfare of his audience is implied in his willingness to share the gospel with them despite great opposition, and in his reminder of the apostles' gentle care. He ends this passage with a direct statement of good will toward the audience.

Paul does not make any claims of the sort we often expect regarding his good sense. However, the Greek word used by Aristotle, *'phronēsis,'* might better be translated as wisdom, and we know from Paul's other writings (for example, 1 Cor. 2:6–16) that true wisdom comes not from what the world thinks of as good sense, but rather from God's revelation. Thus when Paul notes that he has been approved by God to be entrusted with the message of the gospel he has made the strongest possible case for his "good sense."

2.1.3. Pathos

The third of Aristotle's three means of persuasion is the appeal to the audience's emotions. This is done primarily by describing something to which the audience will naturally have an emotional reaction. Often this calls upon the speaker's ability to appeal to the imagination by the use of descriptive, sensory language.

It might be objected that appeal to the emotions is unworthy of the rational beings that we aspire to be. Nonetheless, some emotional appeals have been recognized as among our culture's finest pieces of rhetoric. It may help to note that styles vary from one period to another—not only in attitudes toward the use of pathos in speaking and writing, but toward the emotions themselves.

It may also help in understanding the proper role of pathos to distinguish among different kinds of speeches (or written arguments) and the purposes they intend to serve. The Greeks recognized three types: (1) Forensic oratory is that of the courtroom, intended to convince a judge or jury. (2) Deliberative oratory finds its occasion in politics and aims at decision-making for the future. (3) Epideictic oratory regards praise or blame, and often occurs at ceremonial occasions. We might add to this list, (4) scholarly discourse, whose occasion is the professional society meeting or the lecture hall.

It seems clear that pathos is more appropriate in some of these forms of discourse than others. It is widely accepted in epideictic oratory (consider a nomination speech for a political candidate); it is also an acceptable part of courtroom arguments, where it might be seen as an attempt to overcome bias or indifference that would otherwise interfere with proper judgment. Some might think that while pathos has a reputable role to play in deliberative discourse, it tends to be overused and abused in contemporary politics. Current consensus seems to be that pathos is entirely out of place in scholarly discourse. However, it would be good to bear in mind that it nonetheless occurs.

One of the emotions Aristotle defined was shame: a pain or trouble about those ills, present, past, or future, which seem to tend toward ignominy.[8] In the passage below (an example of epideictic oratory) Jeremiah uses the vivid image of a whore to shame Israel and to attempt to persuade the Israelites to repent.

> The LORD said to me in the days of King Josiah: Have you seen what she did, that faithless one, Israel, how she went up on every high hill and under every green tree, and played the whore there? And I thought, "After she has done all this she will return to me"; but she did not return, and her false sister Judah saw it. She saw that for all the adulteries of that faithless one, Israel, I had sent her away with a decree of divorce; yet her false sister Judah did not fear, but she too went and played the whore. Because she took whoredom so lightly, she polluted the land, committing adultery with stone and tree. Yet for all this her false sister Judah did not return to me with her whole heart, but only in pretense, says the LORD.
>
> Then the LORD said to me: Faithless Israel has shown herself less guilty than false Judah. Go, and proclaim these words toward the north, and say:
>
> Return, faithless Israel, says the LORD.
>
> I will not look on you in anger, for I am merciful, says the LORD;
>
> I will not be angry forever. (Jer. 3:6–12)

2.2. Quintilian and the Five Canons of Rhetoric

By the beginning of the Christian era Greek rhetoric had been amplified by Roman orators. An important contributor to the theory of rhetoric was Quintilian, born in Spain c. 35 A.D. In Quintilian's text, *Institutio Oratoria*, the task of the orator was divided into five parts, called the five canons of rhetoric: *inventio* (invention or discovery), *dispositio* (disposition, arrangement), *elocutio* (style), *memoria* (memory), and *pronunciato* (delivery). We examine the first three of these below. Memory and delivery will not concern us here.[9]

2.2.1. Invention

The subject discussed under this canon is the means for discovering pertinent arguments for the case one intends to make. The knowledge needed for this task, then, includes all that we have discussed above under the heading of Aristotle's three means of persuasion. This part of rhetoric involves gathering information and constructing arguments that the information makes possible.

---

[8]Golden et al., *The Rhetoric of Western Thought*, 38.

[9]Except to note that knowledge of *memoria* is sometimes useful for biblical interpretation, since much of what we find in the Bible began as oral tradition. Recognition of mnemonic devices helps piece together the history of the text.

For guidance in gathering information and thinking of pertinent lines of argument, Quintilian and others discussed the *topoi* (topics)—general headings or lines of questioning that suggested materials from which arguments for the case at hand could be constructed. So, for instance, in constructing arguments for a case in court (forensic oratory), one asks questions about things, actions, persons, motives, means, and time. Answers to these questions provide the material from which arguments can be constructed.

Quintilian believed that ethical appeal required not the assembling of material that would cast favorable light on the orator; rather, the orator must *be* an ethical person. Training and practice in the virtues was a prerequisite to any good speaking. The role of pathos was to keep the audience's attention, and so, for instance, it was appropriate to assemble humorous materials. "There are three things out of which we may seek to raise a laugh," said Quintilian, "others, ourselves, or things intermediate."[10]

2.2.2. Disposition

The Roman rhetoricians expanded Corax's list of the parts of an oration to five, adding a separate section for "refutation," that is, for rebutting the arguments on the other side. The questions to which Quintilian gave attention here included the following: When is an introduction necessary and when can it be omitted or abbreviated? When should the statement of facts be continuous, and when should they be distributed throughout the discourse? Or can the statement of facts be omitted altogether? When should one begin with the arguments of the opponents, and when should one begin with one's own arguments? Should the strongest arguments be presented first or last? How much ethical appeal must be exerted to conciliate the audience? Should the emotional appeals be reserved for the conclusion or distributed throughout? What evidence or documents should be used and where in the discourse will this kind of argument be most effective?[11]

2.2.3. Style

Style is a difficult concept to define, but all might agree to the minimal definition that associates it with the choice and arrangement of words. Quintilian claimed that there are three general styles, each suited to a particular purpose: the plain style for instruction, the middle style for moving people to action, and the high style for charming or delighting the audience.

A major topic addressed under the heading of style is figures of speech. A figure, according to Quintilian, is "any deviation, either in thought or expression, from the ordinary and simple method of speaking, a change analogous to the different positions our bodies assume when we sit down, lie down, or look back. . . . Let the definition of a figure, therefore, be *a*

---

[10]Quoted in Golden et al., *The Rhetoric of Western Thought*, 61.
[11]See Corbett, *Classical Rhetoric*, 280–81.

form of speech artfully varied from common usage."[12] Figures are not mere dressing for what could otherwise be said equally well without them. According to Quintilian, they are another means of lending credibility to arguments, exciting emotion, and winning approval of our character.

Figures can be divided into two classes, *schemes* and *tropes*. Schemes have to do with the arrangement of words; for example, deviation from the usual pattern of word order. Tropes involve deviation from the ordinary meaning or reference of words. Some of the more common schemes are the following:

1. *Parallelism:* similar grammatical structures to highlight similar ideas.
2. *Antithesis:* the juxtaposition of contrasting ideas, often in parallel structure.
3. *Anastrophe:* inversion of the natural or usual word order.
4. *Parenthesis:* insertion of a verbal unit in a position that interrupts the normal syntactical form of a sentence.
5. *Ellipsis:* deliberate omission of words implied by the context.
6. *Alliteration:* repetition of initial or medial consonants in two or more adjacent words.
7. *Anaphora:* repetition of the same word or group of words at the beginning of successive clauses.
8. *Anadiplosis:* repetition of the last word of one clause at the beginning of the following clause.
9. *Climax:* arrangement of words, phrases, or clauses in an order of increasing importance.
10. *Polyptoton:* repetition of words derived from the same root.

Modern rhetoricians have classified and named a vast number of tropes but, again, we mention only a few:

1. *Metaphor:* an implied comparison between two things of unlike nature that yet have something in common.
2. *Simile:* an explicit comparison between unlike things.
3. *Synecdoche:* a figure in which a part stands for the whole.
4. *Antanaclasis:* a pun in which the same word is repeated, but used in two different senses.
5. *Syllepsis:* a pun in which a single word is understood differently in relation to two or more other words that it modifies or governs.
6 *Anthimeria:* the substitution of one part of speech for another.
7 *Periphrasis:* the substitution of a descriptive word or phrase for a proper name or of a proper name for a quality associated with the name.
8. *Personification:* investing abstractions or inanimate objects with human qualities.
9. *Hyperbole:* the use of exaggerated terms for emphasis or heightened effect.
10. *Litotes:* deliberate use of understatement.
11. *Rhetorical question:* asking a question for the purpose of asserting or denying something obliquely.
12. *Irony:* use of a word in such a way as to convey meaning opposite to

[12]*Institutio Oratoria,* 9.1.2. Quoted in Corbett, *Classical Rhetoric,* 425.

the literal meaning of the word.

13. *Paradox:* an apparently contradictory statement that nevertheless contains a measure of truth.[13]

The usefulness of figures for emphasis and emotional appeal cannot be gainsaid. What may be a more startling claim is Quintilian's suggestion that they also serve to lend credibility to arguments. One might go even further and suggest that they sometimes *make* the argument. To see this, compare Jesus' style of argument as represented in the synoptic Gospels with Paul's. Paul's letters contain some figurative language as well as a number of straightforward arguments. Jesus, in contrast, makes most of his important claims by means of figures. Consider, for example, his reply to the question about paying taxes to Caesar:

> "Why put me to the test? Bring me a coin and let me look at it." And they brought one. And he said to them, "Whose likeness and inscription is this?" They said to him, "Caesar's." Jesus said to them, "Render to Caesar the things that are Caesar's, and to God the things that are God's." And they were amazed at him. (Mark 12:15b–17, RSV; cf. Matt. 22:15–22; Luke 20:20–26)

This passage contains all we need to make out Jesus' argument:

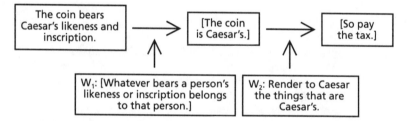

The grounds are provided by Jesus' interlocutor. All Jesus needs to supply to make the argument is the second warrant, since the rest (in brackets) can be filled in from the context. It would have been clear to the original readers, by the way, that the coin, a denarius, was the amount of the tax in question.

The interesting aspect of the argument is the use of *parallelism* and *climax* in Jesus' statement: "and to God the things that are God's." This figure requires the reader to inquire about the more important argument that goes with the parallel warrant. What, exactly, is God's? Is it whatever bears God's likeness? However one fills in the details, it is clear that Jesus' central claim here, as in all his teaching, is about *God's* claims upon *us* (calling into question, by the way, any slavish obedience to Caesar), and his argument is made entirely by means of the figures.

Some of Jesus' most characteristic teaching is found in the parables. A parable is an extended *metaphor* or *simile*. Let us look at the parable of the unforgiving servant:

---

[13]See Corbett, *Classical Rhetoric,* for a more detailed list of figures and for examples of the figures defined here.

For this reason the kingdom of heaven may be compared to a king who wished to settle accounts with his slaves. When he began the reckoning, one who owed him ten thousand talents was brought to him; and, as he could not pay, his lord ordered him to be sold, together with his wife and children and all his possessions, and payment to be made. So the slave fell on his knees before him, saying, "have patience with me, and I will pay you everything." And out of pity for him, the lord of that slave released him and forgave him the debt. But that same slave, as he went out, came upon one of his fellow slaves who owed him a hundred denarii; and seizing him by the throat, he said, "Pay what you owe." Then his fellow slave fell down and pleaded with him, "Have patience with me, and I will pay you." But he refused; then he went and threw him into prison until he would pay the debt. When his fellow slaves saw what had happened, they were greatly distressed, and they went and reported to their lord all that had taken place. Then his lord summoned him and said to him, "You wicked slave! I forgave you all that debt because you pleaded with me. Should you not have had mercy on your fellow slave, as I had mercy on you?" And in anger his lord handed him over to be tortured until he would pay his entire debt. So my heavenly Father will also do to everyone of you, if you do not forgive your brother or sister from your heart. (Matt. 18:23–35)

While one hesitates to state *the* meaning of one of Jesus' parables, it is probably fair to say that at least one of its points can be represented by the following, very simple, argument:

Neither the grounds nor the claim is stated. What we do have, I suggest, is a story that serves as the warrant for this argument. We are presented with an analogy: slaves and their monetary debts compared to Christians and their sins. Our outrage at the unforgiving slave is transferred to ourselves when we think of God's forgiveness of our sins. A great deal of the story's effectiveness comes from its sensuous language; it is concrete and appeals to the imagination. Figural elements also add to the impact; for example, the exact repetition of the two slaves' pleas for mercy draws attention to the similarity of the two situations and sets the reader up to be surprised by the different responses.

So once again we see that figures play an essential role in persuasion—even making up parts of arguments.

3. Conclusion

Rhetoric is a discipline that has been in and out of fashion over the past 2,500 years. Perhaps there is a cycle: the theory of persuasive discourse is widely taught and studied; style disintegrates to the point where it becomes mere decoration, and rhetoric is used for persuasion without regard for truth; rhetoricians come to be held in disrepute; and then the principles of rhetoric must be rediscovered by a new generation.

However well or badly rhetorical theory fares in academia, it is clear that practical reasoning needs to be understood within the broader context of communication. Argument is but a part of persuasive discourse.

And sometimes, as we have seen in the case of Jesus' teaching, arguments themselves cannot be understood without an appreciation for the linguistic devices that are the province of rhetorical theory.

EXERCISE FIVE

1. To which of Aristotle's three categories of persuasion does each of the following belong?

   a. I urge you, brothers and sisters, to keep an eye on those who cause dissensions and offenses, in opposition to the teaching that you have learned; avoid them. For such people do not serve our Lord Christ but their own appetites. (Rom. 16:17–18)

   b. I think that I am not in the least inferior to these super-apostles. I may be untrained in speech, but not in knowledge; certainly in every way and in all things we have made this evident to you.

   Did I commit a sin by humbling myself so that you might be exalted, because I proclaimed God's good news to you free of charge? I robbed other churches by accepting support from them in order to serve you. . . . As the truth of Christ is in me, this boast of mine will not be silenced in the regions of Achaia. And why? Because I do not love you? God knows I do! (2 Cor. 11:5–8, 10–11)

   c. You know the insults I receive, and my shame and dishonor; my foes are all known to you. Insults have broken my heart so that I am in despair. I looked for pity, but there was none; and for comforters, but I found none. They gave me poison for food, and for my thirst they gave me vinegar to drink.

   Let their table be a trap for them, and a snare for their allies. . . .

   Pour out your indignation upon them, and let your burning anger overtake them. (Ps. 69:19–22, 24)

2. Identify the most prominent figure in each of the following (choose the *best* answer):

   a. And not only that, but we boast in our sufferings, knowing that suffering produces endurance, and endurance produces character, and character produces hope, and hope does not disappoint us because God's love has been poured into our hearts through the Holy Spirit that has been given to us. (Rom. 5:3–5) *(anadiplosis, anaphora, parallelism)*

   b. Therefore just as one man's trespass led to condemnation for all, so one man's act of righteousness leads to justification and life for all. (Rom. 5:18) *(antithesis, irony, simile)*

   c. We know that Christ, being raised from the dead, will never die again; death no longer has dominion over him. The death that he died, he died to sin, once for all; but the life that he lives, he lives to God. So you also must consider yourselves dead to sin and alive to God in Christ Jesus. (Rom. 6:9–11) *(alliteration, anastrophe, polyptoton)*

   d. For they that are after the flesh do mind the things of the flesh; but they that are after the Spirit the things of the Spirit. (Rom. 8:5 KJV) *(anthimeria, ellipsis, hyperbole)*

e. We know that the whole creation has been groaning in labor pains until now. (Rom. 8:22) *(irony, litotes, personification)*

f. What then are we to say about these things: If God is for us, who is against us? He who did not withhold his own Son but gave him up for all of us, will he not with him also give us everything else? (Rom 8:31–32) *(climax, parenthesis, rhetorical question)*

g. Then he began to speak and taught them, saying:
"Blessed are the poor in spirit, for theirs is the kingdom of heaven.
"Blessed are those who mourn, for they will be comforted.
"Blessed are the meek, for they will inherit the earth. (Matt. 5:2–5) *(alliteration, anaphora, climax)*

h. He told them another parable: "The kingdom of heaven is like the yeast that a woman took and mixed in with three measures of flour until all of it was leavened." (Matt. 13:33) *(metaphor, personification, simile)*

i. Again I tell you, it is easier for a camel to go through the eye of a needle than for someone who is rich to enter the kingdom of God. (Matt. 19:24) *(climax, hyperbole, periphrasis)*

j. So again Jesus said to them, "Very truly, I tell you, I am the gate for the sheep." (John 10:7) *(irony, synecdoche, metaphor)*

k. Jesus said to her, "I am the resurrection and the life. Those who believe in me, even though they die, will live, and everyone who lives and believes in me will never die. Do you believe this?" (John 11:25–26) *(hyperbole, rhetorical question, paradox)*

l. The LORD God said to the serpent, Because you have done this, cursed are you among all animals and among all wild creatures; upon your belly you shall go, and dust you shall eat all the days of your life. (Gen. 3:14) *(anastrophe, climax, parenthesis)*

3. Read the following passages and answer the questions:

And he said to them, "Suppose one of you has a friend, and you go to him at midnight and say to him, 'Friend, lend me three loaves of bread; for a friend of mine has arrived, and I have nothing to set before him.' And he answers from within, 'Do not bother me; the door has already been locked, and my children are with me in bed; I cannot get up and give you anything.' I tell you, even though he will not give him anything because he is his friend, at least because of his persistence he will get up and give him whatever he needs.
"So I say to you, Ask, and it will be given to you. . . ." (Luke 11:5–9a)

a. What is Jesus' claim?
b. The grounds include an implied comparison. What is it?
c. The story constitutes what part of the argument?

"So I say to you, Ask, and it will be given to you; search, and you will find; knock, and the door will be opened for you. For everyone who asks receives, and everyone who searches, finds, and for everyone who knocks, the door will be opened." (Luke 11:9–10)

d. What is the most prominent scheme here?
e. What is the purpose of this scheme?

> "Is there anyone among you who, if your child asks for a fish, will give a snake instead of a fish? Or if the child asks for an egg, will give a scorpion? If you then, who are evil, know how to give good gifts to your children, how much more will the heavenly Father give the Holy Spirit to those who ask him!" (Luke 11:11–13)

f. Fill in the rest of Jesus' argument.

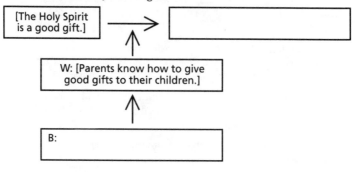

g. Matthew's version of this passage substitutes 'bread' and 'stone' for 'egg' and 'scorpion.' What difference does Luke's use of 'scorpion' make in terms of the emotional impact of the story?
h. An *a fortiori* argument is one that sets up two possibilities, one of which will be more probable than the other. Whatever can be affirmed about the less probable can be affirmed with even greater force about the more probable. Jesus' argument in this passage is clearly of this type. What is the more probable of the two possibilities involved in this argument?

CHAPTER SIX

Academic Papers

We may not all be able to put fire into our writing but we can all put our writing in the fire until a version worthy of a better fate appears.

Louis Gottschalk, *Understanding History*

1. Introduction

The previous chapter complemented our account of argument by placing it within the broader context of communication. This chapter looks at one of the more common communication tasks faced by students—the writing of academic papers. We shall see how insights from previous chapters on reasoning, as well as the foregoing chapter on communication, can shed light on the whys and hows of good academic writing.

2. Reasoning

The most basic requirement for an academic paper is that it make one claim and argue for it. (There are a few exceptions to be noted below.) The following are samples of the types of paper assignments a theology or religion student is likely to encounter:

a. Research paper: for example, write a paper on Augustine's theory of the origin of evil.

b. Book review: describe and evaluate Nancey Murphy's *Theology in the Age of Scientific Reasoning*.

c. Analysis paper: the paper on Augustine's theory of evil becomes an analysis paper when one is asked not only to describe Augustine's position, but to evaluate or criticize it. A paper calling for comparison of two viewpoints (say, Karl Barth and Wolfhart Pannenberg on the doctrine of revelation) is another sort of analysis paper.

d. Constructive paper: write a paper justifying (or criticizing) the practice of infant baptism.

e. Exegesis paper: choose a passage of scripture and write an interpretive paraphrase that expresses its original meaning.

f. Reflection paper: describe a problem you encountered in a recent experience in ministry and reflect on it in light of resources from the course you are taking.

It might be objected that a research paper does not make any claims because it (ordinarily) contains no explicit arguments—it simply reports on its subject. This objection, however, overlooks the fact that all such descriptions are selective and involve judgment about what is important. The presentation of a paper *as* a research paper involves the implicit claim not only that what is reported is true, but also that it represents (1) a fair and balanced account of (2) the most important aspects of the subject in question.

Book reviews not only make implicit claims such as those in a research paper—"this is a fair statement of what the book is about"—but also add explicit claims about how successful the book is in achieving its aims, or how valuable the book will be for a particular audience. So, in our example, one might report that Murphy's book is an attempt to show that theology is a rational enterprise by highlighting its similarities to scientific reasoning, but then go on to claim that the project fails miserably because . . .

An analysis paper, as does a book review, involves both reporting and evaluation. So one makes claims about Augustine's theory of evil, or Barth's and Pannenberg's doctrines of revelation, and then gives grounds for positive, negative, or mixed reviews of those positions.

In a constructive paper the goal is not to evaluate someone else's position or argument but to construct one's own. In a very straightforward way, such a paper ought to make a claim and argue for it.[1]

An exegesis paper may be an exception to the rule of one paper, one argument, since in providing an interpretation of the passage one is in effect making claims about the meaning of each sentence or clause. The claim or claims here are based on a grammatical study of the original language, on studies of the typical uses in scripture of key words, on theories about authorship and editing of the text, and on knowledge of the context of the text, both in terms of its location in scripture and its historical and cultural location.

A reflection paper may be an exception to the rule that all academic papers must make arguments. One might *claim* that the experience being described can be understood in light of some particular aspect of course content. But then one might instead simply show the relevance of the course material by describing the experience in those terms.

A common question students ask when given a writing assignment is, "Should we include our own opinion?" This question makes philosophy professors' hair stand on end, but it reflects an understandable mistake—the failure to note the difference between expressing an opinion and making a claim. The difference, of course, lies in whether or not an argument

---

[1]For further reading, an excellent book is Zachary Seech, *Writing Philosophy Papers*, (Belmont, Calif.: Wadsworth, 1993).

is provided. "I disagree with Augustine's position on the origin of evil" ceases to be mere opinion and becomes a genuine claim when one goes on to say that Augustine is wrong *because* . . . Remember that 'claim' is a functional term; a statement is a claim when it is that for which we argue (see chapter 1).

Writers can err on the side of never getting around to making a claim. But they also (often) err on the side of making too many claims. That is, many student papers bite off more than they can chew—they make a series of loosely related claims, none of which can then receive adequate support. Important questions to ask in planning or evaluating a paper are: Does it make a claim? Does it have one central claim for which the whole paper provides an argument?

Writing is often frustrating because the production of a perfect paper is so elusive a goal. In fact, perfection probably does not even apply here, in part because we have standards of excellence that often work at cross purposes. Two such standards are the importance or interest of the claim versus the quality or solidity of the support we can adduce for it. It may be a fact about human knowledge that the more significant the claim the more difficult it is to provide thorough grounding for it. Students (and other writers as well) are often faced with a choice: to say something interesting but poorly supported, or to provide solid support for a relatively trivial claim. In this author's opinion, the current fashion in professional academia is to prefer the latter. Let the student take note.

2.1. Grounds

In general we can say that the most common sort of grounding for an academic paper is the citation of authorities. And if the purpose of an argument is to move the reader from what is already accepted as true to a new conclusion, this is just exactly what we ought to expect. To recognize someone as an authority is to say that what she or he has written is generally accepted as true. We cite the authorities by means of quotations, summaries of their writings, footnotes, and, to some extent, bibliographies.

Beginning writers are often unsure when and how much to quote sources, where to use footnotes, and how many to include. Perhaps addressing these questions from the point of view of argument (rather than style) will shed some light.

2.1.1. Direct Quotation

Sometimes we use a direct quotation because we admire the way an author has phrased a point and recognize that we could not say it any better. Such quotations must be used *judiciously*.

More often the function of a direct quotation is to supply on the page our grounds for attributing a particular position to that author. So, for instance, suppose we want to argue for the legitimacy of infant baptism by citing Calvin's authority.

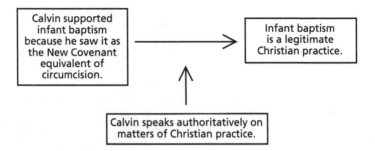

But to say that Calvin supported infant baptism for this reason is already to make an important *historical* claim. If there is reason to suppose one might be misreading or misinterpreting him on this point it may well be appropriate to include a direct quotation to support one's interpretation. We then have a chain argument, where the quotation provides grounds for the statement about Calvin's position.

Part of the task of learning to write well in a given field is learning to recognize when claims *about* the authorities' positions need to be grounded in turn by direct quotations from appropriate texts. One wants neither a paper that is little more than a string of quotations, nor one that leaves the reader wondering how on earth the student got *that* view from that author.

2.1.2. Footnotes

Footnotes, endnotes, or parenthetical citations are a more common method of grounding our claims about the authorities' positions than are direct quotations. Here, rather than placing the evidence on the page as we do with a quotation, we are instead telling the reader where to look to find the grounds for our claims.

Where and how often to use notes? Again a matter of judgment—judgment that the process of education aims to refine. How many and how detailed the references are should be determined by the function they serve. If the purpose is to allow your reader to find evidence for your claims in the books you have read, then a footnote for each sentence is obviously excessive. But to cite a book with no hint as to where in it the points in question have been made will obviously be inadequate.

Common knowledge needs no references at all; one no longer cites Copernicus when claiming that the earth orbits the sun, although at one time it would have been appropriate to do so.

2.1.3. Bibliography

A list of works cited or works consulted at the end of a paper is a more vague way of citing the authorities, but it is often informative nonetheless. A bibliography assures the reader that one has indeed consulted the *authorities* in the field, and has not based one's argument on the writings of eccentrics or 'crack-pots.'

2.2. Warrants and Backing

With regard to warrants used in academic papers it is worthwhile repeating a point made in chapter 2. Warrants are generally left unstated in our arguments (papers) because if they are not generally accepted (and therefore go without saying) they will not do the work required of them in our arguments. There are cases where we do state the warrant because, while we do not believe it will be accepted as a matter of course, we believe we can provide adequate backing for it. But notice that to do so is to make another argument; and we do best to aim for *one* argument per paper. Sometimes this means that we may choose to change the focus of the paper. If we started out to argue that C because of G, and find that there is no readily accepted warrant (W) that will make the argument work, we might instead write a paper arguing for W.

A second point from chapter 2 bears repeating. Much of what is involved in becoming proficient in a discipline is learning what are the accepted warrants in that field. So undergraduate, graduate, and professional papers will be expected to exhibit different degrees of subtlety in knowing when a warrant can be assumed, when it can be used only with appropriate backing, and when it cannot be used at all.

Furthermore, the situation varies from one subgroup to another within disciplines. There are denominational differences (Baptists and Anglicans look differently upon warrants citing the authority of church tradition, for instance). There are 'party' differences, too (for example, differences among liberals, evangelicals, and fundamentalists on the acceptability of warrants employing principles of historical-critical methods in arguments about the Bible).

2.3. Qualifiers and Rebuttals

We said in chapter 2 that while we would always prefer a strong argument to a weak one, the world is such that we must often be content with the weak. A weak argument, however, is not necessarily a poor argument—it simply needs to include an appropriate qualifier and to acknowledge the likely sources of rebuttal. All of this applies equally to papers. A mediocre paper can be turned into an excellent one by including a realistic assessment of the strength of its own argument and by at least mentioning the most threatening of its potential rebuttals.

It is often valuable, also, to note the partial character of one's argument. So, for example, adequate treatment of the grounds for the legitimacy of infant baptism would require biblical exegesis, an investigation of early church history, and the reasons given for the introduction or promotion of the practice. One might also need to consider later church pronouncements, teachings of the reformers, theological arguments, and so on. So in a paper of, say, ten pages, all one can hope to do is to write on one part of the complex and cumulative argument that would be necessary to draw a definitive conclusion. A sophisticated paper does not claim to have settled the issue on the basis of its small contribution to the whole.

In fact, some papers serve only to muddy the waters. A successful rebuttal of a previously accepted argument is an important contribution to the ongoing discussion, even though it provides no positive conclusion. It merely shifts the burden of proof to the other side.

3. Rhetorical Insights

We turn now to considerations from the more inclusive perspective of rhetorical theory.

3.1. Audience

We have already made mention of one important factor that communication theory would keep before us—namely, attention to the audience. We recognized above that acceptability of warrants is relative, to some extent, to the audience being addressed. We mentioned denominational and party differences within Christianity. If we think of the differences between arguing a theological or biblical point with fellow Christians versus trying to make the same point to a Hindu or an atheist we become all the more aware of the extent to which the assumptions of the audience shape the sort of argument we can make.

Papers also have to be adjusted to take account of what the audience is likely to know; articles are sometimes rejected by editors because they include too much information with which the readership of that journal is already familiar.

In doing course work, of course, the audience is either the professor or the teaching assistant—difficult folk to write for, since students often assume that they already know everything! It may help here to think more of the purpose of the paper than of the person who will read it. Ordinarily the purpose is to demonstrate the student's knowledge and comprehension. Consequently the question is not so much What does my audience need to know? as What do I need to show that I know? In practical terms this often comes down to a matter of judgment about what to include, and to the allocation of space according to importance. For example, if the assignment is to criticize Karl Barth's position on revelation, it is not wise to waste a page on a biographical sketch of Barth's life.

3.2. Insights from Aristotle

Recall that Aristotle divided the means of persuasion into three categories: logos, pathos, and ethos.

Logos pertains to the soundness and strength of the arguments—all the issues we have dealt with under the heading of reasoning.

Pathos, persuasion by means of emotion or passion, is generally seen as inappropriate in academic papers. However, it sometimes appears subtly when an author describes one position in terms with positive connotations or its contrary with negatively charged terms. So, for example, in a debate about just-war theory versus pacifism, to characterize the just-war position as "responsible" is to suggest that pacifism is irresponsible.

The reason for a general rejection of persuasion by means of passion in academia is closely related to the issue of ethos. *Ethos* refers to persuasion based on the character of the proposer. We have deeply ingrained attitudes about the values of objectivity and fairness in the academic world. Thus, the most persuasive character is one that comes across as a fair-minded critic. An ill-tempered attack on the opponent's position fails to persuade because we write the author off as biased; and similarly with a too-enthusiastic endorsement. Proper academic style (in our era, at least) requires relatively neutral language.

Ethos, or source credibility, applies also to the sources cited in a paper. It is important to rely on balanced accounts rather than on books written by people with an ax to grind. (For an impeccable source, of course, one cannot do better than notes from the professor's own lectures!)

3.3. Quintilian

We can take each of the five canons or compartments of rhetoric and apply what is said there regarding oral argument to the writing task.

3.3.1. Invention

Invention has to do with the discovery of ideas and so with the research one does before putting the paper together. Often a dialectical process goes on at this stage: one cannot formulate a topic precisely until one knows more about the subject, but one needs to have a precise topic in mind in order to know what to research. A difficult step for student writers is often the elimination of information and arguments that have become irrelevant once the topic is finalized. Louis Gottschalk makes the point well:

> If a historian has failed to understand the proper limitations of his inquiry, he might soon find that he has put hard work into learning many particulars that do not fit neatly into his composition. Still, believing, as historians frequently do, that all facts are created equal and are endowed by their discoverer with an inalienable right to citation, he might try to work them in somehow. If he were trying to establish the truth or falsity of a proposition or to answer a direct question . . . he would perhaps avoid some of the worst irrelevancies.[2]

It may be helpful in writing a paper to consider whether one will begin with a claim and search for grounds to support it, or whether the writing project is more a task of discovery—beginning from the evidence and seeing what claim(s) it can be made to support. Either approach is, in general, legitimate, but different writing assignments may favor one rather than the other. For instance, if you already have a position on infant baptism you will probably hunt for appropriate grounds to support it. However, if

---

[2]Louis Gottschalk, *Understanding History: A Primer of Historical Method* (New York: Knopf, 1951), 201.

the assignment is to review a book it is generally better to start with the grounds—that is, better to read it first and *then* evaluate it.

It is not uncommon to set out to support one conclusion but to discover in the process of writing that the evidence leads in another direction. Some of the best papers are the ones we write after putting the first attempt in the fire.

3.3.2. Disposition

Disposition refers to the arrangement of ideas. Recall that persuasive discourse generally includes four or five parts:

1. The purpose of the introduction is to arouse attention and to orient the audience. Most student writers are well enough aware of the first of these goals, but many fail to realize that their reader (even if that be the professor) needs to be oriented. What is the paper about? Why is the topic important? What is the major claim that will be made and how will it be supported?

2. The narration states the facts of the case. The kind of information that goes into this part of the paper will vary depending on the type of paper. For a book review it will be information about the book; if it is a critique of Barth's doctrine of revelation, the narration will be a description of his position. Remember that the facts need not be collected together into one section; they may instead be distributed throughout the paper.

3. The function of the argument, of course, is to state and support one's claim. It is appropriate to stress here that one good argument, worked out in careful detail, is *much* better than a string of argument-fragments or hints about how one might argue for the claim. This is one appropriate place for qualifiers—statements about the strength and scope of one's argument.

4. There may be a separate section called "refutation" in which one rebuts the opposing arguments.

5. The conclusion should sum up the case that has been made.

The arrangement or organization of the argument section is especially important. Often it is by the organization or structure of the paper that we convey the shape of our argument.

Next time you write a paper, try this method: First diagram your argument in abbreviated form. Then make an outline by deciding, for example, whether you want to state the claim first and then the argument for it, or state the grounds first and work up to your central claim. You can decide on sections and section headings by coordinating sections with the boxes in your diagram. The use of sections and subsections should reproduce the main structure of your outline for the reader.

Transition words and sentences are extremely important since they, along with the actual ordering of the paper, provide the structure of the argument. For instance is the structure intended to be:

paragraph 1 and paragraph 2; therefore paragraph 3

or:

paragraph 1; therefore paragraph 2; and therefore paragraph 3?

The connecting words tell your reader which of the following is the intended structure of the argument:

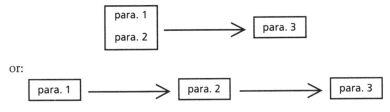

or:

3.3.3. Style

Style in oral presentation as well as in writing refers primarily to the choice of words suitable for the subject matter, for the audience, and for the occasion. We have already mentioned the importance, on the occasion of writing an academic paper, of choosing language that is emotionally neutral. We can add, as well, that the 'colorful' language promoted in creative writing classes is out of place. It would be wonderful if academicians could be persuaded that intradisciplinary jargon were out of place as well.

Among the figures defined in the previous chapter, parallelism may be the single most useful device for presenting one's ideas clearly.

While beautiful style may be a gift, decent style can be acquired by attention to virtues such as *precision* in the choice of words; *clarity* in sentence construction; and *parsimony*—refusing to use many words when few would do. The Bible provides a good model here. Were it not for the careful choice of words by most of its authors, the word studies that help us unlock its meaning would be futile. Notice also the skill with which narrators manage to convey a scene or story with only a few sentences.

3.3.4. Memory

In rhetoric this refers to the devices used by speakers—first, for their own recall and, second, so that the audience does not lose the point part way through. The first of these functions is unnecessary for written communication, but the second is still important for writers. The reader needs to be told (preferably in the introduction) where the argument is going and, in general terms, how it is going to get there. When an argument is long and complex often the reader will need to be reminded along the way of the overall plan and of how the present part fits into it. A summary at the end should review the steps. As one professor puts it: "Tell 'em what you're going to tell 'em; then tell 'em; then tell 'em what you've told 'em."

3.3.5. Delivery

The aspect of writing that corresponds most closely to oral delivery is what we call the mechanics of writing: typing, layout on the page, spelling and grammar. Just as poor delivery of an address can distract the listener from the points being made, so too can sloppy mechanics distract a reader from the author's argument. One should neither judge a book by its cover, nor a paper by its typing—but it happens.

If terrible typing is one pitfall to avoid, there may be an opposite danger. There is a report going around that researchers have found a correlation between fancy computer graphics in student papers and poor content!

Small grammatical mistakes distract the reader as well. Some of the most common in student papers are as follows: (1) The possessive of 'it' is 'its'; 'it's' is a contraction of 'it is.' Since contractions are frowned upon in academic writing, the pestilential 'it's' should *never* appear therein. (2) 'Data' is the plural of 'datum'; 'criteria' of 'criterion'; 'phenomena' of 'phenomenon.' No student of Greek should make these latter mistakes.

4. Conclusion

Two purposes served by a conclusion are to summarize the argument and to conciliate the audience. The first of these is easy to accomplish here: We first examined the standard parts of an argument and considered how each appears in an academic paper. We then took up a number of the issues central to rhetorical theory and examined the requirements they suggest for good academic writing.

The conciliatory task is more difficult. Either of two strategies could be adopted here. One might end with something so engaging as to compensate the reader for patiently plodding through this pedantic chapter, or one might instead apologize for having written such a chapter, perhaps pointing out that writing about writing is often as dull as an education course is poorly taught. Failing the former, I hereby adopt the latter.

EXERCISE SIX

Make a copy of a paper you have written for another class—the shorter the better—and answer the following questions:

a. Does it make a claim? One claim or many? Mark on the paper where the most important claim is stated. (If you do not find a claim, use a different paper.)

b. Indicate on the paper where the grounds for that claim are located. If there are many, choose one or a few of the most important. (If there are none, you had better use a different paper.)

c. Are any warrants stated? If so, mark them. If not, see if you can supply one or more.

d. Did you take account of any potential rebuttals? If so, indicate where; if not, think of one you might have mentioned.

e. Is your claim qualified? If so, mark it; if not, what qualifier would have been most appropriate?

f. Now you should be able to diagram the argument (or one of the arguments) of your paper. You can make the diagram as simple or as complex as you wish—for example, the argument might be a chain argument. However, quality here depends primarily on clarity and accuracy, secondarily on complexity.

g. Write an evaluation of your paper—a paragraph or so—commenting on style, organization, memory devices, mechanics.

PART TWO

Reasoning in Religion

CHAPTER SEVEN

Reasoning in Sermons

1. Introduction

The practice of basing a spoken discourse on a text is an ancient one. Both Old Testament and New Testament preachers based their messages on the scriptures (or on extant oral traditions). The practice of writing about preaching is almost as ancient, and no short chapter can do justice to this body of literature. Our focus will be on the contributions reasoning and rhetorical theory make to the task; our method will be to catch glimpses of the development of homiletics by examining the writings of three figures: Augustine from the fifth century, John A. Broadus from the nineteenth, and Thomas G. Long from the late twentieth century. In the process we will be able to augment the discussions in previous chapters of reasoning and rhetorical theory. In fact, during some historical periods, homiletics was not a mere consumer of rhetorical theory, but itself provided the primary stimulus for developments in that field.

2. Augustine

It was not long after Christianity spread to the Greco-Roman world that rhetorical theory began to be taught explicitly as a basis for homiletics. Augustine of Hippo (354–430), arguably the most influential theologian since the Apostle Paul, believed that the eloquence of the writers of scripture was unsurpassed, but for those whose job was to preach or teach *about* these texts, a knowledge of the theory and practice of rhetoric (including, of course, the theory of sound argument) was essential. Augustine himself had been a teacher of rhetoric before his conversion. His eloquent and rhetorically effective defense of the use of rhetoric by Christian teachers is worth quoting in full:

> Now, the art of rhetoric being available for the enforcing either of truth or falsehood, who will dare to say that truth in the person of its defenders is to take its stand unarmed against falsehood? For example, that those who are

trying to persuade men of what is false are to know how to introduce their subject, so as to put the hearer into a friendly, or attentive, or teachable frame of mind, while the defenders of the truth shall be ignorant of that art? That the former are to tell their falsehoods briefly, clearly, and plausibly, while the latter shall tell the truth in such a way that it is tedious to listen to, hard to understand, and, in fine, not easy to believe it? That the former are to oppose the truth and defend falsehood with sophistical arguments, while the latter shall be unable either to defend what is true, or to refute what is false? That the former, while imbuing the minds of their readers with erroneous opinions, are by their power of speech to awe, to melt, to enliven, and to rouse them, while the latter shall in defense of the truth be sluggish, and frigid, and somnolent? Who is such a fool as to think this wisdom? Since, then, the faculty of eloquence is available for both sides, and is of very great service in the enforcing either of wrong or right, why do not good men study to engage it on the side of truth, when bad men use it to obtain the triumph of wicked and worthless causes, and to further injustice and error?[1]

Augustine believed that the first requirement for the preacher was *wisdom;* the wise are those who "see with the eyes of the heart into the heart of Scripture" (bk. 4, chap. 5). Better to be wise than eloquent, but best of all to be both.

Following Cicero, Augustine taught that the aim of the orator is to teach, to delight, and to move. To each of these aims there corresponds a style of speaking: the subdued style for teaching; the temperate style to give pleasure; and the majestic style to move the hearer to compliance. Christian preachers, accordingly, will treat their subject quietly and humbly when it is being taught; temperately when its importance is being urged; and powerfully when forcing minds averse to the truth to turn and embrace it.

> If the hearers need teaching, the matter treated of must be made fully known by means of narrative. On the other hand, to clear up points that are doubtful requires reasoning and the exhibition of proofs. If, however, the hearers require to be roused rather than instructed, in order that they may be diligent to do what they already know, and to bring their feelings into harmony with the truths they admit, greater vigor of speech is needed. Here entreaties and reproaches, exhortations and upbraidings, and all the other means of rousing the emotions, are necessary (bk. 4, chap. 4).

Augustine emphasized several times the necessity of praying before speaking: first lifting up one's thirsty soul to God, to "drink in what he is about to pour forth, and to be himself filled with what he is about to distribute." For there are many things that may be said and many ways of saying them, and "who knows what it is expedient at a given moment for us to say, or to be heard saying, except God who knows the hearts of all?" (bk. 4, chap. 15). Second, the preacher should pray a (suitably Ciceronian) prayer: to be heard with intelligence, with pleasure, and with a ready compliance (bk. 4, chap. 17).

---

[1]Augustine, *On Christian Doctrine*, bk. 4, chap. 2. The first three books of this work concern "the mode of ascertaining the proper meaning" of scripture; book 4 concerns the proper teaching of Christian doctrine, and makes use throughout of rhetorical theory.

3. John Broadus

Augustine's *On Christian Doctrine* served the church as a guide to biblical interpretation and preaching for a thousand years. Its echoes could still be heard a millennium and a half later in the works of nineteenth-century homileticians such as John Broadus (1826–95), a Southern Baptist preacher and professor of homiletics.

It takes no clever detective work to discover the role of reasoning and rhetorical theory in the homiletic theory of this era. Our investigation will amount to scarcely more than a summary of Broadus's textbook.[2] Along the way we will allow him to make useful additions to our previous accounts of rhetoric and reasoning.

The purpose of preaching, according to Broadus, is to convince the judgment, to kindle the imagination, to move the feelings, and to give powerful impulse to the will in the direction of truth's requirement. In line with these aims, Broadus distinguished six functions of sermons:

1. evangelistic: to convert;
2. theological: to instruct in the truth about God and humankind;
3. ethical: to promote growth in character and spirit;
4. devotional: to enrich the devotional life, sentiments, and ideals;
5. inspiriting: to inspire to Christian action; and
6. actional: to broaden Christians' horizons of interest and responsibility.

While a single sermon might take one of these as its primary focus, most will involve a combination of functions.

3.1. Arguments

The above list of the aims of preaching shows that while arguments are not the sum total of a good sermon, they do have a significant role to play. A diagram will help both to summarize Broadus's view of preaching, and to help locate the role he accords to argument in sermons.

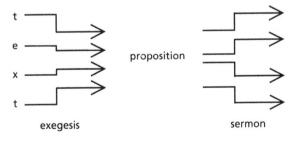

exegesis   sermon

---

[2] John Broadus, *On the Preparation and Delivery of Sermons,* perhaps the most widely used homiletics text; it remained in print for 100 years after its publication in 1870 (when Broadus had commented that "such books do not get a wide sale"). Citations here are to the 1945 edition, ed. J. B. Weatherspoon (New York: Harper and Brothers).

This diagram is meant to show the process by which the preacher moves from the biblical text to the construction of a sermon. The *proposition* is a single assertion, clear and cogent, and as simple as possible. It is derived from study of the text; thus, in our language, the proposition must be a *claim, grounded* in the text itself, and *warranted* by appropriate principles of scriptural interpretation.[3]

The proposition in turn states succinctly the gist of the sermon. It may or may not be stated explicitly, but in any case it must stand behind the sermon, giving it its unity. Each paragraph, Broadus says, must be related in one way or another to the proposition. One author compares the proposition to the trunk of a tree, from which the body of the sermon expands. The root is the "idea" in the biblical text upon which it is based.[4]

The logical relations between propositions and their sermons are varied. Some sermons will be devoted to establishing the proposition by means of biblical arguments. More commonly, though, the exegetical work is left in the study and the sermon instead explicates (expands, elaborates, applies) the claim made in the proposition. The following are some examples of propositions:

> God has a definite life plan for every human person, guiding him, visibly or invisibly, for some exact thing which it will be the true significance and glory of his life to have accomplished.   Horace Bushnell

> Christianity essentially means a spiritual victory in the face of hostile circumstances.   Henry Emerson Fosdick

> The way out of life's frustrations is found, not by resenting our limitations but by accepting the place of frustration as the sphere of God's purpose.
> James Reid

> In the church, relationships take precedence over ritual.
> Fred Craddock

Broadus included in his book a substantial section on argument (something not even mentioned in some recent homiletics texts!). His classification is instructive:

1. Argument from testimony: "In establishing truth in the minds of one's hearers the most direct and simple way is to tell one's own experience of the truth and one's own observation of the truth" (169). One must also draw on the experiences and judgment of others.

2. Argument from induction: "Induction is that operation of the mind by which we infer that what we know to be true in a particular case or cases will be true in all cases which resemble the former in certain assignable respects" (175). The sermon illustration is often not merely an illustration, but rather serves as the *grounds* for an inductive argument. Broadus points to Jesus' own method of using concrete situations familiar to his listeners to lead them to general conclusions.

---

[3]Broadus devotes a section early in his book to the interpretation of texts. We will not summarize this here, since the topic is treated at length in chapter 10.
[4]Austin Phelps, *Theory of Preaching* (New York: Scribner's, 1881), 308.

3. Argument from analogy: Broadus distinguishes these from inductive arguments in that induction works on the basis of *similarity;* analogy depends instead on the two cases exhibiting the same *relation.* That is, the leg of a table is not similar to a human leg, but it bears the same relation to the table as does the leg to the body. Metaphors are often compressed arguments from analogy, but they can lead to both true and false conclusions:

> Thus we call God a Father, and in certain respects Christ reasons from earthly fathers to Him. Yet, if we infer from a father's forgiving his child upon repentance, without satisfaction, that our Heavenly Father will and must forgive us upon repentance, without need of atonement, we extend the analogy more widely than is warranted. God is a Father, but he is also a King (179).

So, as noted in chapter 4 above, arguments from analogy (as well as by induction) warrant conclusions that are never more than probable.

4. Argument from deduction: Doctrinal preaching, says Broadus, has been very largely of this sort.

> Fully expressed, the preacher's syllogism would run somehow thus:
>   All Scripture is true and obligatory;
>   This particular doctrine is Scripture;
>   Therefore this doctrine is true and obligatory.
> The major premise [warrant], All Scripture is true and obligatory, is usually and properly taken for granted (181).

Despite the fact that deductive reasoning in geometry and other formal disciplines certifies the conclusion, Broadus notes that in subjects such as ethics and religion it is possible to be led astray by purely abstract reasoning. "We can very seldom take a general truth and make a series of deductions from it, as is done in geometry, and feel safe as to the results. We must constantly compare our conclusions with the facts of existence and with the teachings of Scripture" (182).

5. Varied forms of argument: Here Broadus discusses an assortment of kinds of argument: argument from cause to effect; from effects to a cause (which would ordinarily be hypothetical arguments, although Broadus does not use this term); *a fortiori* arguments, which he describes as argument from the proposition that has the stronger considerations against it to the proposition that has the weaker considerations against it; and *reductio ad absurdum.* This latter term means literally reduction to absurdity. Such an argument is intended to demonstrate the truth of an assertion by showing that its denial leads to a contradiction. For an example, see Anselm's argument in chapter 13, section 2.1.1.

An interesting type of argument not discussed in preceding chapters he calls the progressive approach. He does not define it, but illustrates it with this example:

> In arguing the being of a God from the general consent of mankind, we observe that in proportion as men have become cultivated and civilized, their ideas of the unity and moral excellence of the Deity have risen higher; that there is a progressive tendency towards the most exalted monotheism, which is hence inferred to be true (185).

Note that this argument depends on an assumed warrant to the effect that in general human understanding progresses toward greater apprehension of truth.

Broadus gives a great deal of attention to "refutation" (in our terms, rebuttals and the defeat of potential rebuttals), and offers some valuable advice: Do not waste time refuting trifling objections. Do not attempt to refute an objection unless it can be done satisfactorily—if not, grant the objection and throw the weight on the positive arguments you are able to provide. When discussing objections, state them fully and fairly. Refutation of erroneous positions or objections can be done by showing that the terms are ambiguous, the premises false, the reasoning unsound, or the conclusion irrelevant. Refutation of an error is sometimes strengthened by showing how the error may have originated.

A few final suggestions for the use of arguments:

1. Arrange a series of arguments so that the strongest comes last (climax).
2. Begin arguments with something your listeners will fully acknowledge.
3. Avoid formality—"have the reality of argument, but as little as possible of its merely technical forms and phrases."
4. Aim for clarity, precision, and force.
5. In general, depend principally on arguments from scripture.

3.2. Rhetoric

In this section we will organize Broadus's homiletic theory under the categories provided by Quintilian's five canons of rhetoric.

3.2.1. Invention

The materials for the sermon come, first of all, from scripture, and in particular from the prior study of the text upon which the sermon is to be based. Other sources of ideas for arguments and illustrations are systematic theology, philosophy and ethics, science, history and biography, literature, other sermons, and personal experience. Systematic theology allows the preacher to speak with boldness, having confidence that a particular doctrinal theme has a place, without contradiction, in a comprehensive system of thought.

3.2.2. Disposition

The arrangement of a sermon requires unity, order, and proportion. Relating each part to the proposition produces unity. Order involves the careful distinction of ideas and their arrangement with an eye both to logical sequence (the order of arguments) and to movement toward a climax. Proportion means giving time to elements of the sermon in accordance with their importance.

The basic form of a sermon is introduction, discussion, conclusion. Broadus claims that the conclusion is the most important part psychologically, rhetorically, and spiritually. The arguments in the discussion should have made it seem the *inevitable* conclusion, and here the emotional appeal is the strongest. Three types of conclusion are recapitulation, application, and direct appeal. The application shows how the proposition applies to the hearer; it may give practical suggestions regarding the best means of performing the duty, and generally involves moral and spiritual appeal for a right response. Such appeals require the excitement of feeling, and this is best done by means of vivid descriptions of things or events that themselves produce the appropriate feelings. Here we find another role for illustrations.

3.3.3. Style

Broadus suggests the following categories as contributors to style: clarity, energy, elegance, and imagination. The most important property of style, he says, is clearness or perspicuity. "Style is excellent when, like the atmosphere, it shows the thought, but itself is not seen" (240). Clarity is achieved by careful choice of words: those that are intelligible to one's listeners and also possess the exact shade of meaning one intends to convey. Sentence structure and proper paragraphing are also important; a pause in speaking can be used to indicate the end of one paragraph and the beginning of the next. Brevity can also contribute to clarity; a good idea can get lost in too many words.

Broadus's judgment regarding the importance of clarity has not been shared by all rhetoricians. Livy is reputed to have directed his students to "darken" the idea. When students complained that they did not know what he meant by this he replied: "So much the better; I did not even understand it myself."[5]

Energetic style cannot be produced except by cultivating an energetic nature. The preacher must be a vigorous thinker, earnest if not passionate in feeling and purpose, and must deeply believe in both the truth and the importance of what is being said. Such energy is expressed by concrete rather than abstract terms, concise statements, and the careful choice of schemes and tropes.

Broadus defines elegant speech as that which is forceful, not flowery. It depends on the use of energetic terms, on suitable arrangement of words and sounds, on the use of figures, and on simplicity.

Imagination is thinking by seeing rather than by argument. Imagination here refers both to the creation of mental images by the use of words, and also to the ability of the preacher to enter sympathetically into the minds and imaginations of others.

---

[5]Quoted by Broadus, *On the Preparation and Delivery of Sermons*, 240, from Quintilian's *Instruction of the Orator*, 8.2.18.

3.2.4. Memory

Under this heading Broadus discusses three methods of delivery—reading, recitation, and extemporaneous speaking—noting the strengths and pitfalls of each.

3.2.5. Delivery

Delivery here refers to both the manner of speech and to what is now called body language. The key to good delivery, according to Broadus, is that one be "possessed with the subject," fully in sympathy with it, and alive to its importance. One must not merely repeat remembered words, but must be "setting free" the thoughts of one's own mind (335).

Notice that we could have arranged much of the foregoing material under the Aristotelian categories of logos, ethos, and pathos. The argument section, of course, corresponds to logos. Under pathos we could have included Broadus's views about the use of vivid descriptions to excite feeling, as well as other remarks about style. Broadus has a great deal to say in his book about ethos—the kind of person the preacher must be in order to be effective. We see just a little of this in his comments about energetic style. He also emphasizes piety as the first requirement for preaching. By this he means a "quality of soul," "earnestness rooted in a continuing experience of fellowship with God," a "reverent devotion of the will to God." "Just rhetorical principles, as well as other and far higher considerations, imperatively require that a preacher of the gospel shall cultivate personal piety. It is *bad rhetoric* to neglect it" (6–7).

4. Thomas G. Long

We now examine the views of Thomas Long, professor of preaching at Princeton Theological Seminary. Long provides several valuable criticisms and emendations of earlier homiletic theory, such as that represented here by Broadus.[6]

4.1. From Exegesis to Sermon

In this generation there has been a reaction against the use of a proposition to bridge the gap between the biblical text and the sermon. The propositional approach, it is argued, reflects the view that what scripture is *for* is primarily to present *ideas*. The idea can be extracted from the text and then explicated (perhaps in a better way than in the scriptural passage itself?). However, this view of scripture is too . . . well, . . . propositional. In addition, it is said, sermons organized around ideas, with their three points and numerous subpoints, tend to be dull; and idea-oriented sermons suggest over time that being a Christian can be boiled down to a set of beliefs.[7]

[6]See Long, *The Witness of Preaching* (Louisville: Westminster/John Knox, 1989).
[7]Long gives much of the credit for this change to Fred Craddock. See Craddock's *As One without Authority* (Nashville: Abingdon, 1971).

So for a time the "central idea" approach to sermons was largely rejected in favor of trying to express in the sermon the many facets of scripture—the variety of "moods, movements, conflicts, epiphanies, and other experiences that cannot be pressed into a strictly ideational mold" (80). In practice, though, homiletics professors found their students producing loosely constructed, vague sermons—"private parables in the name of self-expression."[8]

Long's response to the debate over propositions is to point out that scripture must be understood not only in terms of what it has to say, but also in terms of what it intends to *do*. A general answer to the question, What does scripture intend to do? is that it functions to shape Christian identity. And this is not just the identity of the first readers or hearers; the scriptures are living resources for transforming the lives of Christian communities here and now. Particular texts will do this by means of a variety of other acts: by offering reassurance, by challenging the church's thinking, by evoking faith or hope, by moving to action, and so forth.

Long describes the bridge leading from text to sermon as a "claim"—in the sense of the text's claim *upon* the congregation. The claim has two components: the *focus* statement, which is a concise description of the central, controlling, and unifying theme of the sermon; and the *function* statement, which is a description of what the preacher hopes the sermon will create or cause to happen for the hearers—the change it intends to produce in them. Both should grow directly out of the exegesis of the text, but within the context of an actual Christian community. The claim answers the question, What does this text want to say and do, to and for this particular congregation? For example, Romans 8:28–39, ending with the affirmation that nothing can separate us from the love of God in Christ Jesus, might lead in an openly troubled congregation to the following pair of statements:

> Focus: Because we have seen in Jesus Christ that God is *for* us, we can be confident that God loves and cares for us even when our experience seems to deny it.

> Function: To reassure and give hope to troubled hearers in the midst of, not apart from, their distress (87).

In a different congregation, with a "sunshine and success" view of the gospel, the same text might lead to the following:

> Focus: Trying to hide from the tragic dimensions of life is a sign of lack of faith in God, whose love in Jesus Christ is experienced in the midst of peril and distress.

> Function: To enable the hearers to move from a superficial "sunshine and success" understanding of the faith toward a willingness to trust God in the fullness of their experience (88).

---

[8]Ronald Sleeth, quoted by Long, *The Witness of Preaching*, 83.

Long's emphasis on the doing as well as on the saying reflects an important recent advance in philosophy of language: from a view of language as having one central function—stating facts or ideas—to a view of language as performing any number of kinds of functions. J. L. Austin noted that we *use* language to *do* things: we make promises and requests, we thank, we chide, we confess. To understand the meaning of any utterance we must ask what *speech-act* is taking place. The meaning (the idea, the proposition) is but a part (although an important part) of the doing.[9] For example, in the request "Please pass the bread," the propositional content is *that the bread be passed,* but we miss what is happening if we do not know that this is a request rather than a wish or a description. (We will see more of Austin at the end of chapter 10.)

4.2. Sermon Forms

The view of scripture as a repository of ideas, and of sermons as their explication, very often led to forming sermons by making an outline corresponding to the parts and subparts of the idea. Some went so far as to specify the number of points each sermon should make (three) and to enumerate them explicitly in the sermon itself.

In reaction against the outline approach, recent homiletics texts have offered lists of forms such as the following:

> What is it? What is it worth? How does one get it?
> Explore, explain, apply
> The problem, the solution
> What it is not, what it is
> Either/or
> Both/and
> Promise, fulfillment
> Ambiguity, clarity
> Major premise, minor premise, conclusion
> Not this, nor this, nor this, nor this, but this
> The flashback (from present to past to present)
> From the lesser to the greater[10]

Long points out, however, that the sermon cannot be constructed by first deciding upon the content and then simply selecting a form in which to put it. Rather, he suggests, the form must be chosen to suit the aims of the text. The first step is to break the focus and function statements into component parts, and then to decide what form will best serve each component function. Take, for example, the first set of statements above for Romans 8:28–39:

---

[9]See J. L. Austin's *How to Do Things with Words* (1962; Cambridge: Harvard University Press, 1975).

[10]From Fred Craddock, *Preaching* (Nashville: Abingdon, 1985), 177.

Focus: Because we have seen in Jesus Christ that God is *for* us, we can be confident that God loves and cares for us even when our experience seems to deny it.

Function: To reassure and give hope to troubled hearers in the midst of, not apart from, their distress (87).

If the sermon as a whole is to *say* this, then the tasks along the way are to:

a. Say where and how we have seen in Jesus Christ that God is for us.
b. Name and describe experiences that seem to deny God's love and care.
c. Describe clearly how what we have seen in Jesus is able to create present confidence in God's love and care.

If the sermon as a whole is to *function* as intended it must also:

d. Provide reassurance, based upon God's continuing love and care, to troubled hearers.
e. Evoke a sense of hope for people who struggle with situations that seem to have no future.
f. Call into question all shallow reassurances that do not deal honestly with suffering (107–8).

The form needed, for instance, to describe experiences that seem to deny God's love may well be different from the form needed to provide reassurance of God's continuing care. For some tasks what is needed are quotations from scripture; for others, we need descriptions of theological concepts, or analyses of issues, or accounts of familiar experiences, and so forth.

4.3. Illustrations

Long's discussion of illustrations adds to his account of the forms used in sermons. But first some history: Early homileticians, following the classical rhetorical tradition, assumed that the aim of a sermon was to persuade, and that the stories included in sermons must therefore be devices to make the sermon more persuasive. In the nineteenth and early twentieth centuries a very different view emerged, based on the assumption, already noted, that the purpose of a sermon is to explain an idea. At this point, a variety of 'inclusions'—stories, historical anecdotes, examples, analogies from nature—all came to be called *illustrations*. The etymology of this word fits the perceived function: to throw *light* on the conceptual idea or structure that was the main business of the sermon.

Long acquiesces in the continued use of the single term 'illustration,' but emphasizes the varied functions these elements perform. The illustration in a sermon can serve the same function as a figure of speech in a sentence. He discusses three such figures: simile, synecdoche, and metaphor. The simile is a form of speech that compares two entities not usually thought of as similar in order to create clear and emphatic understanding (for example, George is as slow as molasses). Some sermon illustrations operate like similes and have the same purpose. A relationship or comparison is established between an idea or concept in the sermon and some more familiar, imaginable experience. Long's example is the following:

> As a boy I loved to go puddle gazing, wandering from one puddle to the next, wondering how so much of the sky could be reflected in such small bodies of water. Today I often marvel at how so much of the story of heaven and earth is captured in small biblical tales such as the story of Jesus and the paralytic (162).

Synecdoche is a figure where a part of something stands for the whole. In sermons, when a concept or idea is presented, one sometimes gives an illustration—a concrete case that is not the whole of the theological concept but a suitable instance or taste of it. As an example, Long offers the story of the courageous death of a woman with a brain tumor as a synecdoche-style illustration of Paul's statement (in Rom. 8:18–19) that the creation waits with eager longing for the revealing of the children of God. Her longing for reunion with her husband and freedom from her illness is presented as a taste of the longing to which Paul refers.

Long defines metaphor as calling something familiar by an unfamiliar name. The purpose of metaphor-style illustrations is to invite the hearers to make imaginative connections between the topic of the sermon and some other realm of experience.

Notice how *argument* has crept in the back door of Long's account of sermon illustrations. These figures of speech all present entities or experiences whose structure, characteristics, or functions are known to the hearer. When they are related to ideas in the sermon the characteristics or structure of the illustration is at least tentatively attributed to the idea the preacher is illustrating. So with simile- or metaphor-style illustrations, we have implied arguments from analogy. Synecdoche-style illustrations lay the groundwork for inductive arguments.

5. Summary

We began this chapter with a fairly simple plan: to use the tools developed in the previous chapters to understand what goes on in sermons. We have seen that the role assigned to *argument* has varied through the course of homiletic history, being nearly eclipsed in recent years. However, while classical rhetorical theory has become less prominent in the most recent thinking about sermons, the concerns that rhetorical theory has always addressed have taken center stage: the early rhetoricians studied verbal means of *moving* people (of which convincing by means of argument was but one sort). Contemporary homileticians ask: What kind of movement does this text call for? and, How can the words of the sermon help to bring it about?

6. An Example

In the following pages we look at a sermon preached by Broadus in 1889. It will be interesting to see how well his preaching fits his own homiletic theories, and also to see what we can make of the sermon using Long's somewhat different approach.

Be Careful for Nothing

> Be careful for nothing, but in everything by prayer and supplication with thanksgiving let your requests be known unto God; and the peace of God, which passeth all understanding, shall guard your hearts and minds in Christ Jesus.
>
> Philippians 4:6–7

"Be careful for nothing." We are always telling the children and the servants to be careful of everything. But the word has changed its meaning; originally it meant full of care. In the revised edition of the Bible the word "anxious" is substituted, "in nothing be anxious"; that is the exact, full meaning.

How can we help it? How can any one help being anxious? Our possessions are held by an uncertain tenure. The possessions of the rich are a source of anxiety; and the anxieties of the poor are not proportioned to their possessions. Our very lives are uncertain; and the things that are dear to us awaken anxieties in our minds. We are anxious about those we love better than our lives. Your son stayed out late last night, and made an evasive answer when you questioned him about it. Could you fail to be anxious, as you stole a furtive look at him across the breakfast table? And your husband, you used to hope would become a Christian; but he hasn't, and he does not seem interested of late; he has not been to church in a good many Sundays. The little child in its second summer is sick; and you hear its pitiful wailing in the silence of the night. Can you keep from being anxious about it? Life, property, character, everything is uncertain. How is it possible to avoid being anxious? And yet the Apostle says it, secure in the promise of his Master, "In nothing be anxious."

Be not anxious for tomorrow. Be not anxious for what you shall eat and for what you shall wear; for One knows our needs and it is His purpose to supply all our needs through Christ Jesus our Lord. Worry is the friction of life.

We who live in this fag end of the 19th century find more causes for anxiety than those of any previous age. We want to go fast, walk fast, love fast, sing fast. The danger is that we will die too quickly.

See that man! He wants to catch a train. See how he strains every nerve and muscle until the beads of perspiration stand out upon his brow. Look at him, how fast he is walking! He is afraid he will not get there in time. He is a perfect type of the life of this great American nation.

Sir Arthur Helps, at one time private secretary to Queen Victoria, is the author of a work entitled *Friends in Council*. One of the essays, I remember reading to my wife. It was on the "Kingdom of Worry," and he says: "Worry reigns over more human beings than any other potentate." We wear our lives away with fatiguing, useless worry. Is there no remedy? Let us see:

"In nothing be anxious; but in everything by prayer and supplication let your requests be made known to God." Turn your troubles and anxieties into prayer by supplicating God. Now, the mere fact of telling one about our troubles is sometimes a partial relief. Don't you find it so? You have some dear friend—

Oh, thank God for those friends! some dear friend whose sympathy you can count upon, and it is a comfort that you can tell that friend the cause of your anxiety. They may not have it in their power to aid you, but their sympathy is a great comfort to you. And so, "In everything let your requests be made known to God." It is a greater comfort to go to One with your troubles who understands you, and sympathizes with you, and who will not only listen, but will help you.

One hundred years ago there was a great deal of discussion in England, and in this country also, relative to the Bible. Some said praying to God is like a man in a boat who is given a rope that is fastened to some object on shore. By pulling at the rope he gradually pulls his boat to shore. He does not expect to pull the shore to him. And we can't expect to pull God to us, but we can pull ourselves toward God. But if that were all, the truth is we would never pray. The Bible does not allow us to so limit God's power. When we call upon Him, He will not only hear us; but he will heed and help us.

Will he always give us exactly what we ask for? Not he. He is too wise for that. "If ye who are evil know how to give good gifts to your children, how much more your Heavenly Father." If you who are evil make no mistakes in giving to your children, with how much more wisdom will an All Wise God deal with your requests. Suppose your child should ask for a serpent, thinking it a fish, would you not, instead of complying with the request, give it something else—something better? And so the child can come in its childlike limitations and ask the parent and the parent will know how to give good things to the child. Much more shall not your Father in Heaven know how to give good things to you, for he is not evil?

Suppose that you could have everything you asked, then just in proportion as your experience had been, you would be afraid to ask for those things you think you want. Many of us have lived long enough to see, that those things most longed for are not the things that are best for us to have; and we would be almost afraid to pray, if we were sure of getting just what, in our human judgment, seemed best. But our Heavenly Father knows our needs, and will give us just what is best for us to have.

"In nothing be anxious, but in everything by prayer and supplication, with thanksgiving, let your request be made known to God." "With thanksgiving." Did you notice that I had left that out? Don't ever leave that out. We are very apt to do so. We are so taken up with the affairs of the present that we don't have time to give thanks for the blessings of the past. And our prayers are not often those of thanksgiving. Why, my dear friends, in the greatest misfortunes of life we can still find occasion for thanksgiving.

"And the peace of God which passeth all understanding shall guard your hearts and minds in Christ Jesus."

"The peace of God!" O friends, have you ever been by the bedside of a dying Christian? Can you forget the anguish and suffering of that pale face, from which the life was ebbing? And then some words of comfort which touch the heart were spoken and the anguished face would quiet down, and you would see it filled with peace, "the peace of God." No wonder the Apostle says the peace of God passeth all understanding. There are a great many things impossible for these human hearts of ours to believe, many things we can't understand. The peace of God passeth all understanding, but does not pass possibility of attainment.

But "can the peace of God enter my heart?" some person will ask. Can I, with these strange, passionate emotions ever know the peace of God? How can the peace of God rule my soul?

Mountains of waves are sweeping and raging o'er the sea of Galilee; a little boat with twelve occupants is struggling bravely against the storm; they can manage the boat no longer; it is filling with water. In the rear of the boat lies One sound asleep, while the waves roar around him unheeded. They can manage the boat no longer; and going to him, they say "Master, we are perishing." He arises from his slumber at their call, and noting the looks of fear depicted on their faces says, "Why are ye so fearful? O ye of little faith." And then he commands the waves, saying, "peace, be still." And in obedience to his commands the great waves subsided, the storm ceased, and all was calm. He who calmed the sea at the prayer of his beloved apostles, is he who can calm your storm-tossed soul into peace, if you only trust and ask him, O ye of little faith! The peace of God, which passeth all understanding shall guard your minds and hearts in Christ Jesus. The fort may be old and weak as the one I saw in Mackinac last week, but if it has a strong garrison for its protection, that can "hold the fort"; and so the peace of God shall garrison your hearts, and make them strong to battle with the world's worries and anxieties—there may be sad memories and yet peace.

I remember seeing in Dresden the only picture of Mary Magdalene that I ever saw that seemed at all satisfactory. The ordinary conception is false to the idea. But this was a picture of a woman of middle age, once very beautiful, with deep furrows in her face, left there by terrible experiences. But the suffering is all past and a look of holy peace rests on the countenance. Peace purchased by sorrow and repentance, and yet, peace.

My friends, do you say that it is not possible that all this should be more than a dream? Do you say, "How can I be guarded and protected by something unseen?" I was writing an article on Solomon for the *Baptist Teacher* last week, and was reminded in connection with Solomon's early dreams, of a visit I made to Gibeon with a friend of mine. We were sitting on a housetop looking up some allusions to places of interest in that vicinity in our Bible when a crowd of fifteen or more of the natives, attracted by strangers, came and formed a circle around us. I happened to take out my watch to see the time, while my friend was reading and I noticed the eyes of the men gleam at the sight of the gold. I said to my friend: "Just look at those fellows. Just see how they act," and I took out my watch again. Two of the younger ones started towards me, gazing at the gold with longing eyes; then they drew back. What were they afraid of? We were un-armed and without any means of defense and they could have easily overpowered us. Why were we so secure?

Our names were registered at Jerusalem in a large house over which floated the stars and stripes, and had we come to harm, search would have been made, and as the poor fellows were aware, the Turkish government would rather have destroyed hundreds of their people than offend the great Western power. And thus, something those poor fellows never saw, and never will see, the unseen, far-away power made us safe.

It is a custom of modern medical men to guard against disease by using preventatives, and in proportion as we are wise, we will guard against the disease of anxiety by the preventive of prayer.

Dear friends, the preacher is a stranger among you, and will soon go his way and be forgotten. The best wish he can make for you is, that you may know, living and dying, the meaning of this text: And the peace of God, which passeth all understanding, guard your hearts and minds through Christ Jesus.[11]

---

[11]Reprinted in Clyde E. Fant and William M. Pinson, Jr., eds., *Twenty Centuries of Great Preaching* (Waco, Tex.: Word Books, 1971), 5:66–70.

6.1. Analysis in Broadus's Terms

Let us examine this sermon using some of Broadus's own homiletic terms. Reading the finished sermon suggests that the proposition he had in mind was something like the following:

> Prayers of supplication and thanksgiving will turn anxiety into the peace of God.

The following outline shows that the sermon can be broken down into three major topics, each including explanation, defense, or both:

Introduction
Discussion (three points):
1. Anxiety: how not to be anxious?
    Caused by uncertainty.
    Reflected in constant hurrying.
    All-powerful.
2. Prayer: the cure for anxiety.
    Prayer of supplication.
        Comfort in telling a friend.
        Better to receive help.
            Objection 1: prayer only moves us, not God.
            Reply 1: if that were true no one would pray.
            Reply 2: Scripture contradicts this view of prayer.
            Objection 2: (forestalled) We do not get all that we pray for.
            Reply: God is like a wise parent.
    Prayer of thanksgiving.
3. God's peace: the alternative to anxiety.
    What is it like? Illustration: dying friend.
        Objection 1: Such peace is not possible.
        Replies:
            Analogy 1: Jesus calming the storm.
            Analogy 2: Garrison of the heart.
    What is it like? Illustration: painting of Mary Magdalene.
        Objection 2: Not possible.
        Reply:
            Analogy: Power of U.S. government.
Conclusion
    Final image: prevention of disease.
    Direct appeal.

The *implied* argument of the sermon grounds the proposition's several claims on the authority of the scriptural text. Most of the arguments *stated* in the sermon are "refutations," and nearly all of them involve the use of illustrations.

The first objection (in part 2), that prayer only moves us, is itself made by the use of a simile: "like a man in a boat." Broadus refutes the objection by a *reductio ad absurdum*: *if* this were the case, no one would pray (but obviously many do pray). His second argument is, Such a view of prayer is contradicted by the biblical view of God's power.

The second objection (not stated but implied) is that prayer must not work since we do not always get what we ask for. Broadus uses the scriptural comparison of God to a good parent; here the argument is from analogy.

The first objection to the possibility of God's peace is met, again, with a brief story from scripture. The argument is *a fortiori:* if Jesus can calm the storm, all the more so can he calm your "storm-tossed soul."

The second objection is, How can one be protected by what is unseen? Broadus uses a story from personal experience (the power of the government);[12] again the form of the argument is from analogy.

Some of the more striking *figures* Broadus uses:

1. "With thanksgiving. Did you notice that I had left that out? Don't ever leave that out." This is an instance of antanaclasis. In the first case, "leaving out" regards omission from a sentence. When he repeats it, it refers to omission from one's practice of prayer. Notice that the whole force of the subpoint is carried by this (very effective) play on words.
2. He uses a number of rhetorical questions.
3. To characterize God's peace he uses synecdoche. The peaceful face on the death bed is a representative instance of God's peace.
4. In the conclusion, prayer is implicitly likened to a disease preventative.

More could be said about this sermon from the point of view of Broadus's own understanding of homiletic skill, but it will be interesting to turn now to Long's homiletic theories and see whether we can find a similar number of applications.

6.2. Analysis in Long's Terms

The form of this sermon as a whole could be called "question and answer," or "the problem, the solution." The question or problem is, How can we help but be anxious? The answer is prayer.

Had Broadus distinguished between the focus and the function of this sermon, he might have formulated them in this way:

> Focus: Prayers of supplication and thanksgiving will turn anxiety into the peace of God.

> Function: To encourage the congregation to find greater peace through prayer.

The sub-tasks accomplished by the sermon include the following. The means used are noted in square brackets.

---

[12]This may well have been an effective illustration for the congregation Broadus was addressing. Today, though, the effect would more likely be to distract the listeners, who would spend some time thinking about more charitable accounts of the motives of "the natives."

    a. Evoke typical feelings of anxiety (about family members, feelings of haste). [A series of vignettes expected to reflect the congregation's (women's?) experience. Broadus was a guest preacher so he chose illustrations likely to be familiar to anyone who had ever had a family or had to catch a train.]

    b. Present scriptural words of assurance ("Be not anxious. . . ."). [Repetition of phrases from his own text, and allusions to Matt. 6:25, Luke 12:22.]

    c. Encourage congregation to pray. [Scriptural injunctions; comparison to the relief of talking to a friend.]

    d. Call into question erroneous view of prayer:
        1. that it does not move God; [*Reductio* argument; scriptural authority]
        2. that we should always get exactly what we pray for. [Simile-style illustration: God is like a good parent.]

    e. Remind listeners not to neglect thanksgiving. [Antanaclasis: a figure Long has not discussed.]

    f. Evoke memories of the experience of God's peace. [Synecdoche-style illustration: peace on death-bed as an instance.]

    g. Respond to doubts, encourage faith:
        1. tempestuous emotions; [Metaphor-style illustration: "storm-tossed souls."]
        2. invisible power. [Simile-style illustration: God is like the U.S. government.]

Again, more could be written about this sermon from Long's perspective. But we have seen enough to conclude that Long's theory does provide useful tools for understanding how a sermon works—an understanding that goes beyond earlier theories. However, it is interesting to note that while Long's theory goes beyond that of Broadus, it does *not* go beyond Broadus's skill as a preacher. So what we see here is an advance in homiletic theory that helps it catch up with good homiletic practice. It is often the case that practice precedes theory, but the formulation of adequate theoretical descriptions of practice still pays off by making the practice more consistent in quality and more teachable.

Augustine taught that good preaching requires wisdom and eloquence. We have given some attention here to the demands of eloquence. Broadus taught that wisdom comes from personal piety and from study—study of the Bible and its methods of interpretation, of history, ethics, and theology. It is to these latter disciplines that we turn in the next four chapters.

EXERCISE SEVEN

1. Read the sermon by Marguerite Shuster below and answer the questions that follow.

Beginnings

In the beginning God created the heavens and the earth.

Genesis 1:1 (RSV)

(1) Why, oh why, is there *something* and not *nothing*? There didn't have to be *something*, you know. You're cheating if you start with a cloud of hot gases or a super-dense clump of matter and say that, given enough billions upon billions of years, it just figures that eventually all the possible combinations would occur and, at long last, produce a world like ours, with people like us, who sing hymns (what a strange thing to do!) and build churches (how prodigal!) and hear preachers expound thoughts about a God who got it all going (what possible biological use are preachers?). You're cheating, I say. Maybe your argument is correct and maybe it isn't; but you're still cheating, because whoever said a cloud of hot gases or a dense clump of matter *had* to exist?

(2) Start backwards. Throw out people and everything they feel and everything they make. Throw out plants and animals. Throw out water and earth. Throw out planets and stars. Throw out gases and solids, particles and waves. Throw out time and space. When you're left with absolute emptiness, throw out even that. Now, maybe, you're getting close to talking about *nothing*. Now, maybe, you're ready to ask why *something* should ever appear. For no possible necessity of logic or science, mathematics or metaphysics, could ever produce so much as an atom, so much as a proton, so much as a still tinier quark or gluon out of that nothing. Everything—absolutely everything—is gratuitous. Absolutely everything, including ourselves, *would* not have been, if it were not that. . . .

(3) "In the beginning God created the heavens and the earth." Those simple, majestic words of my text, which serve as a heading or title for the first 35 verses of the book of Genesis, go behind all study and theorizing about the *process* by which our universe and planet and we ourselves came to appear, and assert that apart from God none of these would exist at all. It is a statement of ultimate origins, a statement behind which we cannot go. . . . We do need to know, though, to what or to whom we should attribute all that we see, and whether there is anyone behind it all upon whom we can rely. Thus, these crucial, jam-packed opening words of the whole Bible tell us that God created *the heavens and the earth;* that God *created* the heavens and the earth; and that *in the beginning God* created the heavens and the earth. Let's take these three points separately.

(4) First, God created *the heavens and the earth*. That phrase simply means "everything," the equivalent of the New Testament "all things," as in Ephesians 3:9, where it is said that "God . . . created all things." In a lovely phrase, theologians speak of God finding "cheerful diversion in making all that is." Don't you like that way of thinking about it—seeing God as delighting in making an utterly unbelievable universe, in which components of atoms in some sense act randomly, while they compose galaxies that in some sense behave lawfully? Imagine his bothering with rainbows—not just in the sky but in fishes' scales. Imagine his toying with the idea of the number of legs creatures should have, whether none, or one, like snails, or two or four or six or eight, or however many centipedes really have. Con-

template the difference between plush fur and iridescent feathers. Think of his deciding that mountains and valleys and seas are much better than a perfectly harmonious round sphere. . . .

(5) Not just the complexity, not just the variety, not just the basic orderliness of it all, but the sheer exuberance of the creation boggles the mind.

(6) And God saw that all of it was good—a refrain that sounds a bit too subdued for the marvel of it all. . . .

(7) Second, God *created* the heavens and the earth: the word itself is significant. This particular Hebrew verb is used only of God and is never connected with any statement of any material used in the act. Thus, in itself, it implies creation out of nothing. So does the verse that follows my text, which says, "the earth was without form and void, and darkness was on the face of the deep." Here we do not have a description of some sort of primeval chaos, some amorphous "stuff" that God would take and mold. Many have interpreted the verse that way, but such interpretations go against the sense of verses 1 and 3, as well as not fitting with Hebrew thought. For the Hebrew, talk of formlessness and void was a description of a sort of desert waste and is used here as a way of speaking of the opposite of creation. And "darkness" is to be understood not as a mere phenomenon of nature but as something somehow sinister, dreadful. Thus, these are mythological images for utter nothingness, images that evoke in us the dread we have of nonbeing.

(8) Is it important to stress that God made the world out of nothing? Well, consider the alternative. Contemplate God making use of some material that had intrinsic limitations that he could not overcome, like a sculptor thwarted by the knots in the wood or the cracks in the marble. Or imagine a world with a dark history that would keep encroaching. As an example, Helmut Thielicke relates a Germanic creation story in which

> the world is made of the corpse of the giant Ymir: the sea of his blood, the heaven of his skull, and the clouds from his brains. But this Ymir, from whose body the world was made, was murdered by Odin and his brothers. . . . This Germanic story says that the world was made of curse-ridden matter. The world which is described thus does not bear only divine features; instead the dubious matter of which it is made is constantly breaking through. So whenever guilt and horror appear in the world. . . , it is this prenatal dowry of the world that is erupting. (*How the World Began*, 21.)

We could not then help ourselves, for our fate would be in our origins. We would have been constrained from the very beginning of creation by forces that are absolutely beyond us. Well, we all know that that is not the biblical view—but that is another story. Here, we are only concerned to say that God made his good creation without any such constraints as some sort of preexistent matter would impose.

(9) All God did was speak. He said, "'Let there be light,' and there was light." . . . Creation by speaking—by Word—also makes plain the point that not only did God not use preexistent materials, but also that there is no necessary connection between God and the world. Had he not spoken, it would not have been. The world is not continuous with God, not a part of God, not even like God, any more than a table built by a carpenter is essentially like a carpenter. True, the nature of his workmanship may tell

us something about the character of a carpenter, but only if we have very clearly in mind how utterly different tables and carpenters really are. And we would be hard put to explain the appearing of tables if we were unwilling to suppose the existence of anything fundamentally unlike them. . . .

(10) Finally, the assertion that *in the beginning God* created the heavens and the earth. That phrase contains two components that we have everywhere assumed: that there is a God, and that there was a beginning. Neither, perhaps, can be absolutely proved. Matter could, perhaps, be eternal and everything we see be the result of chance plus vast unthinkable aeons of time. One can believe that if one wishes, but one cannot claim that it is the simplest and most reasonable view of things.

(11) For instance, it has been calculated that to write the figure expressing the likelihood that our universe came to be by a random event would require a chalkboard as large as the entire universe. At the level of physics, the forces that hold the world together are so incredibly finely tuned that infinitesimally small changes would make life as we know it wholly impossible. . . . Thus, scientists report having their "atheism shaken" at the unlikeliness of it all, seeing a "hidden principle at work"; "or they say. . . I cannot abide the notion of purposelessness and blind chance in nature, and yet I do not know what to put in its place for the quieting of my mind." Apart from God, scientists are baffled.

(12) And to say just a word on the other issue—the matter of beginnings—the Big Bang theory of the origins of the universe—the currently favored model—brings scientists what they sometimes consider "perilously close" to positing a first moment.

(13) Still, one doesn't logically *have* to posit a God, or a beginning. But it helps. And add the consideration with which we started: there could have been just nothing. Nothing at all. For all who believe, Genesis 1 tells us why there is, instead, something: we ourselves, everything we love, the whole remarkable universe.

(14) In the beginning God created the heavens and the earth. And they were good. Let us seek better to love this beautiful world, even as we seek more confidently to rest our hope and trust in the mighty God who made it and us.[13]

a. Which paragraph(s) make up the introduction?
b. Which paragraphs make up the discussion?
c. Which paragraph(s) make up the conclusion?
d. Does the sermon as a whole fit one of the forms listed in "Sermon Forms" above (sec. 4.2), or does its form better fit the model of a sermon as the explication of an idea?
e. Does the introduction fit one of the forms in "Sermon Forms" above (sec. 4.2)? Which one?
f. How many major points does the discussion contain?
g. Which of the six functions of preaching listed by Broadus is most prominent?
h. Which of Cicero's three styles of speech would best suit this sermon?

    i. Which two paragraphs are most clearly aimed at "kindling the imagi-
nation"?

    j. If we take the text itself "In the beginning God created the heavens
and the earth" to be the proposition or the focus statement, does the
sermon explicate it, argue for it, or both?

    k. Does Shuster *apply* the proposition? If so, where?

    l. What mistaken view of creation is refuted in paragraph 7?

    m. What is the purpose of the Ymir story?

    n. Outline paragraphs 7 and 8.

    o. What role does the figure of the carpenter play?

    p. What is the function of paragraph 11?

    q. List the four main sources of materials for this sermon.

2. Read the following excerpts from sermons and choose from the list
below a function that the excerpt was most likely designed to serve.

    a. The God that holds you over the pit of hell, much as one holds a spider, or
some loathsome insect over the fire, abhors you, and is dreadfully pro-
voked: his wrath towards you burns like fire; he looks upon you as worthy
of nothing else, but to be cast into the fire; he is of purer eyes than to bear
to have you in his sight; you are ten thousand times more abominable in
his eyes, than the most hateful venomous serpent is in ours. You have
offended him infinitely more than ever a stubborn rebel did his prince;
and yet it is nothing but his hand that holds you from falling into the fire
every moment.[14]

    b. How often, my brethren, we pray, and our thoughts are elsewhere, as though
we forget in whose presence we are standing or before whom we are kneel-
ing? If all our faults are reckoned together against us, do they not over-
whelm us, even though they are small? Lead is all one mass, and sand
consists of tiny grains, yet the latter by their number weigh down heavily
upon you. So, too, your sins are little. But do you not see how the rivers are
filled and the lands wasted by little drops of water? They may be little, but
their number is great.[15]

    c. Men's hearts harden, and their guilt increases apace at such a day as this,
they neglect their souls; and never was there so great a danger of such
persons being given up to hardness of heart and blindness of mind. God
seems now to be hastily gathering in his elect in all parts of the land; and
probably the greater part of adult persons that ever shall be saved, will be
brought in now in a little time, and that it will be as it was in the great out-
pouring of the Spirit upon the Jews in the apostles' days; the election will
obtain, and the rest will be blinded. If this should be the case with you,
you will eternally curse this day, and will curse the day that ever you were
born, to see such a season of the pouring out of God's Spirit, and will wish
that you had died and gone to hell before you had seen it. Now undoubtedly it is, as it was in the days of John the Baptist, the axe is in an extraor-
dinary manner laid at the root of the tree, that every tree which brings not
forth good fruit, may be hewn down and cast into the fire.[16]

[14]Jonathan Edwards, "Sinners in the Hands of an Angry God."
[15]Augustine, "The Lord's Prayer Explained."
[16]Edwards, "Sinners in the Hands of an Angry God."

d. Now do not mistake and suppose that embracing the gospel is simply to believe these historical facts without truly receiving Christ as *your* saviour. If this had been the scheme, then Christ had need only to come down and die; then go back to heaven and quietly wait to see who would believe the facts. But how different is the real case! Now Christ comes down to fill the soul with His own life and love.[17]

e. To begin with, the face is not gentle. Here is how John of Patmos pictures the face of the Lord Christ as he speaks to the churches in the opening chapters of the Book of Revelation: "Then I turned to see the voice that was speaking to me, and on turning I saw seven golden lampstands, and in the midst of the lampstands one like a son of man, clothed with a long robe and with a golden girdle around his breast; his head and his hair were white as wool, white as snow; his eyes were like a flame of fire, his feet were like burnished bronze, refined as in a furnace, and his voice was like the sound of many waters . . . from his mouth issued a sharp two-edged sword, and his face was like the sun shining in full strength."[18]

f. They that lie back on the water of life and wait on the Lord between strokes shall renew their strength. They that lie trustingly in the bosom of providence, knowing that God will care for them while they recuperate—these are they that shall renew their strength in every way, physically, mentally, and spiritually. They shall even mount up with wings as eagles and soar through life in joy and victory. They shall both run and swim marathon distances, and not get weary. They shall walk and walk and walk and not faint.[19]

g. There was a time when we thought that the world could be a better place. We were capable of visions, you see. We could imagine a world of green lawns rather than a street full of junk, a world where neighbors greeted one another rather than pass silent with hidden faces.[20]

h. "Jesus loved him and said, 'Go, sell all you have and give it to the poor!'" He lacked "one thing needful," something beyond the bounds of conventional morality and realistic, practical ethics.

   Of course, if I had been Jesus that day, that's not what I would have said. I might have asked the well-heeled young man for an endowed fund for student scholarships, a bigger pledge for the church budget, not everything. This I call pastoral care, compassion. Unlike Jesus, if I had looked upon the young man, I would have been sensitive to his personal limitations, his need for some earthly security.[21]

i. To put it another way, Paul's word is advising us to make wise choice of our reruns. Whatever previously aired programs you may see this summer, you may be sure they are the best and not the worst of any series. It occurs to me that my ancestors had just such a selective process at work. They were instinctively seeking things to praise God for, largely as a result of their African religious roots. That made them live it over and over again. One small blessing lived through a hundred times could make a huge difference in the quality of their lives, if not the variety.[22]

[17]Charles Finney, "God's Love for a Sinning World."
[18]Edmund Steimle, quoted by Long, *The Witness of Preaching,* 123.
[19]Quoted by Long, 154.
[20]John Vannorsdall, quoted by Long, 125.
[21]William Willimon, quoted by Long, 120.
[22]Henry Mitchell, quoted by Long, 121.

j. November 30: the first Sunday in the Christian year, the first Sunday in the season of Advent, when we recall—and anticipate once again—God coming to be among us. God, among us. What in the world are we daring to say when we say that? On the face of it the whole idea is preposterous, like the cartoon I have in front of me. Dennis the Menace stands at his easel, diligently drawing away with his crayons. His mother stands in the background, throwing up her hands and inquiring, "How can you draw a picture of God? Nobody knows what he looks like." In the next frame Dennis replies confidently, "They will now."[23]

Functions
1. Attack the tendency to suppose we can capture God in human words and ideas.
2. Evoke feelings of crushed hopes.
3. Replace a popular misunderstanding of Jesus.
4. Replace a popular misunderstanding of faith.
5. Attack the tendency to tone down the gospel.
6. Impress upon the hearer the urgency of conversion.
7. Evoke feelings of trust in God.
8. Impress upon the hearer the gravity of sin.
9. Impress upon the hearer the gravity of small sins.
10. Communicate the idea that Christians can use memories to participate in creation of the world in which they live.

[23]Marguerite Shuster, "A Fire and a Name."

CHAPTER EIGHT

Reasoning in Ethics

1. Introduction

We engage in moral reasoning every day—making judgments about good and evil, right and wrong. Ethics is the name of the philosophical discipline that studies, systematizes, and attempts to justify moral reasoning. In chapter 1 we noted that morality is an important element in religious observance, and that the theological discipline that studies Christian morality is called theological ethics or moral theology. So ethics today is done by both philosophers and theologians.

Christian ethical thought has two intellectual ancestors: the Hebrew tradition and Greek philosophy. Already in the writings of Paul we find traces of Greek thought. By the time we reach Augustine the philosophical influences are quite strong. During the Middle Ages it is fair to say that for Christians there is no clear distinction between philosophical and theological ethics; the two traditions are thoroughly knit together. However, in the modern period philosophical ethics emerges once again as a discipline independent of theology.

2. Philosophical Ethics

Because of their constant relations through the centuries it is not possible to understand moral theology without some knowledge of philosophical ethics. So let us take a look at some of the history of the latter.

2.1. Classical Greece

In the classical Greek period (fifth and fourth centuries B.C.) ethical reasoning was often based on judgments about the *purposes* of things; this sort of ethics is called teleological, from *telos,* meaning end or purpose. The purposes of things could be determined by reflection on their natures. Another important concept was that of *virtue*. A virtue was understood as an acquired character trait or disposition that enables the possessor to attain his or her true end. Thus, Aristotle was able to argue that rationality is the essential characteristic of human nature (it is what distinguishes us from other animals). Therefore the highest virtue for humans is theoretical wisdom. Whatever characteristics aid in the achievement of this excellence are also virtues. An Aristotelian argument in schematic form would look something like this:

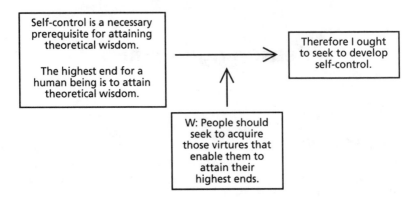

The recognition that self-control is necessary for attaining the higher virtue of theoretical wisdom comes from experience. Knowledge of the highest goal for human life comes, as noted above, from reflection on the nature of human beings, in particular on what differentiates them from other sorts of beings. The backing for this warrant cannot be summarized adequately here, since it involves a great deal of Aristotle's philosophy. It can be hinted at, though, by noting that for the Greeks in general there was no sharp differentiation between the way things are and the way they ought to be—between what we today might call 'facts' and 'values.' The cosmos for Aristotle is a rational *order;* order is *good;* filling one's proper niche in that order, therefore, is good. So to be good is simply to be what one (intrinsically) *is.* This is the intuition behind much ethical thought based on *natural law,* which we find appearing in various forms in both theological and philosophical ethics up through the early modern period.

2.2. The Modern Period

As noted above, philosophical ethics came into its own again in the modern period, distinguishing itself from the moral teaching of the churches. It was hoped that by turning to *reason* a common basis for personal and political life could be secured in the wake of the wars and turmoil following the Reformation. Two schools of thought have been particularly important. The most familiar is utilitarianism; the other is called deontological, or Kantian for its most prominent founder.

2.2.1. Utilitarianism

Stated simply, this is the view that one ought to choose the course of action that brings about the greatest good for the greatest number of people ("act utilitarianism"); or one ought to follow the rule of conduct that in general brings about the greatest good for the greatest number ("rule utilitarianism"). Jeremy Bentham (1748–1832) and John Stuart Mill (1806–73) were influential in formulating this way of thinking.

Let us look at the form of a typical utilitarian argument—act-utilitarian, in this case. Suppose Granny is slowly dying of an incurable disease and is suffering from uncontrollable pain. The doctor sees two options: to allow nature to take its slow, painful (and expensive) course, or to administer a lethal dose of morphine. The latter course would end Granny's pain, save the emotional trauma for the family watching her suffer, and avert the bankruptcy that her long illness will cause. On the other side, there is a slight chance that the doctor will be caught and punished. It becomes clear that in this case, at least, euthanasia will bring about the greatest good for the greatest number of people, so this is the *right* thing to do. Schematically:

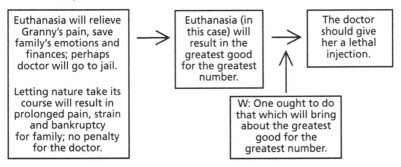

Despite serious problems with utilitarianism as a system of ethics (for example, should the greatest good be thought of in terms of pleasure, long-term happiness, eternal salvation?), we often find it difficult to think in any other way about moral matters. But note how the sort of claims that are made has changed since the days of the Greek philosophers, for whom moral reasoning had to do first of all with what constituted a *good person;* how to act in particular situations was secondary and to be judged on the basis of wisdom about how the virtues could be cultivated. Now the focus of moral reasoning is on the acts themselves, and in particular on how to make decisions when faced with moral dilemmas.

A very common kind of argument, both within and outside of ethics, is what is called the slippery slope argument. We treat it here because it often involves imagined *consequences* of a policy or position. Arguments against euthanasia often take this form: Allowing doctors or family members to decide that some terminally ill patients should be assisted in dying will be the first step toward making judgments about others' "quality of life" and deciding that they, too, should be "put out of their misery"; we will end up being just like the Nazis. So this form of euthanasia must not be permitted.

Arguments of this sort are often effective, but we need to be wary of them. An argument of similar form can be constructed to support (or rebut) practically any claim. The weak point of this one is the assumption that killing terminally ill patients *will lead to* killing in other cases, that the imagined sequence of stages is inevitable. Well, maybe so, maybe not.

Another frequently heard argument concerns abortion. It is obviously wrong to kill a newborn infant; there is no intrinsic difference between a newborn and a child in the womb just before birth, so it must be wrong to kill an unborn baby, too. There are only differences of degree between an unborn baby and an embryo; therefore, it must be wrong to abort an embryo or a fetus at any point from conception on.

This argument is an instance of what is also sometimes called the black-and-white fallacy. It is misleading in that it assumes that a large number of differences, each in itself too small to matter, still do not matter when added together. Thus, one can move gradually from black to white through shades of gray that are so similar that they cannot be distinguished, and conclude that there really is no difference between black and white. Moral reasoners, beware!

2.2.2. Deontological Ethics

The second predominant approach to ethics in modern philosophy is called deontological, from the Greek stem *deont-*, meaning that which is binding. The reader who objected to the utilitarian conclusion above with the protest that euthanasia is murder and is just *wrong*, whatever the consequences, was displaying the sort of moral intuition central to deontological ethics. Here the emphasis is on the fact that we often know what our moral duty is apart from calculating the consequences, and sometimes even in the face of adverse consequences.

According to Immanuel Kant (1724–1804), moral arguments were all to be *backed* by a principle called the *categorical imperative*. Kant expressed this principle in several forms, one of which is the following: "Act only according to that maxim by which you can at the same time will that it should become a universal law."[1]

Thus, a doctor who is a deontologist might argue:

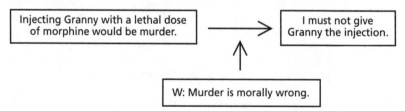

---

[1]Immanuel Kant, *Foundations of the Metaphysics of Morals*, trans. Lewis White Beck (New York: Liberal Arts Press, 1959), 39.

So far the argument is rather dull. The interesting feature added by Kant is the backing provided by the categorical imperative, and by the reasoning used to justify it in turn. Kant's insight is that there is really no distinction between being moral and being reasonable. It is unreasonable to make ourselves exceptions to general moral principles (why should I be allowed to commit murder if no one else is?). The mark of a moral principle is exactly its generality—its universalizability. Some actions cannot be undertaken as a general policy because attempting to do so would destroy the very possibility of such actions. We cannot all be murderers because in the end there will be no one left to do it; we cannot all lie because consistent lying destroys the very possibility of communication; we cannot all steal because there would no longer be personal property to steal. Note that the problem is not that it is bad for people not to have property or to be able to communicate; rather, it is that the policies in question cannot be carried out consistently.

A deontological and a utilitarian ethicist might argue for the same claims (for example, against lying, in favor of the protection of private property), but we can see that the warrants and backing they would provide will be radically different. To some extent, the existence of these two different approaches to ethics accounts for the intractability of some public moral debates. For example, "pro-choice" advocates may argue their case on the basis of the *consequences* for mother and child of an unwanted pregnancy. "Pro-life" advocates may be arguing on the basis that abortion (as murder) is *categorically* wrong. But in addition to these differences in style of reasoning, we can see here that there are also differences in judgment about the truth of the assertions that are used in the grounds of the arguments: for example, *Is* the fetus a person or not? *Is* abortion murder or not?

3. Theological Ethics

Moral arguments and ethical systems produced in the course of Christian history have been at least as varied as those in philosophy—perhaps more so—often because Christians have found *varied* ways to make use of the *variety* of concepts provided by the philosophers. Since a comprehensive survey of systems is not possible here, we will proceed by offering some representative examples from different historical periods.

As mentioned above, ethical thought within the Christian tradition draws mainly from two sources: the Hebrew tradition and Greek philosophy. So throughout we find echoes of the Jewish emphasis on divine law. Theological ethics at its simplest and most basic employs warrants of the sort: "God said . . . " While divine command may rightly be the beginning of Christian ethics, it can never be the sum total, even in Hebraic thought, for there is always the problem of interpretation and application. As a rabbi friend has pointed out, it is not clear whether the command "Do not boil the kid in its mother's milk" (Exod. 23:19—said to be the root of Kosher dietary law) implies that one must prepare meat and milk dishes with separate utensils, or only that one should avoid cheeseburgers.

3.1. Moral Reasoning in the New Testament

Let us look first at an example from Jesus' teaching:[2]

> You have heard that they were told, "Love your neighbor and hate your enemy." But what I tell you is this: Love your enemies and pray for your persecutors; only so can you be children of your heavenly Father, who causes the sun to rise on the good and bad alike, and sends the rain on the innocent and the wicked (Matt. 5:43–45 REB).

Jesus' command to love enemies and pray for persecutors is a general precept rather than a claim regarding a particular person and situation, so we might best construe it as a *warrant* for Jesus' followers to apply in various situations as they arise:

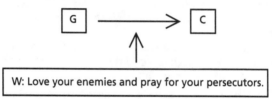

Next, Jesus supplies backing. Why should his followers love their enemies? Because in doing so they become children of the heavenly Father, who does good for both the innocent and the wicked. So the assumption that backs Jesus' moral teaching here is that his followers are to be like their Father. God's character is known from his provident care for all creatures, whether they be pleasing to him or not.

A few comments are in order about the content that might be filled in as grounds and claim in the above argument form. It is important to note from the context that the teaching is addressed to the disciples, not to all people everywhere. So appropriate arguments will be about the morality of the disciples. Second, as noted above, we in the modern (or postmodern) West are accustomed to thinking of ethical arguments as having to do solely with decisions about actions. So we are apt to think that the arguments governed by this warrant will be of the following sort:

Notice, though, that while loving actions can sometimes be undertaken upon command, the context of the sermon makes it clear that outward actions alone do not satisfy the demands of the new law. Jesus' disciples must not only act lovingly, they must also have love in their hearts—which is another way of saying that they must *be* the sort of people who can love their enemies and pray with genuineness for their persecutors.

---

[2]At least as the early church remembered it. We will address questions of historical authenticity in chapter 10.

So the ethic of Jesus, at least as we see it here, makes claims first of all about the sort of person one must be, and only secondarily about the kinds of actions one must undertake. More particularly, the teaching Jesus provides here is intended to warrant arguments about the kind of person a *disciple* is to be, and it is backed in this instance not by a command of the Father, but rather by Jesus' insight into the *character* of the Father.

3.2. Medieval Christian Ethics

One of the most notable accomplishments of Thomas Aquinas (1225–74) was his synthesis of Augustinian theology with the recently rediscovered philosophy of Aristotle. His ethical thinking, therefore, provides an interesting example of medieval theologians' use of concepts drawn from philosophical ethics to support Christian moral claims. Consider the following excerpt:

> Since the best thing for man is to become attached in his mind to God and divine things, and since it is impossible for man intensively to busy himself with a variety of things in order that man's mind may be applied to God with greater liberty, counsels are given in the divine law whereby men are withdrawn from the busy concerns of the present life as far as possible for one who is living an earthly life. Now, this detachment is not so necessary to man for justice that its absence makes justice impossible; indeed, virtue and justice are not removed if man uses bodily and earthly things in accord with the order of reason. And so, divine admonitions of this kind are called *counsels,* not *precepts,* inasmuch as man is *urged* to renounce lesser goods for the sake of better goods.
>
> Moreover, in the general mode of human life, human concern is devoted to three items: first, to one's own person, what he should do, or where he should spend his time; second, to the persons of those connected with him, chiefly his wife and children; and third, to the acquisition of external things, which a man needs for the maintenance of life. So, to cut off solicitude for external things the counsel of *poverty* is given in the divine law, that is to say, so that one may cast off the things of this world with which his mind could be involved with some concern. Hence, the Lord says: "If thou wilt be perfect, go sell what thou has and give to the poor . . . and come, follow me" (Matt. 19:21). And to cut off concern for wife and children there is given man the counsel of *virginity* or *continence.* Hence, it is said in 1 Corinthians (7:25): "Now, concerning virgins, I have no commandment of the Lord, but I give counsel." And giving the reason for this counsel, he adds: "He that is without a wife is solicitous for the things that belong to the Lord: how he may please God. But he that is with a wife is solicitous for the things of the world: how he may please his wife, and he is divided" (1 Cor. 7:32–33). Finally, to cut off man's solicitude even for himself there is given the counsel of *obedience,* through which man hands over the control of his own acts to a superior. Concerning which it is said: "Obey your prelates and be subject to them. For they watch as being ready to render an account of your souls" (Heb. 13:17).[3]

As in most instances of ethical reasoning, Thomas is arguing for a *warrant,* which might be used in a moral argument such as the following:

[3]*Summa Contra Gentiles,* bk. 3, chap. 130.

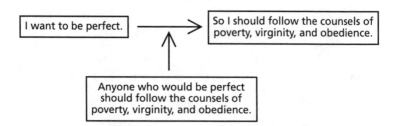

Thomas believed that much of what is revealed in scripture could also be known independently by reason. This view is illustrated by the way he argues in backing his warrant: in effect he says that the counsels are enjoined by scripture *and* it is apparent on the basis of reason that they should be. His argument employs an overriding Aristotelian principle that one ought to give up lesser goods in order to attain the highest goods. According to Thomas's theology, the highest good for humankind is knowledge of and love for God; this is the *end* or *purpose* of human life. But we also know from experience that concerns of the present life get in the way of devotion to God; these concerns center around one's person, one's family, and one's possessions. It is reasonable, therefore, to free oneself, insofar as possible, from these concerns. The means of attaining such liberty is by making vows of poverty, virginity, and obedience. Note in the following schematization how the warrants are backed by quotations from scripture. That the greatest human good (perfection) is to be found in God, and in addition that one ought to renounce lesser goods for God's sake, are both supported (later in the passage) by scriptural quotations: "The kingdom of heaven is like to a merchant seeking good pearls, who, when he had found one pearl of great price, went his way and sold all that he had and bought it" (Matt. 13:45); and "the things that were gain to me . . . I counted them but as dung, that I might gain Christ" (Phil. 3:7–8).

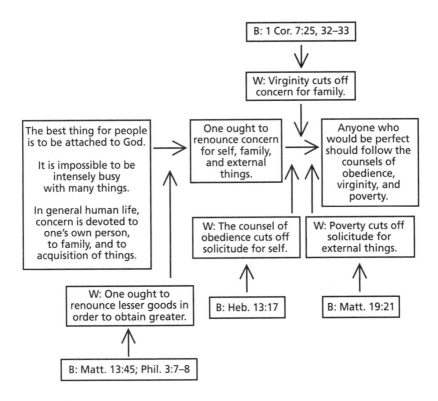

One last point to note about Thomas's argument concerns the second half of the first paragraph. Here he is *qualifying* the sort of argument his warrant will allow. The three counsels are not obligatory, so the qualifier 'necessarily' is not appropriate. One can only argue something of this sort: If I wish to be perfect, *ideally* I should follow the counsels of poverty, obedience, and virginity.

3.3. Reformation Ethics

Martin Luther shared with many of his medieval predecessors the view that God's will could be known by reflecting on the orders of creation. However, this knowledge of natural law is often obscured by sin, so scriptural precepts are needed to reawaken it. Luther's dual reliance on scripture and the observable order of things is nicely illustrated in the following argument, written to encourage Wolfgang Reissenbusch, a monk in Saxony, to set aside the very vow of celibacy we have just seen Thomas supporting.

Reverend and esteemed Sir:

I am moved by several good friends and also by the esteem in which I hold you to write this letter on the estate of matrimony. I have often spoken to you about it and have observed that you are not only suited for and inclined toward marriage but are also forced and compelled to it by God himself, who created you therefor.

I do not think that you should be kept from it by the rule of your order or by a vow, for you should be fully convinced that no vow can bind you or be valid except under two conditions.

First, the vow must be possible of fulfillment and within our power to perform. For who will vow an impossible thing? Or who will demand it? All vows are therefore described in the Scriptures in terms that are within our power, such as to give God cattle, sheep, houses, land, and so on. Now, chastity is not in our power, as little as are God's other wonders and graces. But we are all made for marriage, as our bodies show and as the Scriptures state in Gen., ch. 2: "It is not good that man should be alone; I will make him a help meet for him" (2:18).

Whoever, therefore, considers himself a man and believes himself to be included in this general term should hear what God, his Creator, here says and decrees for him: he does not wish man to be alone but desires that he should multiply, and so he makes him a helpmeet to be with him and help him so that he may not be alone. This is the Word of God, through whose power procreative seed is planted in man's body and a natural, ardent desire for woman is kindled and kept alive. This cannot be restrained either by vows or by laws. For it is God's law and doing. . . .

For this reason such a vow against God's Word and against nature, being impossible, is null and void. And God also condemns it, just as if somebody should vow to be God's mother or to make a heaven.

Secondly, to be valid a vow must not be against God and the Christian faith. Everything that relies on works and not on God's grace is against God and the Christian faith; as it is written in Heb., ch. 12, "The heart must be established with grace, not with meats" [Heb. 13:9]—that is, not with works and laws that pertain to food, drink, and the like. Of this sort are all monastic vows; they establish hearts and consciences on works and not on grace, and by this reliance on works men deny Christ and lose faith. . . .

Why should you delay, my dear and reverend sir, and continue to weigh the matter in your mind? It must, should, and will happen in any case. Stop thinking about it and do it right merrily. Your body demands it. God wills it and drives you to it. There is nothing that you can do about it.[4]

Luther's letter serves as a *rebuttal* to Reissenbusch's (unstated) argument that because he had made a vow of chastity and because vows should not be broken he must remain chaste rather than marry. Luther's rebuttal consists in pointing out that there are exceptional cases wherein vows are invalid.

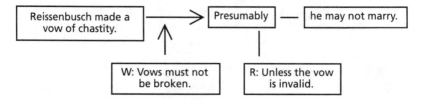

[4]*Luther: Letters of Spiritual Counsel,* ed. and trans. Theodore Tappert, Library of Christian Classics 18 (Philadelphia: Westminster Press, 1955), 273–74.

To establish that Reissenbusch's vow is in fact invalid Luther argues that there are two grounds for breaking a vow: one when what has been promised is impossible, and the other when what has been promised is contrary to the Christian faith. Reissenbusch's vow of chastity is invalid on both counts. It is impossible because we were made for marriage. We know this both from scripture (Gen. 2:18) and by observation—male and female bodies are obviously designed for intercourse and procreation. This is an instance of inferring God's will from observation of the "orders of creation."

In addition, celibacy is judged to be "against God and the Christian faith" because it is an instance of works righteousness. Here we see brought to bear the central theme of Luther's theology—salvation by grace alone.

Luther's two arguments can be summarized as follows:

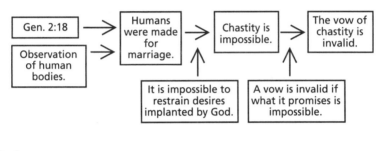

And:

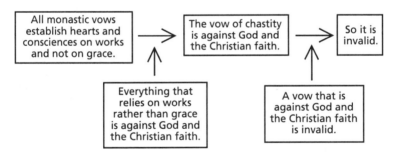

3.4. Modern Theological Ethics

To a great extent modern theological ethicists have attempted to appropriate the basic patterns of reasoning established by modern philosophers and turn them to Christian purposes. The writings of J. Philip Wogaman provide an interesting example of the influence of utilitarianism.

Wogaman's system revolves around the notion of a *presumption*. Christian ethical presumptions function in ethical arguments the way the presumption of innocence does in a legal argument, where innocence must be assumed until adequate evidence to the contrary is produced. In other words, *the burden of proof* rests with the prosecution. In the Christian moral sphere we have presumptions such as the goodness of created existence, the value of individual life, the equality of persons in God. Anyone who would choose to act against such a presumption bears the burden of proof to show why an exception should be made in this case. For example:

> The article of faith, the presumption, remains: God has created the world and the creation is good. How, exactly, can such a faith claim serve as a methodological presumption to help guide Christians in their moral judgments?
>
> In a general sense, the answer to this is that in any issue of judgment where the postulated goodness of creation is itself the matter in question, our presumption should always lie with actions reaffirming that goodness. Potential suicide is an obvious illustration. Excluding deliberate acts of martyrdom or heroism, which are not really suicidal, taking one's own life always suggests that existence has become intolerable. . . . Nevertheless, the presumption of the goodness of creation necessarily places a burden of proof against such a desperate act. To put this differently, our initial presumption must be that suicide is incompatible with Christian faith since such an act always suggests that for the individual involved existence is no longer good.
>
> Some forms of alleged suicide may be excluded from this assessment because they are in no sense based upon suicidal intent. . . . In war there have been reported instances of soldiers hurling themselves on live grenades in order to absorb the lethal impact of the explosion, thus saving the lives of comrades. . . . The word suicide ought to be reserved for those actions which have the termination of one's own existence as their primary end—and not for those actions which, while inevitably self-destructive in effect, are designed to save the lives of others.
>
> Still, the burden of proof ought to be against even generous actions which will inevitably result in personal loss of life. Among those who love life, who find created existence good, this presumption functions automatically and can only be overcome when some greater good than one's own continued physical existence is at stake. The burden of proof may then have been met. A tragic incident which occurred in California during the mid-1960s can illustrate the problem. A small aircraft crashed into the home of a minister who lived near an airport and exploded into flames. Miraculously, this man escaped uninjured through the front door. Without his knowledge, his wife and mother escaped through the back door, also uninjured. Frantically looking about for his loved ones, he dashed back into the burning house to save them. As a result of this unnecessary act of bravery he received severe burns from which he later died. What should be said concerning such an instinctive act of self-sacrifice? . . . It might be said that the burden of proof justifying this exceptionally perilous act had been met. However, the objectively needless waste of this good man's life should remind us that heroic self-sacrifice where there is virtually no hope of achieving the good sought must have a burden of proof placed against it.[5]

So, according to Wogaman, all interesting ethical argument involves potential *rebuttals*. In this case, self-destructive acts are ordinarily proscribed by the presumption of the goodness of created existence, which functions as a warrant in the argument:

---

[5]J. Philip Wogaman, *A Christian Method of Moral Judgment* (Philadelphia: Westminster, 1976), 73–74.

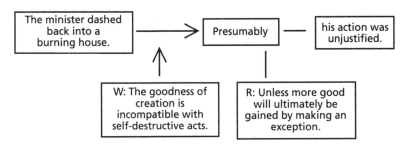

The *backing* for Wogaman's presumption (mentioned briefly in the quotation above but spelled out at length elsewhere) is the theological conviction that the world is God's creation, and is therefore good. Note that when it comes down to making judgments about concrete cases (the minister and the burning house) Wogaman's thinking is *thoroughly utilitarian.* He states explicitly that "one general criterion is involved in all thought about exceptions. This is that more good will ultimately be gained by making an exception than by remaining faithful to the presumption itself (51). So Wogaman's argument for the acceptability of the minister's action is as follows:

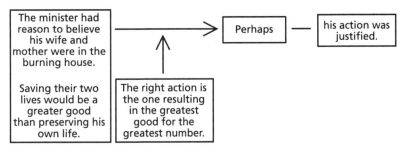

3.5. Current Changes in Theological Ethics

Some more recent moral theologians see modern philosophical ethics (utilitarian and deontological) as an inadequate framework for Christian thought and have returned to an emphasis on character and virtue. Stanley Hauerwas and James Wm. McClendon, Jr. are two examples. Both are influenced by the work of philosopher Alasdair MacIntyre, who has attempted to provide a more usable definition of 'virtue.' According to MacIntyre, a virtue can be understood in terms of a *practice*—a coherent and complex form of socially established cooperative human activity.[6] Virtues are skills or qualities one needs in order to attain the goods that are internal to such practices. In the following argument we see McClendon first defining the Christian virtue of *presence* and then arguing for its necessity for the practice of evangelism.[7]

---

[6]Alasdair MacIntyre, *After Virtue,* 2d ed. (Notre Dame: University of Notre Dame Press, 1984), 187.

[7] James Wm. McClendon, Jr., *Ethics* (Nashville: Abingdon, 1986).

To epitomize several of these points, and to bring the threads of the chapter together at the close, let us attend to a particular Christian virtue, . . . *presence.* By presence is meant quite simply the quality of *being there* for and with the other. Exactly because it is not on the classic lists of virtues, it may be easier to approach without preconceptions. We remember that God's presence with us is one of the great gifts of the gospel, associated with the incarnation of the Word, the giving of the Spirit, and the return of the Lord; we recall that in Christian history his presence is celebrated in every eucharistic meal, invoked at every baptism, and claimed anew at every gathering of disciples. What we want now, however, is to understand presence as a dimension of the Christian life. Clearly *being there* is for us a function of our embodied existence; it is only by metaphor or analogy that we can speak of a disembodied presence. Still, that very analogy is important, for if a Paul whose bodily presence is judged "weak" (2 Cor. 10:10) can, though absent in body, be "present in spirit" to judge a flagrant case of misconduct (1 Cor. 5:3f.), so can we, though bodily present, *fail* to be there for those who need us. One thinks of an estranged couple sitting at a table for two and staring moodily past one another. . . .

But is presence, even in this extended sense, really a virtue, or is it like left-handedness or curiosity, merely somebody's quality or distinguishing feature? Earlier in this chapter the black church was set forth as displaying the quality of presence. When black slaves had no other earthly resource, they knew how to be present to and for one another, and knew that Another was present for them as well. . . . To characterize this presence as a virtue is to say that it is a strength or skill, developed by training and practice, which is a substantive part of (the Christian) life. . . . This strength meets the needs, fulfills the goals, carries the meaning of Christian living (106–7).

This brings us to the next important concern, the relation of virtues to practices. In Chapter Three we met the question whether some general human virtues, understood as skills for living, might be merely the enhancement of our organic psychological and physical equipment, and thus pretty much the same for all organically similar people. The answer offered there, however, was that our skills for living are embedded in the several stories of which we are a part and so cannot be understood apart from these stories. . . . Now we can say more clearly how that is so; many virtues have their home in connection with particular practices whose pursuit evokes exactly those virtues. For example, if we are members of a community one of whose practices is Christian witness or evangelism, it will be plain to us that the virtue of presence, first discussed in Chapter Three, is required by that practice—in MacIntyre's words, is "appropriate to, and partially definitive of, that form of activity," while the 'perversions' of and vices contrary to presence (e.g., nosiness) will be condemned in part just because they defeat the practice of evangelism. For one who will not be present to and for the neighbor cannot effectively witness to that neighbor, even though witness consists in a good deal more than presence alone (169).

Note that precedent for presence is found not only in scriptural accounts of early church members (in the case of the Apostle Paul), but even in God's own story. So there is the hint of an argument for the cultivation of such a skill on the basis of the warrant that Christians today must reproduce in their own communities not only the character of the early church, which took its moral guidance from Jesus, but ultimately, the character of God.

The explicit argument here is in the second passage, and is a fairly simple one:

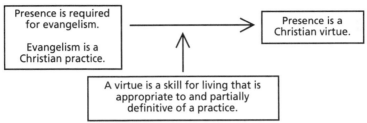

We end with one other example of an argument for the cultivation of virtues warranted by their necessity for a practice central to Christian life. In the following passage we have a report (by Stanley Hauerwas) of John Howard Yoder's account of gifts and virtues required for the practice of moral discernment:

> Yoder's characterization of how practical reason should work to inform Christian conscience directs our attention to questions of how our community works, rather than leading us to concentrate on how ideas or principles work. Practical reason is not a disembodied process based on abstract principles, but the process of a community in which every member has a role to play. Such a process does not disdain the importance of logical rigor for aiding in their deliberation, but logic cannot be a substitute for the actual process of discernment.
>
> The conversation made possible by such a community draws from people of different gifts and virtues. For example, certain people have the charisma of prophecy, whose primary focus is neither prediction nor moral guidance but stating and reinforcing the vision of the place of the believing community in history in which any moral reasoning gains intelligibility. Equally important are what Yoder calls "agents of memory," who do not pretend to speak on their own but as servants of communal memory. These "scribes" are practical moral reasoners who do not judge or decide anything but remember "expertly, charismatically, the store of memorable, identity-confirming acts of faithfulness praised and of failure repented." Scripture is crucial for moral reflection, as texts inform the community's memory through the "charismatic aptness of the scribe's selectivity." Such selectivity, however, must be informed as well as critically related to the tradition which is essential to the church's interpretation of Scripture. The community of practical discourse also depends on what Yoder calls "agents of linguistic self-consciousness." These are those teachers who are charged with the steering of the community with the rudder of language. Such people, realizing at once the power and danger of language, will be attentive to the temptations to use verbal distinctions and/or purely verbal solutions to "solve" substantial problems. Also crucial are "agents of order and due process" who have the task to oversee and lead the community. Their task is to insure that everyone is heard and that conclusions reached are genuinely consensual.
>
> That such agents are required in the Christian community is but a reminder that the existence of such a people is not determined by a series of decisions

but rather requires the development of virtues and the wisdom gained from those in the past as well as the present who have attempted to follow Jesus.[8]

Yoder's views are tightly compressed here, but we can construct the following argument for the charism or virtue of prophecy by making explicit some of his assumptions. The same could be done for the other virtues he mentions.

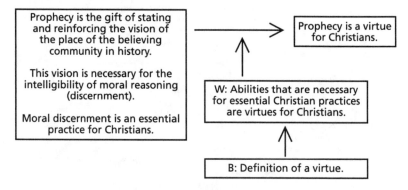

This is a good example with which to end. It serves as a reminder that there is more to the skill of Christian moral reasoning than abstract thought. It reminds us as well that moral judgment has traditionally been a function of the Christian *community* under the guidance of the Holy Spirit.[9]

4. Concluding Remarks

Christian ethicists, it seems, have to combat two quite different temptations. One is to suppose that genuine moral reasoning must have a universal character, and that any argument that depends essentially on the beliefs of a particular religious tradition is not a genuine moral argument. This view is epitomized in the work of Immanuel Kant. In response, it might be noted that all moral reasoning will need to be grounded on *some* assertions about the way things are; and all knowledge, we recognize today, is dependent upon some tradition. To illustrate, I remind the reader of the parenthetical criticism of utilitarianism above. To determine the greatest good in a particular situation one has to have some idea about the kinds of goods that are possible for human beings. Anyone who makes utilitarian calculations that *omit* the factor of eternal happiness is thereby assuming the truth of the assertion that the present life is all there is.

On the other hand, some may object to the reliance on philosophy that the tradition demonstrates, assuming that Christian ethics would be more Christian if theologians would just stick with the kind of reasoning found in the Bible. In response, I suggest a quick look at the New Testament with

[8]Stanley Hauerwas, *Christian Existence Today* (Durham, N.C.: Labyrinth Press, 1988), 73–74.

[9]See my *Theology in the Age of Scientific Reasoning* (Ithaca, N.Y.: Cornell University Press, 1990), chap. 5, for a discussion of the practice of communal discernment.

an eye for the different kinds of moral arguments included there. While there may be considerable agreement there on matters of content, there is no single form of argument to be discerned and emulated.[10]

The distinction between form and content is not entirely clear, but in a rough way we can understand the Christian ethical tradition as a series of attempts to organize and understand the *content* of New Testament morality according to conceptual *forms* provided by the succession of cultures in which it has been taught. However, it is always necessary to be careful that the tradition does not lose its distinctiveness when the new wine fails to fit the prevailing wineskins.

EXERCISE EIGHT

The passages in this exercise and in all succeeding chapters are chosen both to provide practice in reasoning skills and to familiarize students with the writings of important thinkers in the various fields. In some cases they will be authors already described in the chapter; in other cases they will have been chosen to provide broader exposure. Brief notes provide some context when it seems necessary.

Read each passage carefully several times, then answer the questions that follow.

1. This passage is not an argument, but rather a report on Luther's reasoning. We could, however, reconstruct an argument from the information presented here.

   > (1) Because the offices, particularly the political offices, have been instituted by God as the indispensable form of serving our fellow man, (2) Luther encourages Christians to make themselves available for such offices wherever there is a lack of people to administer them properly. (3) Christians ought always to be available whenever they have the opportunity to serve others, no matter what form such service may actually take. (4) They should not selfishly ask whether a particular service is important in the eyes of the world or attractive to them personally, but only how necessary it is.[11]

   a. Which sentence or clause tells us what Luther claimed?
   b. Where do we find grounds for Luther's argument?
   c. Which sentence or clause provides a warrant?
   d. If we take 4 as a reply to a potential rebuttal, what is the rebuttal?

2. Accept anyone who is weak in faith without debate about his misgivings. For instance, one person may have faith strong enough to eat all kinds of food, while another who is weaker eats only vegetables. (1) Those who eat meat must not look down on those who do not, and those who do not eat

---

[10]See John Howard Yoder, *The Politics of Jesus* (1972; Grand Rapids: Eerdmans, 1994), for one account of the unity of New Testament ethical teaching.

[11]Paul Althaus, *The Ethics of Martin Luther,* trans. Robert Schultz (Philadelphia: Fortress, 1972), 71.

meat must not pass judgment on those who do; (2) for God has accepted them. (3) Who are you to pass judgment on someone else's servant? (4) Whether he stands or falls is his own Master's business (Rom. 14:1–4a REB)

a. If 1 is the claim, which statement provides the grounds?
b. 3 suggests a warrant for the argument. Write it in a more 'warrant-like' form.
c. From this warrant we can see that there is a step missing in Paul's argument. Fill in the missing parts.

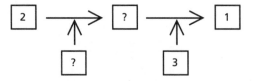

3. This passage from a textbook on philosophical ethics summarizes Socrates' reply to the question why he should allow himself to be executed. Socrates (469–399 B.C.) was Plato's teacher (who, in turn, taught Aristotle). Socrates was the main character in Plato's *Dialogues*.

> Suppose that all your life you have been trying to be a good person, doing your duty as you see it and seeking to do what is for the good for your fellow men. Suppose, also that many of your fellow men dislike you and what you are doing and even regard you as a danger to society, although they cannot really show this to be true. Suppose, further, that you are indicted, tried, and condemned to death by a jury of your peers, all in a manner which you correctly consider to be quite unjust. Suppose, finally, that while you are in prison awaiting execution, your friends arrange an opportunity for you to escape and go into exile with your family. . . .
>
> This is the situation Socrates, the patron saint of moral philosophy, is in at the opening of Plato's dialogue, the *Crito*. The dialogue gives us his answer to our question and a full account of his reasoning in arriving at it. . . . Socrates first lays down some points about the approach to be taken. We must not let our decision be affected by our emotion, but must examine the question and follow the best reasoning. We must try to get our facts straight and to keep our minds clear. Questions like this can and should be settled by reason. We cannot answer such questions by appealing to what people generally think. They may be wrong. We must try to find an answer we ourselves can regard as correct. We must think for ourselves. We ought never to do what is morally wrong. The only question we need answer is whether what is proposed is right or wrong, not what will happen to us, what people will think of us, or how we feel about what has happened.
>
> Having said this, Socrates goes on to give, in effect, a threefold argument to show that he ought not to break the laws by escaping. We ought never to harm anyone. Socrates' escaping would harm the state, since it would violate and show disregard for the state's laws. If one remains living in a state when one could leave it, one tacitly agrees to obey its laws; hence, if Socrates were to escape he would be breaking an agreement, which is something one should not do. One's society or state is virtually one's parent and teacher, and one ought to obey one's parents and teachers.

In each of these arguments Socrates appeals to a general moral rule or principle which, upon reflection, he and his friend Crito accept as valid: (1) that we ought never to harm anyone, (2) that we ought to keep our promises, and (3) that we ought to obey and respect our parents and teachers. In each case he also uses another premise which involves a statement of fact and applies the rule or principle to the case in hand: (1) if I escape I will do injury to society, (2) if I escape I will be breaking a promise, and (3) if I escape I will be disobeying my parent and teacher. Then he draws a conclusion about what he should do in his particular situation. This is a typical pattern of reasoning in moral matters and is nicely illustrated here.[12]

a. Write the claim for which Socrates is arguing.
b. Diagram Socrates' three arguments, supplying any missing warrants or grounds. Note that two of the arguments are slightly more complex than Frankena may lead you to believe. Also, you may wish to reformulate the claim slightly in each case.

4. This passage by Thomas follows the one quoted in "Medieval Christian Ethics" above (sec. 3.2).

There have been some people who, in opposition to the teaching of the Gospel, have disapproved the practice of voluntary poverty. The first of these to be found is Vigilantius, whom, however, some others have followed later, "Calling themselves teachers of the law, understanding neither the things they say, nor whereof they affirm" (1 Tim. 1:7). They were led to this view by these and similar arguments.

Natural appetite requires every animal to provide for itself in regard to the necessities of its life; thus, animals that are not able to find the necessities of life during every period of the year, by a certain natural instinct gather the things needed for life during the season when they can be found, and they keep them; this practice is evident in the case of bees and ants. But men need many things for the preservation of life which cannot be found in every season. So, there is a natural tendency in man to gather and keep things necessary to him. Therefore, it is contrary to natural law to throw away, under the guise of poverty, all that one has gathered together.
. . .

Moreover, if it be evil to possess the substance of this world, but if it be good to deliver one's neighbors from evil and bad to lead them into evil, the conclusion is that to give the substance of this world to a needy person is an evil and to take from an owner is a good. Now, this is not right. So, it is a good thing to possess the substance of this world. Therefore, to throw it away entirely is an evil thing.

Furthermore, occasions of evil are to be avoided. But poverty is an occasion of evil, since some are induced, as a result of it, to acts of theft, of false praise and perjury, and the like. Therefore, poverty should not be embraced voluntarily; rather, should care be taken to avoid its advent.[13]

a. In what relation do the arguments here stand to Thomas's argument discussed earlier in this chapter?

[12]William Frankena, *Ethics* (Englewood Cliffs, N.J.: Prentice-Hall, 1963), 1–2.
[13]Thomas Aquinas, *Summa Contra Gentiles,* bk. 3, chap. 130.

b. Diagram the argument in the fourth paragraph. (You need to supply one missing warrant.)

c. The refutation of an assumption by showing that it leads to an absurd conclusion is a type of argument called *reductio ad absurdum*. In which paragraph does Thomas make such an argument?

d. Diagram the argument in the second paragraph.

5. This passage from Wogaman's ethics illustrates his use of the concept of a moral presumption.

> (ii) The Value of Individual Life
>
> Thus, the burden of proof falls against any action or policy or social movement which has as its rationale the alleged unimportance or disvalue of any individual lives. Grosser illustrations which leap to mind [such as genocide] need not detain us. . . . Other kinds of problems may pose more difficulty for sensitive Christians in our time. There is, for instance, the problem of capital punishment. . . . There are Christians who still strongly believe in it. . . . I believe that such Christians should reflect more deeply upon the meaning of the presumption of the value of each life. The Christian moral presumption ought to be against capital punishment even when it is punishment for the crime of murder. I find it conceivable that under extreme historical circumstances some form of capital punishment might be necessary as a deterrent. The burden of proof should still be against it. It should not be used unless there is very strong evidence that it is necessary as a way of saving lives and as a way of affirming the sanctity and security of all life in community. . . . Capital punishment rests on the postulate that the criminal is no longer fit to live.[14]

Diagram the argument discussed here for which the presumption of the value of individual life serves as a warrant.

---

[14]Wogaman, *A Christian Method of Moral Judgment*, 82.

CHAPTER NINE

Reasoning in History

1. Introduction

Historical reasoning shows up in a surprising variety of ways in the broad range of theological and religious studies. Historical critical methods are applied to the texts of scripture; the knowledge derived from historical studies of ancient Israel and its neighbors, of the early Christian church and its milieu, contributes further to the interpretation of these formative texts. Historians also study the institutional history of the church, as well as the history of the development of doctrine and of theology. In some seminary curricula and in college and university religion departments a major focus is the history and phenomenology of world religions.

Historical records of various sorts have been written since the beginning of recorded history (is this sentence necessarily true?). But critical or scientific history—defined by one author as "a type of historical thinking in which the historian made up his mind for himself instead of repeating whatever stories he found in old books"[1]—became a recognizable academic discipline only in the early modern period.

We saw in chapter 8 that there is a great deal of disagreement about reasoning in ethics: Are moral claims to be warranted by appeals to utility, or by their generalizability, or in one of several ways by a religious tradition? But in historical studies of all kinds, both secular and in the various disciplines within the church, there is a great deal of agreement about certain aspects of historical reasoning. We shall look first at the areas of agreement among historians and then at the issues where conflict arises. Both in this chapter and the next (on biblical studies) we shall see how historical reasoning is applied by scholars in the church.

---

[1]R. G. Collingwood, *The Idea of History* (1946; New York: Oxford University Press, 1956), 1.

2. Historical Claims and Grounds

Roughly speaking, historians make two kinds of claims: The first is claims to the effect that particular events happened in the past (e.g., the Exodus took place early in the reign of Ramses II; the Roman emperor Constantine issued the Edict of Milan in A.D. 313). People often speak here of the "facts" of history, and we will follow this usage, but with the note that this may be confusing. We generally use 'fact' in such a way that it is interchangeable with 'datum' or 'grounds,' but these 'facts' are, in fact, claims (reconstructions of the past), and are themselves based on more basic sorts of grounds or data. The second kind of claim historians make regard *explanation* of the 'facts' so reconstructed—that is, claims about the events' conditions and causes, about the actors' motives, reasons, and influences (e.g., the Protestant Reformation was politically as well as theologically motivated; Augustine's theology was affected both by Neoplatonism and by the impending collapse of the Roman Empire).

Again speaking roughly, we can say that there are two kinds of grounds used in (first-order) historical arguments: (1) One important *source* of grounds is documents that contain testimonies, records, reports of various sorts from or about the past. (2) Another important category of grounds depends on physical traces from the past: coins, pottery, tools, buildings, and the like. I say "first-order" here to call attention to the fact that, as in all scholarly disciplines, arguments in history often turn out to be arguments about other historians' arguments, whose grounds often come from the others' writings as much as from original evidence (i.e., primary documents and traces).

It is important to notice that traces and documents are the *source* of grounds for historical arguments, not the grounds themselves. Grounds must be statements or sentences, not things. (This is true for any argument, and is a point that needs to be made about scientific reasoning as well.) So, for example, a historian may examine a coin, noting that it bears the inscription "In God we trust," and argue that the society whose coin it is sponsors some sort of civil religion. But it is not the coin itself, or even the sentence "In God we trust," that serves as grounds for the argument. Rather it is the sentence: "Americans print 'In God we trust' on their coins" that grounds the argument.

3. Warrants for Evaluating Documents

The area within historical reasoning where much agreement is found regards the use of primary documents (grounds of type 1) for making claims about past events (claims of type 1). The following are some of the most common warrants that go into such arguments.[2]

---

[2]This information is readily available in works on historiography. I have followed very closely Louis Gottschalk, *Understanding History: A Primer of Historical Method* (New York: Knopf, 1951), an older book but lucidly written.

3.1. Assessing Authenticity

An authentic document is what it claims to be—that is, it is not a forgery; it is not falsely attributed to its purported author; it was written when it purports to have been written and for its ostensive purpose. There are enough forged documents in existence to make techniques for recognizing them an important part of historical method. The following is a list of clues that help to distinguish authentic documents from forgeries:

1. Materials that do not correspond to those likely to be used when the document is supposed to have been written: For example, paper was rare in Europe before the fifteenth century. A corresponding warrant would be: It is *unlikely* that a document is authentic if it is produced on or by means of materials or processes known to be used only rarely during the period when it purports to have been written. Similarly: A document can certainly be taken to be a forgery if it is produced with materials unknown at the time it was supposed to have been written.

2. Anachronisms of style, spelling, handwriting, punctuation, grammar: As with anachronistic materials, these clues can be used to argue that a document was not written when it is claimed to have been written.

3. Anachronistic references to events: A document that refers to an event whose date we know cannot have been written before the date of that event.

4. The absence of trivia and otherwise unknown details: Sometimes a document is taken to be a forgery because the author was too careful to include only information that historians would recognize as being from the appropriate period—that is, it may be too pat, too perfect.

5. Provenance: A document's being found where it ought to be (such as in the archives of the family concerned or in a government bureau's records) creates the presumption of its genuineness.

No text on historical reasoning should fail to mention the unmasking of the Donation of Constantine, which purported to be a grant by Constantine of temporal power in Italy and elsewhere to the papacy. Lorenzo Valla showed in 1440 that the document was a fake; it was probably written in the eighth century, and therefore about 400 years after the death of Constantine. Excerpts of his argument follow:

> As for the text of the document, it is still more absurd and unnatural that Constantinople should be referred to as one of the patriarchal sees, when it was not yet either patriarchal or a see or a Christian city; it was not yet called Constantinople; it had not yet been founded or even planned. In fact, the privilege was supposedly granted three days after Constantine was converted to Christianity, when Byzantium still existed and not Constantinople. . . . Who fails to see, therefore, that he who drew up the privilege lived a long time after the age of Constantine? . . .
>
> Now, let us speak to this deceiver about his crude language. Through his babbling, he reveals his most impudent forgery himself. . . . Where he deals with the gifts, he says "a diadem . . . made of pure gold and precious jewels." The ignoramus did not know that the diadem was made of cloth, probably silk. . . . He thinks it had to be made of gold, since nowadays kings usually wear a circle of gold set with jewels. But Constantine was not a king and he

would never have dared to call himself a king or to adorn himself in regal fashion. He was Emperor of the Romans, not a king. . . .

Is the barbarousness of his style not sufficient proof that such a piece of nonsense was forged not in Constantine's day but much later? . . .

The text ends with the words "Dated at Rome, the third day before the Kalends of April, in the fourth consulate of Constantine Augustus. . . ." The word "dated" [Latin *datum*, "given"] is used only in letters and nowhere else, except by the ignorant. For letters are given to the addressees or to the courier who brings them to the addressees. But since the so-called privilege of Constantine was not to be delivered to anyone, one should not have said it was "dated." Thus it is plain to see that the person who wrote this was lying and was unable to feign what, according to verisimilitude, Constantine would have said and done.[3]

So here we see Valla calling attention to three anachronisms: Constantinople would not yet have been known by that name; diadems in those days were cloth, not gold; and the word 'dated' was not used in such a way in Constantine's day. These are very clear pieces of evidence for the forgery.

The claim that the "barbarousness of his style" argues against the genuineness of the document is, of course, more of a judgment call, and Valla does not provide us with the evidence to show that the style is barbarous. Note that he must be assuming as a warrant something about the deterioration of Latin style since the time of the Roman Empire.

3.2. Textual Criticism

Documents may be on the whole authentic but contain parts that are not, due to errors or deliberate alterations. Textual criticism aims at establishing the original text of documents that have been changed, for example, in the course of repeated copying or translating, or both. This kind of historical reasoning was developed primarily for dealing with biblical texts, where we have no original documents and the copies in existence show some variation.

One begins by collecting and comparing as many copies as possible. Regarding each variation one then has to decide which version is more likely to represent the original form. For example, if a passage in one text is missing from another, one has to decide if an addition has been made to the longer text, or whether its absence in the shorter text is due to a later omission. Two general rules are: (1) when the age of the two copies is known, the earlier text is presumed to be closer to the original, and (2) anachronisms or other clues suggesting different authorship may be used to argue that the variant passage is a later insertion.

We will consider rules for textual criticism in greater detail in chapter 10.

---

[3]Lorenzo Valla, *The Profession of the Religious and the Principal Arguments from The Falsely-Believed and Forged Donation of Constantine,* trans. and ed. Olga Z. Pugliese (Toronto: Centre for Reformation and Renaissance Studies, 1985), 70–71.

3.3. Assessing Credibility of Testimony

Once the historian is satisfied that the document in hand is what it purports to be (in whole or in part) the next step is to assess the credibility of its contents. Commonly accepted rules (warrants) for assessing the reliability of testimony found in documents include the following:

1. An eyewitness (primary) source is to be preferred over a secondhand report. (Notice that a single document often contains both primary and secondary material. Consider, for example, a newspaper story, part of which is based on the reporter's own observations and part on the reports of those the reporter has interviewed.) The backing for this warrant is the simple observation that reports of events change as they are passed from one person to another.

2. The closer the time of making the document to the event it records, the more reliable it is likely to be. This warrant is backed by the general observation that memory fades and becomes less accurate as time passes.

3. The more serious the author's intention to make a mere record of an event, the more dependable the document is likely to be as a historical source. This warrant is backed by the observation that the purpose for which one writes affects the accuracy of the report. If one is writing a memorandum for one's own use, one has very little motivation to distort or suppress facts. However, such motives do sometimes play a role in writing reports for others, ranging from unintentional 'fixing-up' of the facts to deliberate propaganda.

4. In general, the smaller the intended audience for a document the more reliable its content is likely to be. The reasoning behind this warrant is that "the effort on the one hand to palliate the truth or, on the other, to decorate it with literary, rhetorical, or dramatic flourishes tends to increase as the expected audience increases."[4]

5. The greater the expertise of the author in the matter being reported, the more reliable the report. The backing here is the obvious fact that one can better report what one understands, and also the fact that an expert is likely to notice details that the novice will pass over.

6. The less the witness had to gain by reporting falsely, the more reliable the report may be expected to be. So the report of a disinterested party can be given more credence than that of an interested party. However, the report of facts prejudicial to a witness or someone near to the witness can be given high credibility. The reasoning behind this warrant is that someone is very unlikely to say something damaging to self or to loved ones except for the sake of the truth.

7. Statements contrary to the witness's known expectations or biases are likely to be true.

8. Statements about incidental facts are likely to be true. The backing here is that a witness would not think to lie about or have motive to misrepresent something that is merely incidental to the matter at hand.

---

[4]Gottschalk, *Understanding History*, 90.

Two warrants used in assessing the credibility of testimony are so prominent in historical reasoning that they need to be set off from the rest. One involves the weight of independent corroborative testimony; the other is the principle of analogy. The warrant (9) that independently corroborated testimony is to be preferred to uncorroborated testimony is too obvious to require further comment.

10. The principle of analogy can be stated as follows: Testimony regarding events that conform to other known historical or scientific facts is to be given greater weight than testimony that does not. Put the other way around: Testimony regarding events that are thought of as impossible or highly unlikely is to be taken with due skepticism. All historians make great use of this principle. However, there has been considerable discussion in theology and biblical studies about whether or not it is to be given final authority. Many scholars have concluded that it requires the denial of the historicity of all miracle accounts in scripture, including the resurrection. Others have argued that, while the principle has its place in historical reasoning, there are cases where other considerations may be taken to override it.

4. The Status of Historical Facts

While there is considerable agreement among historians about how to establish historical 'facts' on the basis of testimony found in documents (i.e, to make claims about what happened when), there is less agreement about the status of those claims. Notice, first of all, that we use 'history' in two ways: one is to refer to the past itself; the other is to refer to the verbal reconstruction or description of it that historians write. When we speak of establishing historical facts, we can *only* be referring to the bits and pieces that go into the latter. That is, we never actually reproduce or make contact with the past events themselves.

So one can now ask about the relation between past events and the historians' 'facts.' "Objectivists" stress the close approximation of description to past event. For example, Leopold von Ranke (1795–1886) argued that written history is an exact scientific reconstruction of the past. On the other side, "subjectivists" stress the extent to which the selection, interpretation, and value judgments involved in reconstructing the past make history a creative endeavor. Wilhelm Dilthey (1833–1911), R. G. Collingwood (1889–1943), and Benedetto Croce (1866–1952) have all contributed to an understanding of history that sees it more as contemporary reflections—abstract and subjective thought—about the past. Such reflections are bound to change with new generations of historians, who look at the past from a different point of view.

We will not pursue the arguments of these two schools of thought. The important point to remember, and one upon which all agree, is that however closely the historians' 'facts' are taken to represent actual past occurrences, they are not to be confused with or mistaken for those past events. In the language of this text, historical facts are *claims*—they are the end product of historians' arguments grounded on testimony in documents and on other surviving traces. So despite our calling them facts, and often recognizing them to be very well grounded, their epistemological status is more like that of a scientific theory than a fact or datum of observation. They belong to the realm of human thought, not to the world of things and events.

5. Arguing from Facts to Explanations

Historians argue about individual historical facts because they give different weight to the various grounds and warrants upon which they are based. These arguments are minor compared to the fights that arise when one comes to explaining the whys and hows of the past—for example: Why did the Roman Empire collapse? What caused the Protestant Reformation? One reason for such lengthy debates is the sheer complexity of the issues, but another is an underlying disagreement about the very nature of historical explanation. Let us look at a few of the most important positions on this issue.[5]

Carl Hempel and others have argued that explanation in history works the same way as explanation in science.[6] We have an observation or event to explain. We find a universal law under which it falls. Showing that it is an instance of such a regularity is what it means to explain a particular event.

I believe we can understand Hempel's point by considering how we might diagram an argument such as the following:

> The Jewish religious authorities wanted Jesus put to death because they perceived him to be a threat to the establishment.

Here the claim is about the *causal connection*. In diagramming the argument we have as grounds a collection of established historical facts. (Remember that the 'facts' themselves are claims from previous arguments.) The relevant facts here would have to be that the religious leaders did want to put Jesus to death and that they perceived him as a threat to their authority.

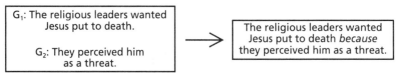

The difficulty in such arguments is exactly in warranting the *causal* connection. Hempel's point can now be made easily: What we *mean* in asserting a causal connection rather than a coincidental connection is that *whenever* an event of the first type occurs, an event of the second will, too.

---

[5]For further reading see William H. Dray, *Philosophy of History* (Englewood Cliffs, N.J.: Prentice-Hall, 1964).
[6]See chapter 4, above, for Hempel's views on scientific explanation.

Therefore, we can only make justifiable causal arguments in history (or any other discipline) if we have in mind a *generalization*, either universal or statistical, that will serve as a warrant, such as:

> W_1: Whenever the establishment sees its power threatened it will act to remove the threat.

Or:

> W_2: Sometimes people who threaten the power structures in their society will be executed.

These warrants are backed by observations of other instances.

Other historians (or philosophers of history) have argued that history is essentially different from science. Perhaps the most noted is Collingwood, whose position can be expressed by saying that historians use different *kinds* of warrants and backing than scientists. Collingwood emphasizes that history has to do with human actions. We do not understand human acts by noting regularities but rather by intuiting *reasons*. To understand an action the historian must rethink or reenact the agent's thoughts. To discover the thought behind an action in this way is already to understand the action. The reenactment requires knowledge of the agent's conception of the relevant facts, of the agent's purposes, of what the agent took to be the available means, and so forth.

So the sort of argument Collingwood envisions might be represented as follows: The grounds are, first of all, the action and, second, the facts about the agent's purposes, the situation, the means available. The claim will be about the agent's reason for so acting. To rephrase our previous example:

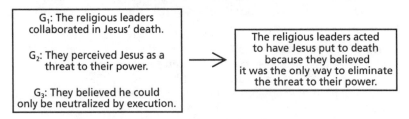

The warrant needed for this argument might be expressed as follows:

> *W:* There is an understandable connection between the religious leaders seeing Jesus as a threat to their power and attempting to remove him by any available means.

The interesting feature of Collingwood's position is the manner in which a warrant such as this one is backed. It is not, in Collingwood's view, a particular instance of an observed regularity (as for Hempel). Rather, it is backed by putting oneself in the shoes of the religious leaders and seeing what one would have done (or would have wanted to do) in that same situation. So the backing might be expressed as follows:

B: In the situation of the religious leaders of Jesus' day I would have wanted him out of the way and would have seen execution as the only option.

6. Philosophies of History

An even more basic issue in historiography (i.e., theory about the writing of history) than the general nature of historical explanation is whether or not it is legitimate to invoke God as a historical explanation. From the beginning, Jews and Christians have believed that the course of history is guided by the acts and plans of God. Augustine gave definitive form to the storyline into which Christians ever since have fit their own histories. This is the story of creation, fall, redemption, and final consummation.[7]

According to Collingwood, Christian presuppositions had four principal effects on the understanding of history: (1) History must be universal history—it cannot be merely the history of one's own people, since all people are a part of God's plan. (2) Historians will ascribe events to the working of divine wisdom (providence) rather than to the wisdom of human agents. (3) History will be seen to fall into an intelligible, overall pattern. (4) Having subdivided all history into two periods, before and after Christ, historians will be inclined to subdivide it further into other epochs and periods as well.[8]

While there was an attempt during the Renaissance to turn historical thought away from its God-centered Christian pattern and concentrate instead on humanity, the providential view of history continued to have many supporters well into the eighteenth century. For example, Joseph Priestley wrote:

> Let an historian, therefore, attend to every instance of improvement, and a better state of things being brought about, by the events which are presented to him in history, and let him ascribe those events to an *intention* in the Divine being to bring about that better state of things by means of those events.[9]

From the eighteenth century on, opposing voices argued against the providential view of history in favor of a naturalistic approach. Historical events and historical changes needed to be accounted for on the basis of principles internal to those processes—especially on the basis of human motives and human actions.

Today the naturalistic approach has entirely supplanted the providential view among academic historians. This does not mean, necessarily, that Christian historians have ceased to believe in a God who acts in history. Rather it is that the discipline of history is now *defined* as a study of the

---

[7]See especially Augustine's *City of God.*
[8]Collingwood, *The Idea of History,* 49–50.
[9]Joseph Priestley, *Lectures on History and General Policy* (Dublin, 1778), 454. Quoted by Donald Livingston in *Hume's Philosophy of Common Life* (Chicago: University of Chicago Press, 1984), 288.

past to see what can be explained naturalistically. It may be that some historians of history date the beginning of the discipline in the nineteenth century because it was only then that naturalism was firmly established. A similar change resulted in the birth of natural science. It was only when students of nature decided to see what could be explained about the world without invoking God that science became a discipline independent of theology.[10] So, at present, when either historians or scientists invoke God or providence as an explanation they become by definition theologians!

7. An Example

The following passage, part of Wolfhart Pannenberg's argument for the historicity of Jesus' resurrection, illustrates some of what has been said above:[11]

> The Easter traditions of primitive Christianity divide into two different strands: the traditions about appearances of the resurrected Lord, and the traditions about the discovery of Jesus' empty grave. In the historical development of the traditions in the Gospels a tendency is at work to draw the two complexes of tradition closer together to an increasing extent. Mark still offers an unadulterated account of the empty tomb; Luke, at any rate, still holds discovery of the grave and the appearance of the resurrected Lord apart. Matthew connects the discovery of the grave with a report of an appearance; John and the Gospel of Peter then allow appearances to take place at the grave. In the oldest stratum of tradition, however, both strands are still separate: Mark reports only the empty tomb (ch. 16); Paul reports only appearances of the resurrected Lord (I Cor. 15). Historically, then, one must investigate both traditions separately. I will begin with a summary of the tradition of the appearances.
>
> The historical question of the appearances of the resurrected Lord is concentrated completely in the Pauline report, I Cor. 15:1–11. The appearances reported in the Gospels, which are not mentioned by Paul, have such a strongly legendary character that one can scarcely find a historical kernel of their own in them. Even the Gospels' reports that correspond to Paul's statements are heavily colored by legendary elements, particularly by the tendency toward underlining the corporeality of the appearances.[12]

There are two interesting arguments here. One claim is that the appearance tradition and the empty-tomb tradition need to be considered separately in terms of the evidence they provide for Jesus' resurrection. Pannenberg grounds this argument on the fact that in the earliest texts the two traditions are distinct. His assumed warrant is that traditions and documents closer to the event are more reliable than later ones (see war-

---

[10]To read more on this issue, see C. T. MacIntire, ed., *God, History, and Historians: An Anthology of Modern Christian Views of History* (New York: Oxford University Press, 1977).

[11]We saw another part of the argument in chapter 4, section 4.2. The passage there follows this one in Pannenberg's text.

[12]Wolfhart Pannenberg, *Jesus—God and Man*, trans. Lewis L. Wilkins and Duane Priebe (Philadelphia: Westminster, 1968), 88–89.

rant 2 in "Assessing Credibility of Testimony" above [sec. 3.3]). Notice
that in making this argument he is accepting a prior set of conclusions
about the relative ages of these New Testament texts—1 Corinthians and
Mark as the earliest, John's Gospel as the latest.

Pannenberg's second claim is that the Gospel appearance accounts can
scarcely be taken to provide historical information (i.e., "one can scarcely
find a historical kernel"). The grounding for this claim is a statement to
the effect that these accounts are heavily colored with legendary elements.
Pannenberg's reasoning here has to do with the kind of report he takes
these Gospel accounts to be. The style of language indicates that their
purpose is not straightforward historical reporting—rather they have been
embellished in ways intended to make a point (see warrant 3, sec. 3.3
above). Pannenberg claims (elsewhere) that this is an appropriate use of
the principle of analogy: these documents bear a resemblance to other
documents we know to be legendary in nature. Those other documents
are not historically reliable; therefore these documents cannot be considered historically reliable. Thus, he turns in the following passage to Paul's
account in 1 Corinthians.

> In I Cor. 15, Paul enumerates the basic appearances of the resurrected Jesus:
> first the resurrected Lord appeared to Peter, then to the Twelve, then to five
> hundred Christian brethren at once, then to James, the brother of Jesus, then
> to all the apostles, and finally to Paul himself. The intention of this enumera-
> tion is clearly to give proof by means of witnesses for the facticity of Jesus'
> resurrection. The intent to prove is especially clear in v. 6 where the reference
> to the appearance to the five hundred brethren at once is supplemented by
> the notice that some of them have fallen asleep, although most are still alive
> (89).

Here Pannenberg is noting Paul's own sense that firsthand testimony,
corroborated by a number of witnesses, is more convincing than the testimony of a single witness (see warrants 1 and 9 in sec. 3.3 above).

> In judging the Pauline report one must, in the first place, emphasize that it is
> very close to the events themselves. This involves, first, the person of Paul
> and, second, the age of the formula as such. First Corinthians was probably
> written in the spring of 56 (or 57?) in Ephesus. However, Paul speaks from a
> still older, personal knowledge. According to Gal. 1:18, he was in Jerusalem
> three years after his conversion and there visited at least Peter and James. The
> particular mention of the appearance to James may well go back to this visit.
> If Paul's conversion is to be dated, from the information in Gal. 1, in the year
> 33 (35?) and if Jesus' death is to be put in the year 30, then Paul would have
> been in Jerusalem between six to eight years after the events. From this the
> statements in I Cor. 15 are very close to the events themselves. This observa-
> tion is strengthened by a further finding. Not only does the author of this text
> stand very close to the events, but in addition he uses formulations coined
> previously. Thus he does not create his statements *ad hoc* from a possibly
> inaccurate memory, but he appeals to a formulated tradition, for whose for-
> mulation little time remains between the event and the composition of First
> Corinthians. For various reasons, one must even suppose that this tradition
> arose very early, namely, prior to Paul's visit in Jerusalem (90).

So here Pannenberg sets up the grounds for arguing that Paul's report is highly credible, not only because it comes from eyewitness reports but also because the reports themselves are more likely to be accurate if they were made soon after the event. So, while Paul is not working from a document written immediately after the events, he did have access to an oral tradition that arose within a few years of them (cf. warrant 2 in sec. 3.3 above).

> It is questionable whether or not the kernel of Paul's statement involves a unified formula. Generally the first is asserted. According to this view, the kernel of the enumeration in I Cor. 15 consists of an old, originally Aramaic formula that, however, may have included only vs. 3b–5: "That Christ died for our sins in accordance with the scriptures, that he was buried, that he was raised on the third day in accordance with the scriptures, and that he appeared to Cephas, then to the twelve." Paul himself then would have expanded this old formula with the appearances reported in vs. 6f., presumably in accordance with the information he received in Jerusalem. The formula itself, if Paul had received it soon after his conversion, must have reached back to the first five years after Jesus' death.
>
> Recently, Ulrich Wilckens has offered a different analysis of the section in I Cor. 15:1–11. In his view, vs. 3b–5 do not involve one single formula, since the connection of the individual parts by *kai hoti* is not otherwise attested within closed formulas and suggests, rather, a free enumeration. To be sure, the parts connected in such a way were already available to Paul as formulated material. Wilckens thinks the same is true for the basic contents of the following sentences as well. The formal elements that Paul has brought together involve, according to Wilckens, "legitimation formulas for the justification of the special authority of particular Christians who were honored by an appearance." Although the original intention of such formulas may have been the legitimation of an individual or of a group under presupposition of the reality of Jesus' resurrection, the Christian mission and, in any case, Paul in the text under consideration, collected such formulas in order to prove their presupposition, the resurrection of Jesus (90–91).

Here Pannenberg raises a complicating factor (and one from the province of textual criticism): stylistic features suggest that Paul has quoted an existing tradition listing those to whom Jesus appeared. However, it is not clear how much of Paul's text is quoted from such a source, and how much is added to the tradition by Paul himself.

We can recognize from the summary of Wilckens's argument a warrant that he uses for answering such questions about oral traditions. He assumes a high degree of regularity in verbal formulations of this sort, and notes that the conjunction *kai hoti* is not found in any of the others. So his warrant is something like the following: One can infer that a passage is a traditional formula if its elements closely resemble other recognized formulas.

At this point Pannenberg could have made yet another argument for the reliability of the testimony in Paul's text. Recall the warrant listed above to the effect that statements about incidental facts are likely to be true (warrant 8, sec. 3.3 above). If Wilckens is correct in claiming that the original purpose of the appearance tradition(s) was to legitimate the person who had been granted the appearance, then attestation of the *fact* of the appearance is incidental.

Finally, we reach Pannenberg's conclusion:

> In view of the formulated traditions used by Paul and of the proximity of Paul to the events, the assumption that appearances of the resurrected Lord were really experienced by a number of members of the primitive Christian community and not perhaps freely invented in the course of later legendary development has good historical foundation (91).

So Pannenberg has now presented his argument for the *fact* that the early disciples had experiences of the Lord after his death. The next question is what to make of this fact or, in other words, how to explain it. The passage we examined in chapter 4 contains Pannenberg's argument that the major competing hypothesis to explain the disciples' experience (a hallucination resulting from their excitement) conflicts with the facts, and therefore must be rejected. The only remaining hypothesis to explain the experience is that Jesus did indeed rise from the dead.

Next, Pannenberg answers a potential rebuttal based on the principle of analogy: Resurrection as a historical event is impossible since it violates the laws of nature. Pannenberg answers:

> First, only a part of the laws of nature are ever known. Further, in a world that as a whole represents a singular, irreversible process, an individual event is never completely determined by natural laws. Conformity to law embraces only one aspect of what happens. From another perspective, everything that happens is contingent, and the validity of the laws of nature is itself contingent. Therefore, natural science expresses the general validity of the laws of nature but must at the same time declare its own inability to make definitive judgments about the possibility or impossibility of an individual event, regardless of how certainly it is able, at least in principle, to measure the probability of an event's occurrence. The judgment about whether an event, however unfamiliar, has happened or not is in the final analysis a matter for the historian and cannot be prejudged by the knowledge of natural science (98).

Here we see a small part of Pannenberg's argument against taking the principle of analogy as a final measure of the historicity of purported events. Pannenberg is not timid about disagreeing with the mainstream of philosophy of history. His theological position is based on the claim that we cannot ultimately make sense of history—of its unity, regularity, and openness—without postulating that God is the "all-determining reality." Thus, divine action comes once again, in his work, to be the focus of historical explanation.

8. Concluding Remarks

A distinction has worked its way into theological literature based on the fact that German has two words for our English word 'history': *Historie* is used by some theologians to refer to that which is public and accessible on generally accepted standards of historiography. *Geschichte* is used to refer to the interpretation or significance attributed to historical facts. Thus it is possible to say, for instance, that God's action in Jesus is historical in the sense of *Geschichte*, but only a few details of Jesus' life are historical in the sense of *Historie*. It is important to note, however, that there can be no absolute distinction between these two senses of 'history,' since the verbal description of what we take to have happened in the past already involves interpretation, as does the selection from all past happenings those that are important (significant) enough to record.

Nonetheless, we can make a rough distinction (as we have above in sec. 2) between the record of past events, which may remain largely unchanged from one generation to another, and historians' interpretations of those events, which are likely to vary from one cultural perspective to another, and to change over time as perspectives and interests shift. So while participants are the best recorders of facts, some say that it is impossible to write about the history (significance) of one's own times. In fact, the shifts in historical perspective mean that we can write the history of the historical reinterpretations of events (revisionist history).

One of the most important developments in recent thought (since the nineteenth century) has been the recognition of our total and inescapable immersion and participation in historical reality. Present thought is conditioned by historical antecedents, and the past itself can only be viewed from a historically conditioned perspective. This has led some to conclude that all knowledge is relative and therefore worthless. We might instead contend that to want a perspective on human history that somehow stands outside of that history is to fail to recognize and accept our creaturely status.

EXERCISE NINE

Read the following passages and answer the questions.

1. Adolf von Harnack, an influential nineteenth- and early twentieth-century church historian was interested in distinguishing the original "kernel" of Jesus' teaching from later theologizing. In the following two passages he is discussing the historical reliability of the witness to Jesus' teaching.

> Our authorities for the message which Jesus Christ delivered are—apart from certain important statements made by Paul—the first three Gospels. Everything that we know, independently of these Gospels, about Jesus' history and his teaching, may be easily put on a small sheet of paper, so little does it come to. In particular, the fourth Gospel, which does not emanate or profess to emanate from the apostle John, cannot

be taken as an historical authority in the ordinary meaning of the word. The author of it acted with sovereign freedom, transposed events and put them in a strange light, drew up the discourses himself, and illustrated great thoughts by imaginary situations. Although, therefore, his work is not altogether devoid of a real, if scarcely recognizable, traditional element, it can hardly make any claim to be considered an authority for Jesus' history; only little of what he says can be accepted, and that little with caution. On the other hand, it is an authority of the first rank for answering the question, What vivid views of Jesus' person, what kind of light and warmth, did the Gospel disengage?[13]

    a. What, according to Harnack, are the main sources for historical claims about Jesus?

    b. Which of the warrants discussed in this chapter is most heavily relied upon in rejecting the fourth gospel as an historical source?

    c. What are the grounds used to support Harnack's assessment of the nature of the fourth gospel?

    d. So Harnack's argument for the unreliability of the fourth gospel is a two-step chain argument. Diagram it. (The first *claim* and the warrants are assumed; you will have to supply them.)

2. Harnack continues:

> Another point: this tradition [the gospel accounts of Jesus' ministry] is, apart from the story of the Passion, almost exclusively Galilean in its character. Had not the history of Jesus' public activity been really bounded by this geographical horizon, tradition could not have so described it; for every historical narrative with an eye to effect would have represented him as working chiefly in Jerusalem. That is the account given by the fourth Gospel. That our first three evangelists almost entirely refrain from saying anything about Jerusalem arouses a good prejudice in their favour.[14]

    a. What claim is in question here?

    b. What are Harnack's grounds?

    c. What warrant (discussed in this chapter) is assumed?

3. David Hume was an eighteenth-century British philosopher and historian. In this passage he is working on a rebuttal to an important apologetic strategy of his day—the claim that the scriptures were authenticated as the word of God by the miracles that occurred in biblical times.

> In the foregoing reasoning we have supposed that the testimony upon which a miracle is founded may possibly amount to entire proof, and that the falsehood of that testimony would be a real prodigy. But it is

---

[13]Adolf Harnack, *What Is Christianity?* trans. T. B. Saunders (1900; Gloucester, Mass.: Peter Smith, 1978), 19–20.
[14]Harnack, *What is Christianity?* 22–23.

easy to show that we have been a great deal too liberal in our conces-
sion, and that there never was a miraculous event established on so
full an evidence.

For, *first,* there is not to be found, in all history, any miracle attested by a sufficient number of men of such unquestioned good sense,
education, and learning as to secure us against all delusion in themselves; of such undoubted integrity as to place them beyond all suspicion of any design to deceive others; of such credit and reputation in
the eyes of mankind as to have a great deal to lose in the case of their
being detected in any falsehood, and at the same time attesting facts
performed in such a public manner and in so celebrated a part of the
world as to render the detection unavoidable—all which circumstances
are requisite to give us a full assurance in the testimony of men.

Secondly, we may observe in human nature a principle which, if
strictly examined, will be found to diminish extremely the assurance
which we might, from human testimony, have in any kind of prodigy.
The maxim by which we commonly conduct ourselves in our reason-
ings is that the objects of which we have no experience resemble those
of which we have; that what we have found to be most usual is always
most probable; and that where there is an opposition of arguments,
we ought to give the preference to such as are founded on the greatest
number of past observations.[15]

a. What is Hume's claim?
b. From paragraph 2 it is possible to identify three (implied) warrants
   that Hume sees as appropriate in weighing testimony. List them.
c. Diagram the argument using grounds found in paragraph 2.
d. There is one very important warrant stated in paragraph 3. What is
   it?
e. With which warrant in section 3.3 does Hume's warrant in paragraph 3 correspond?

4. Michael Sattler was one of the most important leaders of the Radical
   (Anabaptist) Reformation in the early 1500s. The meeting at Schleitheim
   was convened to establish the points on which the radicals differed
   from mainline Protestantism. Yoder is arguing here that Sattler was the
   main author of the Schleitheim document.

> Sattler may well have been quite conscious that little time now re-
> mained to consolidate the movement he had planted. Just as October–
> December 1523 marked the first self-awareness of the Zürich radicals
> and December 1524–January 1525 the first formal breach, so early 1527
> must be recognized as the coming-of-age of a distinct, visible fellow-
> ship taking long-range responsibility for its order and its faith.
>
> Pressure from the outside, confusion from the inside, loss of the
> guiding influence (which had never been especially clear or authorita-
> tive) of the Zürich founders, and the growing realization that instead
> of holding forth a vision for widespread renewal the young movement
> would have to accept a continuing separate, suffering identity, com-

[15]David Hume, "Of Miracles," in *An Enquiry concerning Human Understanding*
(1784).

bined to make it quite possible that the entire movement might now filter away into the sand.

It was to this need that the Schleitheim meeting spoke. We know nothing of how the meeting was called, the precise provocation which led it to take place just at this moment, or who participated. The tradition according to which Michael Sattler was the leading spirit in the meeting, and the author of the document reproduced below [the Schleitheim *Brotherly Union*], is so widespread as to be worthy of belief, even though none of the early traditions to that effect are eyewitness reports. This tradition is confirmed by obvious parallels in thought and phrasing between the Schleitheim text and the other writings known genuinely to be from Sattler's hand.

The *Seven Articles,* which are the heart of the text, were presumably discussed, rewritten, and approved in the course of the meeting. Here Sattler's contribution may well have been some drafting prior to the meeting. The *Seven Articles* are imbedded in a letter written in the first person after the meeting, which is presumably altogether from the pen of Sattler.[16]

a. Yoder includes an argument to the effect that the *Brotherly Union* was written by Sattler. Two standard warrants for accepting testimonies are balanced off against one another in his argument. What are they?

b. What additional evidence does Yoder supply to 'break the tie'?

c. Write out the warrant that is assumed which makes the additional evidence relevant.

5. In the following passage Yoder is describing the documents from which his translation of the Schleitheim confession was made, and describing the history of these documents as far as it is known. The original document no longer exists.

The textual basis of the present translation is that prepared by Dr. Heinold Fast in his edition of the *Täuferakten* for eastern Switzerland, graciously communicated before publication. The effort to establish the original text by critical conjecture must work with four sources: (a) Zwingli's *Elenchus,* within which the full text is translated into Latin on the basis of the four copies Zwingli had in hand. This was the basis for the earliest translations into English. (b) The manuscript preserved in the Berner Staatsarchiv, reproduced once partially by Ernst Mueller, *Geschichte der Bernischen,* Frauenfeld, 1895, Täufer, 38 ff., and more fully but still not with complete accuracy (cf. Fast), by Beatrice Jenny, *Bekenntnis.* There are good reasons to believe that this was one of the four texts Zwingli had before him, but it does not always coincide with his Latin translation and a few times the other reading reflected in his translations seems preferable. (c) The early print reproduced by Böhmer in 1912. (d) The early print reproduced by Köhler in 1908.

The two early prints are very similar. They were the basis for all the later printings, for the translations into French and Dutch, and for the

[16]John Howard Yoder, ed., *The Legacy of Michael Sattler* (Scottdale, Pa.: Herald Press, 1973), Introduction to the *Brotherly Union,* 29–31.

manuscript copies preserved by the Hutterian Brethren and later re-printed by Wolkan, Beck, and Lydia Müller. Köhler's reprint is the basis as well of the widely used English translation by J. C. Wenger.[17]

a. To what category of historical reasoning does this passage belong?
b. What is the aim or purpose of the reasoning being discussed here?
c. Which three of the documents described here must be the earliest *existing* texts (i.e., the ones closest to the original)?
d. Among his four copies, Zwingli probably had (at least) two different versions. How do we know this?
e. List two factors that might be cited in order to rebut the argument that Zwingli had two different versions.
f. Let us call the original text the "first generation" and any copies of this "second generation," and so on. On the basis of information in this passage, what is the earliest possible generation of documents in existence? Which of the four oldest texts might be of this generation?

---

[17]Yoder, *The Legacy of Michael Sattler*, Introduction to the *Brotherly Union*, 33–34.

CHAPTER TEN

Reasoning in Biblical Studies

1. Introduction

It is difficult to imagine another set of texts that have been pored over and examined from so many points of view for so many years as those comprising the Bible. The goal of this chapter is to introduce some of the most important of the subdisciplines within biblical studies in order to see what sorts of claims they make about the Bible and the methods they use for establishing them. We can sort out some of the methods by making the following *rough* distinctions. First, the Bible may be treated either as most like a historical document or as most like a literary work. This gives us two broad categories: historical criticism and literary criticism. If we treat the texts as historical documents we can further distinguish between forms of criticism that aim at discovering the history *of* the texts and those that aim at discovering the history *in* the texts—that is, the events the texts purport to describe. 'Historical criticism' is used to refer to both of these endeavors.

A number of subdisciplines have developed within historical criticism. We shall look at textual criticism (also discussed in chapter 9), source criticism, form criticism, and redaction criticism—all aimed at reconstructing the history of the texts.

While 'historical criticism' could be used to refer to all of the above, we shall use the term to refer specifically to the discipline that makes claims about the historical events described by the texts. Since the reasoning used here has also been dealt with in chapter 9, we shall concentrate on one specific area, the determination of the "authentic sayings" of Jesus.

Finally, we shall include a brief section on literary criticism.

2. Textual Criticism

Anyone who has played the child's game "gossip" is aware of the outrageous possibilities for distortion as the message is passed from one set of ears to the next. The texts that make up the Bible have gone through nearly as tortuous a process, as indicated in the following passage:

> From the very beginning the books that now make up the New Testament were copied and recopied. Possibly Paul himself had his letter to the Romans copied and sent to churches other than Rome. Certainly churches having letters from him circulated them to other churches, and it was not long before there was a Pauline corpus, a collection of his letters, in general circulation. Similarly, the other books now included in the New Testament were copied and circulated. Copies of the gospel of Mark, for example, were available to the authors of Matthew and Luke. Indeed, constant copying and circulation could almost be described as a prerequisite to final inclusion in the New Testament, for books not found generally useful, and hence not copied and circulated, would not have found their way into the canon. But all this was going on in circumstances that made any kind of control over the texts very difficult. For the first three centuries the church rarely had the resources to employ professional scribes, or sufficient peace and stability to be able to establish careful control of the texts being copied. Moreover, for a large part of this time the books did not have the status of sacred Scripture and its consequent reverential handling. It was not until the epoch of the great uncials [papyrus books copied in capital letters in the fourth century and after] that these conditions prevailed, and by this time the damage had been done. Scribal errors of all kinds had crept into the manuscripts, devotional and theological factors had affected them in numerous places, reminiscence of one passage had influenced the text of another, and so on.[1]

All we have to go on in retracing the steps back to the original are copies of copies of copies of . . . The earliest fragment of the New Testament in existence is a scrap with four verses of John 18 dating from the first half of the second century. The earliest complete (or nearly complete) texts of the New Testament date from the fourth century. We are, of course, much further removed from the original texts of the Old Testament.

In 1707 John Stuart Mill reported no less than 30,000 variants among the New Testament texts available to him. However, it is important to note that these variations are generally rather small—much less significant than the history in the quotation above would lead us to expect. Since Mill's day, great progress has been made toward the goal of producing an eclectic text (called a critical text) that more accurately reflects the wording of the originals than any single surviving manuscript. The methods of reasoning used for this task fall within the discipline of textual criticism.

2.1. Grounds and Warrants in Textual Criticism

So it is easy to see what sort of *claims* textual critics make. Regarding a given passage in the existing texts, they make claims that one version is (probably) the original wording, and that others represent errors or corruptions of one sort or another.

The first task for textual critics is to sort manuscripts into families ac-

---

[1]Norman Perrin and Dennis Duling, *The New Testament: An Introduction* 2d ed. (New York: Harcourt Brace Jovanovich, 1982), 450–51.

cording to resemblances. If the ages of the texts are known, it is the oldest member of each family that is of greatest interest. So here we see the first warrant used in textual criticism: Older manuscripts are to be preferred to more recent ones. It is backed by the assumption that errors are introduced over time and hence grow in number in later manuscripts. The evidence here (called external evidence) is anything that contributes to the dating process; for example, the material on which the words are written, even the form of the letters or the handwriting.

However, while we can certainly say that older *readings* (variants) are to be preferred to later ones, it is not always the case that the oldest texts contain the oldest readings. Theoretically, a relatively late manuscript could be an accurate copy of a first-century text and a second-century manuscript could be a poor copy of the same first-century text. In this case, the wording of the later copy would come closer to the original. So, in addition to the external evidence used to establish the age of the documents themselves, textual critics rely on internal evidence. We can see the sorts of factors that serve as grounds here by considering some of the standard warrants upon which the arguments turn:

1. Prefer the least harmonized variant. The assumption backing this warrant is that scribes might be expected to fix up a passage, making it fit better theologically with the rest of the text, or with other New Testament or Old Testament writings (in the case of quotations); but they would not have motives for making deliberate changes in the other direction.

For example in the New Revised Standard Version, Acts 8:35ff. reads:

> [35]Then Philip began to speak, and starting with this scripture, he proclaimed to him the good news about Jesus. [36]As they were going along the road, they came to some water; and the eunuch said, "Look, here is water! What is to prevent me from being baptized?* [38]He commanded the chariot to stop, and both of them, Philip and the eunuch, went down into the water, and Philip baptized him.

The note reads, "Other ancient authorities add all or most of verse 37, And Philip said, 'If you believe with all our heart, you may.' And he replied, 'I believe that Jesus Christ is the Son of God.'"

The fact that verse 37 is in a footnote indicates that the editors of this version have concurred with the arguments claiming that it is a later addition rather than a part of the original. This claim is grounded in part on the fact that the verse fits so well with the early church's teaching about baptism—it appears to have been added to harmonize this story with a theology of baptism such as Paul's.

A second warrant that comes into play in this example is: (2) Prefer the shorter reading. The backing here is the assumption that a copyist is more likely intentionally to add material than to leave it out; a sacred text may be thought to need interpretation or clarification, but it is unlikely that any of that text would be omitted intentionally, unless it was considered objectionable for some reason. One way material was added was by copying into the text explanatory remarks or notes that were at one time written in the margins.

So in this passage from Acts we have two independent arguments:

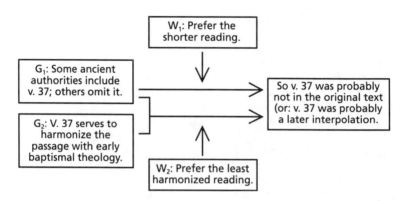

A third warrant used by textual critics is: (3) Prefer the more difficult reading. Again, the assumption is that scribes would 'fix' passages in various ways. For example some texts of John 1:18 read as follows: "No one has ever seen God; the only *God,* who is in the bosom of the Father, he has made him known." Other manuscripts have "the only *Son* who is in the bosom of the Father." Scholars claim that in fact "only God" (*theos*) rather than "only Son" is the more primitive version since it is the more difficult reading: "The unique *God* who is in the bosom of the Father" does not make much sense. Since "unique Son" (*monogenēs huios*) appears elsewhere, a scribe might easily have taken *monogenēs theos* to be a copying error and have 'fixed' it. It is interesting to note that the NRSV has solved the problem with a deliberately interpretive translation that makes use of both English words: "It is God the only Son, who is close to the Father's heart."

Another warrant is: (4) Prefer the reading that is most characteristic of an author's style. Here grounds would involve preferred vocabulary, good or bad grammar, typical constructions, and so forth. To get a sense of different styles of thought, read several different New Testament authors and compare them on the extent to which *arguments* appear in what they have written.

While different grounds and warrants often point in the same direction, it is sometimes the case that they lead to opposite conclusions. For example, a third version of John 1:18 omits both *theos* and *huios,* so *monogenēs* (only-begotten) stands as a noun in the sentence. Warrant 2 (prefer the shorter reading) supports this version's claim to be the original. But there is another warrant: (5) Prefer the most widely attested (most common) reading. With this warrant we can argue to the opposite conclusion, since it happens that very few ancient manuscripts have the shorter form. (In addition, this variant text is itself explained by the difficulty of "only-begotten God.")

Thus, there is an overarching warrant: (6) Choose the reading that best explains all the others.

3. Source Criticism

Source criticism is an important aspect of historical criticism. This enterprise seeks to determine whether the authors used earlier sources, either written or oral. We can deal with this topic briefly because two of its most important findings have already been discussed: the documentary hypothesis regarding the four traditions woven into the Pentateuch (see "The Documentary Hypothesis" [chap. 4, sec. 4.1]); and the Q hypothesis regarding a non-Markan source for Matthew and Luke (see Exercise 4).

You will recall that in both cases the reasoning involved was hypothetical; that is, the existence of earlier sources was *hypothesized* in order to account for characteristics of the texts: In the Old Testament case, to account for stylistic features such as repetition of stories, for different theological points of view, and others. In the case of the synoptic Gospels, the fact to be accounted for is the large quantity of similar or identical material in Luke and Matthew that did not come from Mark.

These are the most striking results of source criticism, but in understanding any of the received documents it has been helpful to look for evidence of the use of previously formulated material. However, as the documents are analyzed into smaller and smaller units, the clues used to detect inclusions of earlier material tend to fall under the heading of another branch of biblical criticism called form criticism, to which we now turn.

4. Form Criticism

The intent of this discipline is to recognize literary units that the authors have incorporated into their writings: for example, laws, priestly instruction, prophetic oracles, hymns, royal psalms, and national laments in the Old Testament; hymns, prayers, confessions of faith, and miracle stories in the New Testament.

The name 'form criticism' (from *formgeschichte*, literally, 'history of forms') makes it clear that the primary sort of grounds for arguments here will be the *forms* of the literary units. Warrants for the most basic arguments will be general statements about the features of the various literary forms.

The easiest forms to recognize are poems and hymns, not because they are written as such in the early texts, but on the basis of clues such as structure, rhythm, alliteration and parallelisms. One example is Philippians 2:5–11. The following paragraph explains in technical detail the clues that led scholars to conclude that it was a hymn already in existence when Paul wrote the letter:

> Into this hortatory context Paul inserts a hymn to Christ, possibly of Jewish-Christian origin, which he has modified slightly by adding the words, "even death upon a cross." The hymn represents an early kerygmatic confession. The hymnic interpretation of this section is based on the rhythmic quality of the sentences, on the use of parallelism (found in OT psalms and poetry), and on the rare, characteristically un-Pauline expressions (*kenoun*, meaning "to

empty," *harpagmos, hyperypsoun, morphē, schēma, isa thēo einai*). Though there appear to be two periodic sentences, each is composed of nine cola and the whole is conveniently divided into six strophes. Each strophe has a main verb and two subordinate determinations. . . . In the first three strophes Christ is the subject; in the last three, God. Strophes 3 and 6 begin in Greek with *kai*. The version [below] follows the arrangement of E. Lohmeyer.

> 6 Who, though of divine status,
>   did not treat like a miser's booty
>   his right to be like God,
> 7 but emptied himself of it,
>   to take up the status of a slave
>   and become like men;
>   having assumed human form,
> 8 he still further humbled himself
>   with an obedience that meant death—
>   even death upon a cross!
> 9 That is why God has so greatly exalted him
>   and given him the name
>   which is above all others:
> 10 that everyone at Jesus' name
>   should bend his knee
>   in heaven, on earth, and under the earth!
> 11 that every tongue should proclaim
>   unto the glory of God the Father
>   that Jesus Christ is LORD![2]

So there are three arguments alluded to here. One, for the non-Pauline authorship, is based on the assumption that authors can be expected to use a fairly standard set of vocabulary. Another argument is based on the warrant that poetry is often characterized by its rhythm; and the third on the warrant that Hebrew (and therefore also Jewish-Christian) poetry exhibits parallelisms. These two warrants come from comparison with other biblical texts, especially the Psalms. Notice how extrabiblical knowledge of poetics provides the concepts that allow for the recognition and description of the regularities and rhythms in this piece. In general, warrants for form criticism come from noticing similarities among assorted passages of scripture along with outside information about literary forms from Jewish, Greek, and other cultures.

Let us look at another example, which nicely illustrates the use of nonbiblical forms to interpret biblical passages:

> The next significant step was taken by G. E. Mendenhall in *Law and Covenant in Israel and the Ancient Near East*, 1955. Hittite treaty documents of the fourteenth and thirteenth centuries B.C. had long been known: it was left to Mendenhall to direct attention to their form, and to draw from this certain conclusions of relevance to the Decalogue. The Hittite treaty documents contained certain common recurring elements.

[2] Joseph A. Fitzmyer, "The Letter to the Philippians," in *The Jerome Biblical Commentary*, ed. Raymond Brown, Joseph Fitzmyer, and Roland Murphy (Englewood Cliffs, N.J.: Prentice-Hall, 1968), 2:250.

(1) A Prologue identifying the great king of the Hittite empire and giving his titles.
(2) A statement of the past gracious acts of the king towards his vassals.
(3) A statement of the conditions upon which the treaty is made, prominent among them a prohibition on any trafficking with the king's enemies.
(4) The provision that the treaty document be deposited in a temple and regularly read to the community.
(5) A list of the gods cited as witnesses to the treaty.
(6) Blessings and curses consequent upon the keeping or violation of the treaty.

The Decalogue, which Old Testament tradition claims to be the character of the covenant between Yahweh and his people at Mt. Sinai, probably in the thirteenth century B.C., is remarkably similar to such treaties in form.
(1) There is a prologue identifying this god and giving his title, "I am Yahweh your god."
(2) There is a statement of his past gracious act: "who brought you out of the land of Egypt, out of the house of bondage."
(3) There is a statement of the conditions inherent in this covenant headed by "you shall have no other gods before me."
(4) The cultic *Sitz im Leben* of this type of law had been stressed by Alt, and everything points to the Decalogue having been read in Israel at some regular covenant renewal ceremony.
(5) Deuteronomy 27–28 has a series of curses and blessings connected with the people's disobedience or obedience to the commandments.

The exclusiveness of Yahweh in Hebrew tradition naturally prevented any direct parallel to gods being cited as witnesses.

  Mendenhall concluded that the Decalogue must be described as a formal treaty covenant regulating the relationship between Yahweh and his vassal people, and further that it must come from the same general period as the Hittite treaties. . . . Although Mendenhall's conclusions have been challenged, his and subsequent studies heave breathed new life into discussions concerning the concept of the covenant and the place which it occupies in Israel's religious traditions.[3]

So in this argument, the list of features of the Decalogue and the list of features of a Hittite treaty constitute the grounds. The claim, of course, is not that the Decalogue *is* a Hittite treaty, but rather that, because such documents served as a model, conclusions about the significance of the Decalogue can be drawn from knowledge of the treaties. The warrant employed would be something like: Similar forms are used for similar purposes. So knowledge of form and knowledge of use go hand in hand. An important term used here is, in German, *Sitz im Leben,* the life situation in which the form arose and was used. Hermann Gunkel (1862–1932), the first to apply this form of reasoning to the Old Testament, says,

  Every ancient literary type originally belonged to a quite definite side of the national life of Israel. Just as among ourselves the "sermon" belongs to the pulpit, while the "fairy-tale" has its home in the nursery, so in ancient Israel

---

  [3]Robert Davidson, "The Old Testament," in *Biblical Criticism,* ed. R. P. C. Hanson (Middlesex, England: Penguin Books, 1970), 78–79.

the Song of Victory was sung by maidens to greet the returning war-host; the Lament was chanted by hired female mourners by the bier of the dead; the Thora was announced by the priest in the sanctuary; the Judgment (*mishpat*) was given by the judge in his seat; the prophet uttered his Oracle in the outer court of the temple; the elders at the gate gave forth the Oracle of Wisdom. To understand the literary type we must in each case have the whole situation clearly before us and ask ourselves, Who is speaking? Who are the listeners? What is the *mise en scène* at the time? What effect is aimed at?[4]

5. Redaction Criticism

The recognition that much of what we read in the Bible has been pieced together from earlier sources rather than written fresh by the authors puts us in position to ask another set of questions. These have to do with the purposes of the author-editors in including and modifying the materials they have used.

When it was recognized that biblical 'authors' (the Evangelists, in particular) were often in fact editors, their job was at first viewed as fairly uninteresting, almost mechanical. However, more recently they have been recognized as creative theologians in their own right. Redaction criticism aims at establishing the theology of the biblical writers by analyzing the way they accepted or rejected, expanded or otherwise modified traditions, reordered materials, and composed new materials.

An example of redaction criticism is the following, where Norman Perrin and Dennis Duling make claims about Luke's theological interests by comparing his account of Jesus' baptism to the one in Mark—assuming that Luke worked from Mark's account and made changes in order to convey his own point of view.

> In those days Jesus came from Nazareth of Galilee and was baptized by John in the Jordan. And when he came up out of the water, immediately he saw the heavens opened and the Spirit descending upon him like a dove; and a voice came from heaven, "Thou art my beloved Son; with thee I am well pleased" [Mark 1:9–11].

> Now when all the people were baptized and when Jesus also had been baptized and was praying, the heaven was opened, and the Holy Spirit descended upon him in bodily form, as a dove, and a voice came from heaven, "Thou art my beloved Son; with thee I am well pleased" [Luke 3:21–22].

> A consideration of Luke-Acts as a whole combined with Luke's version here shows that all the emphasis is on the descent of the Spirit on Jesus. His baptism has become but one of the three circumstances (a general baptism ["all the people"], his baptism, the fact that he was praying) that set the stage for the descent of the Spirit, whereas in Mark the baptism and the descent of the Spirit are equally significant. Incidentally, the introduction of the theme of Jesus at prayer is characteristic of Luke's gospel. He does it in at least six places

---

[4]Quoted by John H. Hayes, *An Introduction to Old Testament Study* (Nashville: Abingdon, 1979), 128.

where it is not to be found in his sources. . . . The emphasis in Luke's gospel is on the fact that the ministry of Jesus began not with his baptism but with the descent of the Spirit on him. This becomes important when we recall that in Acts, his second volume, the ministry of the church begins in exactly the same way. In Acts 2 the ministry of the church begins with the descent of the Spirit at Pentecost, which in Acts 1:5 is interpreted in advance as baptism. The author clearly intends to set these two things—the ministry of Jesus and the ministry of the church—in close and formal parallelism with one another, and this becomes an important clue to his theology. . . . The parallelism helps to explain why the descent of the Spirit at the beginning of Jesus' career receives the emphasis it does in Luke's gospel.[5]

Perrin and Duling's first claim is that Luke has made the descent of the Spirit the main emphasis of this passage. We might reconstruct the argument as follows:

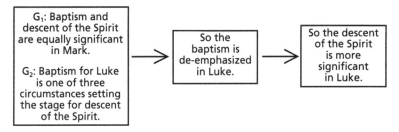

The authors assume a simple warrant to the effect that the de-emphasis of one member of a set entails additional emphasis on the remaining member(s).

G_1 and G_2 are already *interpretations* of the respective passages in Mark and Luke. Let's see what evidence we can find in the texts for these interpretations. Notice that there is an important difference in the construction of sentences. For Mark the information about Jesus' baptism is expressed in a complete sentence; in Luke the information is presented in a dependent clause—a grammatical technique that de-emphasizes the contents of the clause.

Perrin and Duling might also have made use of the fact that Luke adds more detail to the description of the Spirit with the phrase, "in bodily form." The more elaborate description indicates greater interest and emphasis.

The authors have another argument tucked into this paragraph:

| Luke describes Jesus at prayer in at least six places where it is not found in his sources. | | A characteristic theme of Luke's gospel is an emphasis on Jesus at prayer. |

We can infer that they are using a warrant such as: Whenever an author frequently adds to the sources material relating to a particular theme, that theme can be taken as theologically significant.

---

[5]Perrin and Duling, *New Testament,* 236–37.

Having called attention to the emphasis on the descent of the Spirit and on Jesus at prayer, the authors then situate these two points within the larger context of Luke's theology by introducing the idea of a parallel treatment of the inaugurations of the ministries of Jesus and the church.

6. Historical Criticism

Historical criticism (as we are using the term) seeks to establish the accuracy of the texts as historical witnesses. We have already dealt in the previous chapter with some of the methods of reasoning used here. This leaves us free to consider one aspect of historical criticism that has gained wide attention of late—the attempt to establish the *authentic* sayings of Jesus. Scholars have long supposed that some of the sayings attributed to Jesus are not in fact his own words, but are put into his mouth by the Gospel writers; the long discourses in John are among the most highly suspect.

In the process of considering which sayings could be taken as actual memories and which were the work of the early church, scholars have devised a number of criteria, such as the following, that serve as warrants in their arguments.[6] The first three are the ones most commonly used.

1. The criterion of multiple attestation (or the cross-section method). This criterion states that the appearance of a saying, teaching, or activity in independent strands of the New Testament tradition points to its authenticity.

2. The criterion of dissimilarity (or discontinuity). A saying that has no parallels in the Jewish tradition, or in the faith, practice, and situations of the early church, as we know them from outside the Gospels, has greater claim to authenticity.

For example, the Gospels report Jesus as beginning statements with "Amen, amen." In Judaism and the Old Testament, 'amen' is used as a response to someone else's statement; in New Testament writings its use parallels that of the Old Testament and, in addition, Paul adds it at the end of doxologies. This criterion warrants the conclusion that because Jesus' *reported* usage differs from both Judaism and the early church it has claim to authenticity. So the argument goes like this:

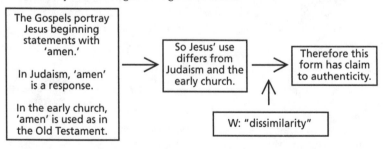

[6]This list was compiled by Marianne Meye Thompson from a variety of sources. See, for example, R. H. Stein, "The 'Criteria' for Authenticity," in *Gospel Perspectives: Studies of History and Tradition in the Four Gospels,* ed. R. T. France and D. Wenham (Sheffield: JSOT Press, 1980), 1:225–63.

3. The criterion of coherence (or consistency). By the application of the other criteria, one can arrive at a body of authentic material by which additional material may be judged authentic insofar as it coheres or is consistent with this body of material.

4. The criterion of multiple forms. Attestation of a motif (a characteristic teaching or activity) in multiple forms (e.g., miracle stories, pronouncement stories, parables, sayings) argues for authenticity.

5. The criterion of Aramaic linguistic phenomena. Since Jesus' native tongue was Aramaic, traces of Aramaic linguistic characteristics in the Greek gospel materials argue in favor of the primitive nature of those particular traditions; the more primitive the tradition, the more likely that it comes from Jesus.

An interesting example here comes from Matthew 23:23–24:

> Woe to you, scribes and Pharisees, hypocrites! For you tithe mint, dill, and cumin, and have neglected the weightier matters of the law: justice and mercy and faith. It is these you ought to have practiced without neglecting the others. You blind guides! You strain out a gnat but swallow a camel!

In Aramaic the word for 'gnat' is *galma,* and the word for 'camel' is *gamla,* so "you strain out a gnat and swallow a camel" is a play on words. However, the pun is lost in the Greek. This strongly suggests that the original saying was in Aramaic, and on the basis of this warrant, has greater claim to authenticity.

6. The criterion of Palestinian environmental phenomena. Closely related to the previous warrant, this criterion argues that evidence of Palestinian social, domestic, agricultural, and religious customs in a tradition indicates its origin in a Palestinian environment; hence, it is more likely that the tradition is primitive and authentic.

7. The criterion of the tendencies of the developing tradition. Because certain 'laws' govern the transmission of tradition during the oral period, we can, by understanding these laws, determine with some probability which tradition is early and which is late and inauthentic.

8. The criterion of modification by Jewish Christianity. Very much like the criterion of dissimilarity, this states that the authenticity of a saying is more probable especially when Jewish Christianity has lessened the rigorousness or boldness of the tradition.

For example, the modification of the Markan statement on divorce by the exception clause in Matthew 5:32 and 19:9 ("except on the ground of unchastity") suggests that the Markan form is earlier.

9. The criterion of divergent patterns from the redaction. When an evangelist includes material which does not otherwise fit with his emphases (for example, the story of the Syro-Phoenician woman in Mark 7:24–30) it indicates that the tradition is of such a lineage that he did not feel free to omit it; hence it is more likely primitive and authentic.

10. The criterion of environmental contradiction. If a saying or motif in the gospel material presupposes a situation in the life of Jesus that was impossible, then it is inauthentic.

11. The criterion of contradiction of authentic sayings. A saying is inauthentic if it contradicts a recognized authentic saying.

As with the preceding list of warrants for textual criticism, we some-times find cases where two or more warrants allow for the construction of contradictory arguments. For example, warrant 8 (the criterion of modifi-cation by Jewish Christianity) leads us to conclude that Mark's report of Jesus' teaching on divorce is probably the authentic one, since Matthew's version is less rigorous. However, warrant 6 (the criterion of Palestinian environmental phenomena), allows us to argue that Matthew is more likely to be authentic because it presupposes Jewish divorce law (women not allowed to divorce their husbands), while Mark presupposes Roman law, wherein women were allowed to do so.

The fact that these criteria do often work at cross purposes (think espe-cially of the criterion of difference versus the criterion of Palestinian envi-ronmental phenomena) indicates that we must be on guard against con-fusing two questions: (1) What actually happened in the past? and (2) For what can we provide reasonable arguments, using these warrants and the evidence available to us today? When we recognize how fragmentary the evidence is for reconstructing the history of Israel or the life of Jesus, and when we see, as well, how limited and crude are the warrants that can be used in our historical arguments, we must give up the hope of identifying the results of historical study (history in the sense of what historians write) with history in the sense of what actually happened. This is good news and bad news. The bad news is that there is much about our actual past that can never be known. The good news is that we need not be terribly dismayed if we find that historians' results give us a less robust picture of Jesus (or Israel) than we would like. The historian's claim, "This much only can we know of the life of Jesus from historical reasoning," does not entail that there *was* no more to the life of Jesus than the portraits they present.

This is a good place to stress a general point that pertains to the whole of practical reasoning. The confidence we can have in a claim can never be stronger than our confidence in the warrant. So, in this case, a claim for the authenticity *or* inauthenticity of a statement attributed to Jesus can never be made with more certitude than the level of trust we place in one or several of the warrants listed in this section. In matters connected with our faith we would like to have very definite answers. But in biblical criti-cism, as in all scholarly disciplines, the quality of the results depends on the quality of our human investigative procedures.

7. Literary Criticism

It is difficult to say anything brief yet comprehensive about literary criti-cism. A wide variety of approaches have been developed here, and in most cases the methods of reasoning are less clear-cut than in the various forms of historical criticism. A partial list will suggest the variety: genre criticism, narrativist interpretation, rhetorical criticism, structuralist interpretation, new criticism, reader-response criticism, deconstructionist interpretations, and others. Two very tentative generalizations can be made. One is that in all cases the texts are approached with methods of study germane to departments of literature rather than departments of history, and in most cases the biblical books are treated as literary units, rather than broken down into the smaller units studied by form critics. To some extent the development of literary criticism was a reaction against the atomizing of the text by historians, and also expressed the frustration of those who believed that the equation of the meaning of the text with the history behind it was reductionistic.

Since the territory of literary approaches to the Bible is too vast and chaotic to summarize, we will content ourselves with one example—Phyllis Trible's rebuttal of the argument that Genesis 2–3 supports male dominance.

> Concern for sexuality, specifically for the creation of woman, comes last in the story, after the making of the garden, the trees, and the animals. Some commentators allege female subordination based on this order of events. They contrast it with Genesis 1:27 where God creates 'adham as male and female in one act. Thereby they infer that whereas the Priests recognized the equality of the sexes, the Yahwist made woman a second, subordinate, inferior sex. But the last may be first, as both the biblical theologian and the literary critic know. Thus the Yahwist account moves to its climax, not its decline, in the creation of woman. She is not an afterthought; she is the culmination. Genesis 1 itself supports this interpretation, for there male and female are indeed the last and truly the crown of all creatures. The last is also first where beginnings and endings are parallel. In Hebrew literature the central concerns of a unit often appear at the beginning and the end as an *inclusio* device. Genesis 2 evinces this structure. The creation of man first and of woman last constitutes a ring composition whereby the two creatures are parallel. In no way does the order disparage woman. Content and context augment this reading.[7]

The argument that Trible rebuts in this passage is actually the conflation of two arguments:

| Woman was created after man. | ⟶ | Therefore woman is subordinate. |

The implied warrant for this argument is that second in order of creation implies subordination and inferiority.

The other argument is as follows:

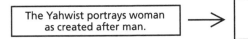

| The Yahwist portrays woman as created after man. | ⟶ | So the Yahwist intended to portray woman as subordinate and inferior. |

The implied warrant here is somewhat different: The order of creation shows the author's view of dominance and submission, superiority and inferiority.

---

[7]Phyllis Trible, "Eve and Adam: Genesis 2–3 'Reread,'" *Andover Newton Quarterly* 13 (1973): 251–58. Quotation on pp. 251–52.

Note the different order of claim being made in these two arguments: one about 'the way things are,' and one about the author's intent. Trible replies at the level of authorial intent, rebutting the argument by contesting the warrant. She supplies two somewhat different arguments:

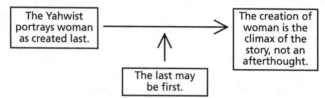

We might take as backing for Trible's warrant the reference to Genesis 1, where humans are obviously the climax of creation, since it is a particularly apt example illustrating (and thereby supporting) the general principle that what is recounted last is often the most important focus of the story.

Trible's second argument can be paraphrased as follows:

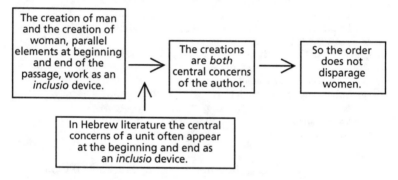

8. The 'Meaning' of the Text

The difference noted above between claims about the way things are and claims about the author's intent points up an important issue regarding biblical interpretation. A key goal of biblical criticism, of course, is to ascertain the meaning of the texts. But has one adequately grasped the meaning when one knows what it is (outside the text) that the passage describes? Or does one grasp the meaning of the text when one has adequately deciphered what the author intended to communicate? Or is it yet some third thing?

Different answers to this question have been prevalent in different periods of Christian history. The modern answer was that the meaning lies in the actual history that is revealed in (or concealed behind) the text. Edgar McKnight suggests that for earlier Christians the meaning also lay in a referent outside the text, but here it was a spiritual world, not human history:

> Augustine's world allowed, or even required, that signs be interpreted in light of realities beyond the visible world of phenomena, and symbolic interpreta-

tion was often required to go beyond plain meaning. . . . But the world transformed by the Enlightenment required that origin and meaning be seen in the light of this world.[8]

Trible's approach to literary criticism, as we have seen, concentrates instead on what the author intended to communicate. However, it is currently debated whether the meaning is fixed by the author's intent (and by what the intended audience would have understood if the communication was successful) or whether the meaning is really constituted afresh as each generation appropriates the text and sees in it something new.

The issues at stake here can perhaps be made clear by reference to the theory of language developed by philosopher J. L. Austin.[9] Austin analyzed language as "speech-acts"—things we *do* in the world by means of language. All speech-acts have four ingredients: (1) a conventional aspect; (2) a referential or representative dimension; (3) an intentional or affective dimension; and (4) a dimension he referred to as "uptake." We can illustrate these with a simple example. If I say "Please pass the bread," certain conditions have to be met in order for the speech-act to be successful: (1) I must be speaking a language known by my audience, and I must be using it correctly—*conventionally*. (2) There must be such a thing as bread, and it must be in such a location that it can be passed to me— neither too far away nor already on my plate—the *referential* dimension. (3) I must actually want the bread and I must intend to convey that want to you by means of my (conventional) sentence—otherwise the sentence does not in fact convey my *intention*. (4) Finally, you must *'get the message'* by means of what I say, or else the speech-act fails.

All biblical study begins with the conventional aspect—study of the meanings of words, of grammatical structures, of typical, conventional forms of speech from the relevant period. The further question of meaning, about which there is disagreement, can now be expressed as follows: Is the meaning to be found in the referent, in the author's intent, or in the uptake? Austin, of course, would insist that all three must receive equal attention. But when we apply his complex theory of language to the scriptures rather than to a simple speech-act like requesting bread, the complexities multiply. We have textual problems, and translations, and historical gaps of *thousands* of years, and intentions of oral historians and poets and editors and scribes—as well as authors—all to consider. No wonder biblical criticism has become a bewildering *assortment* of disciplines!

---

[8]Edgar McKnight, *Post-Modern Use of the Bible: The Emergence of Reader-Oriented Criticism* (Nashville: Abingdon, 1988), 53.

[9]For a clear interpretation of Austin and an application of his insights to religious language, see James Wm. McClendon, Jr. and James M. Smith, *Understanding Religious Convictions* (Notre Dame: University of Notre Dame Press, 1975), reissued as *Convictions: Defusing Religious Relativism* (Valley Forge, Pa.: Trinity Press International, 1994).

For an application of Austin's theory to the problem of textual interpretation, see my essay, "Textual Relativism, Philosophy of Language, and the baptist Vision," in *Theology without Foundations: Religious Practice and the Future of Theological Truth*, ed. Nancey Murphy, Mark Nation, and Stanley Hauerwas (Nashville: Abingdon, 1994), 244–69.

EXERCISE TEN

Read the following passages and answer the questions.

1. This passage describes the characteristics that Old Testament scholars use to differentiate the four major traditions found in the Pentateuch.

> Yahwist Tradition: The earliest discernible tradition in the Pentateuch, called "Yahwist" (or "J" from the German form) because of its anachronistic use of "Yahweh" [written 'LORD' in most translations] in the Genesis material, is more commonly dated about the 10th century in the southern kingdom. . . . The constants distinguishing the tradition include a characteristic vocabulary, a stylistic elegance reflected in its colorful presentation of scenes, especially the dialogues, a perceptive psychology, deep theological insights, and a bold use of anthropomorphisms [in reference to God]. . . .
>
> Elohist Tradition: The sister tradition of J is called "Elohist" (E) because of its careful use of "Elohim" [for God] in the pre-Sinai material. . . . E avoids the more striking anthropomorphisms; God speaks to man generally in dreams or from clouds or the midst of fire or, finally through the medium of angels. . . . His morality is stricter than J's. . . .
>
> Deuteronomic Tradition: The third tradition is somewhat more easily distinguished and dated. In its pentateuchal form it is restricted, with possibly small exceptions, to the book of Deuteronomy, whence its name and abbreviation (D). The marked hortatory style, expressed in a distinctive vocabulary, points to a period of religious crisis for its composition. . . . Salvation could be had, in D's outlook, only by a loyal response to Yahweh's covenant laws and by a return to pure worship of God at the one sanctuary in Jerusalem. . . . The urgency of D's appeal is marked by the constant reference to "you" and to the "now" or "today" of their decisions. . . .
>
> Priestly Tradition: The attribution of the fourth tradition, with its obvious concern for liturgy, to the Priests of Jerusalem accounts for its title, "Priestly" (P). Like D it can be easily distinguished in the Pentateuch. Its style is abstract and redundant; it is fond of genealogies, chronological precision, and minute description of ritual elements; it avoids anthropomorphisms even more carefully than E.[10]

Using the information above, identify the probable tradition to which each of the following passages belongs:

a. Then the LORD said to Noah, "Go into the ark, you and all your household, for I have seen that you alone are righteous before me in this generation (Gen. 7:1).

b. In the six hundredth year of Noah's life, in the second month, on the seventeenth day of the month, on that day all the fountains of the great deep burst forth, and the windows of the heavens were opened (Gen. 7:11).

c. Take care that you do not forget the LORD your God, by failing to keep his commandments, his ordinances, and his statutes, which I am commanding you today (Deut. 8:11).

d. When Israel set out on his journey with all that he had and came to Beersheba, he offered sacrifices to the God of his father Isaac. God spoke to

---

[10]Eugene Maly, "Introduction to the Pentateuch," in *Jerome Biblical Commentary*, ed. Brown et al., 1:3–4.

Israel in visions of the night, and said, "Jacob, Jacob." And he said "Here I am" (Gen. 46:1–2).

e. Realizing that their father was dead, Joseph's brothers said, "What if Joseph still bears a grudge against us and pays us back in full for all the wrong that we did to him?" So they approached Joseph, saying, "Your father gave this instruction before he died, 'Say to Joseph: I beg you, forgive the crime of your brothers and the wrong they did in harming you'" (Gen. 50:15–17).

Now write one or more warrants (based on the information above about the four traditions) that you can use to argue for the authorship you assigned to each text.

2. This is an entry from the *Interpreter's Dictionary* on a name found in two different forms in Greek texts of Romans.

> JUNIAS . . . ['*Iounias*] (Rom. 16:7); KJV JUNIA ['*Iounia*]. A Jewish Christian, fellow prisoner of Paul. If the name is masculine (so RSV), it is found nowhere else than in this passage, and must be a short form of Junianus. Grammatically it might be a feminine (so KJV), though this seems inherently less probable, partly because the person is referred to as an apostle.[11]

   a. What is the textual question at issue here?
   b. Gingrich apparently favors the conclusion that the masculine reading is correct. What warrant is he assuming?
   c. There are grounds for a counterargument in the paragraph. What are they?
   d. What information in the paragraph could be used as the most relevant rebuttal to the argument for the feminine reading?
   e. Other things being equal, what conclusion on this issue follows from the warrant: "Prefer the more difficult reading"?

3. The following passage from a book on the Gospel of Matthew presents a theory about the author's intentions based on the overall structure of the Gospel and other clues.

> First, then, what is the structure of Matthew? A tradition going back to Papias . . . has been much revived in our time. The view has been urged that apart from the 'prologue' in i–ii, and the epilogue in xxvi–xxviii, the remainder of the material in the Gospel falls into five groups or books, as follows:
>
> Preamble or prologue: i–ii: The birth narrative.
>
> Book I: (*a*) iii.1–iv.25: Narrative material.
> (*b*) v.1–vii.27: The Sermon on the Mount.
>   Formula: vii.28–9: '*And when Jesus finished these sayings,* the crowds were astonished at his teaching, for he taught them as one who had authority, and not as their scribes.'

---

[11]F. W. Gingrich, *The Interpreter's Dictionary of the Bible*, (Nashville: Abingdon, 1962), 2: 1026–27.

Book II: (*a*) viii.1–ix.35: Narrative material.
(*b*) ix.36–x.42: Discourse on mission and martyrdom.
    Formula: xi.1: '*And when Jesus had finished instructing his twelve disciples. . . .*'

Book III: (*a*) xi.2–xii.50: Narrative and debate material.
(*b*) xiii.1–52: Teaching on the Kingdom of Heaven.
    Formula: xiii.53: '*And when Jesus had finished these parables. . . .*'

Book IV: (*a*) xiii.54–xvii.21: Narrative and debate material.
(*b*) xvii.22–xviii.35: Discourse on church administration.
    Formula: xix.1: '*Now when Jesus had finished these sayings. . . .*'

Book V: (*a*) xix.2–xxii.46: Narrative and debate material.
(*b*) xxiii.1–xxv.46: Discourse on eschatology: farewell address.
    Formula: xxvi.1: '*When Jesus finished all these sayings,* he said to his disciples. . . .'

Epilogue: xxvi.3–xxviii.20: From the Last Supper to the Resurrection.

Each of the books, isolated in the above table, is closed by a formula which, as can be seen, occurs in almost identical forms at vii.28, xi.1, xiii.53, xix.1, xxvi.1. And the five blocks of material naturally call to mind the five books of the Law at the beginning of the OT, namely, Genesis, Exodus, Leviticus, Numbers, Deuteronomy. The Law consists of these five books of the commandments of Moses: in each book each body of law is introduced by a narrative largely concerned with the signs and wonders which Jehovah had wrought in redeeming his people from Egypt. Roughly the same schematization appears in Matthew's Gospel. Each of his five books begins with an introductory narrative and closes with a stereotyped formula linking its discourse with the next narrative section. The suggestion is, therefore, natural that Matthew was concerned to present his Gospel in the form of a new Pentateuch, or a new book of the Law. And as a corollary to this he thought of Jesus as a New Moses. . . .

    There are difficulties in this theory that are too seldom noticed. First, is it correct to assume that the words which occur at the close of the five discourses constitute anything more than a connecting formula, a merely literary link? Perhaps the formula was insignificant in the mind of Matthew and should not be given much weight in the interpretation of his work. Secondly, it is possible that Matthew derived this fivefold division from his sources. Such a division is common in Jewish tradition. . . . It may therefore be that the fivefold division was merely traditional and had no profound significance for Matthew: it is a division of convenience, not of theological intention. And again, thirdly, any rigid parallelism between the arrangement of the material in Matthew and in the Pentateuch on examination breaks down. Had Matthew had a strictly detailed schematic parallelism with the Pentateuch in mind, it would have been far more obvious.

    How shall we evaluate these difficulties in the Pentateuchal theory of Matthew? The formula at the close of each discourse must, I think, be taken seriously: its regular introduction points to a peculiar import and its length gives it an unmistakable deliberateness; it does not seem to be a mere connecting link or a mere liturgical formula. As to the fivefold structure being a derivative merely borrowed by Matthew from his sources, it is difficult to find either in Q or in M anything like a fivefold division. It is when we come to the third objection that we are on dangerous ground. The parallelism between Matthew and the five books of Moses can be over-emphasized.[12]

a. What is the main claim being assessed here?
b. What are the three potential rebuttals for this argument?
c. What function is played in the overall argument by the following sentence: "The formula at the close of each discourse must, I think, be taken seriously: its regular introduction points to a peculiar import and its length gives it an unmistakable deliberateness; it does not seem to be a mere connecting link or a mere liturgical formula."
d. The sentence quoted above (in c) is actually a short argument in itself. What two warrants is Davies assuming?
e. Davies will conclude later in this book that some form of the Pentateuchal parallel theory does hold up, and that the Sermon on the Mount corresponds to the giving of the Law on Mt. Sinai. Look, now, at the two passages below and see what you can explain of the difference between them on the basis of Davies' theory.

> He came down with them and stood on a level place, with a great crowd of his disciples and a great multitude of people from all Judea, Jerusalem, and the coast of Tyre and Sidon. . . . Then he looked up at his disciples and said: "Blessed are you who are poor, for yours is the kingdom of God" (Luke 6:17, 20).

> When Jesus saw the crowds, he went up the mountain; and after he sat down, his disciples came to him. Then he began to speak, and taught them saying: "Blessed are the poor in spirit, for theirs is the kingdom of heaven" (Matt. 5:1–3).

f. What kind of criticism is involved in making the judgment called for in question e?

4. In these two passages, Michael Cook is entering the current debate about appropriate warrants to use in assessing the authenticity of sayings attributed to Jesus.

> The basic assumption is that the gospels are kerygmatic and confessional. They have arisen out of the needs of the early communities and their primary purpose is to proclaim Jesus as Christ and Lord in light of the resurrection. The form-critical view is correct that they are directly and immediately sources for knowledge of the early Christian communities. Any and every saying and/or action *could* simply be the product of those communities, e.g., through Christian prophets speaking in the name of the Lord or through the development of exegetical insights into the Old Testament or through the theology of the Evangelists as developed by their particular communities. These are the actual phenomena that one finds in the sources and they force one to the conclusion that the burden of proof rests upon anyone who would claim historical authenticity.

---

[12]W. D. Davies, *The Sermon on the Mount* (Cambridge: Cambridge University Press, 1966), 6–9.

> Jeremias works on the assumption of historicity unless proved otherwise, but in the light of Harvey's discussion on the morality of historical knowledge this would seem to be an unacceptable assumption. The biblical historian must be especially cautious in the claims he makes precisely because the sources he is using are so thoroughly oriented to an apologetic and confessional stance. This necessitates the use of oblique criteria, especially of unintentional data, in order to attain reasonable certainty. Perrin makes use of three . . . [13]

    a. According to Cook, what is the basic warrant used by Jeremias?
    b. What basic assumption about the documents does Cook propose instead?
    c. *Without* the aid of "oblique criteria and unintentional data" what are the main kinds of claims that can be supported using New Testament texts?
    d. What part of an argument would Cook's unintentional data constitute? His oblique criteria?

5. The passage continues:

> Perrin makes use of three which we will now consider. The fundamental criterion is the *criterion of dissimilarity,* which he [Perrin] formulates as follows: "the earliest form of a saying we can reach may be regarded as authentic if it can be shown to be dissimilar to characteristic emphases both in ancient Judaism and of the early Church. . . ."
>
> The second criterion, which builds on the first, is the *criterion of coherence:* "material from the earliest strata of the tradition may be accepted as authentic if it can be shown to cohere with material established as authentic by means of the criterion of dissimilarity." A good example of this, in my opinion, is the question of whether and in what sense Jesus made use of the late Jewish apocalyptic title "Son of Man." One can only establish such usage if it can be shown to harmonize with Jesus' proclamation of the Kingdom which will already have been more solidly established on the basis of the criterion of dissimilarity. . . .
>
> The final criterion, which is even more supplemental in that its usefulness lies in arriving at general characteristics rather than at specific elements, is the *criterion of multiple attestation:* "a motif which can be detected in a multiplicity of strands of tradition and in various forms (pronouncement stories, parables, sayings, etc.) will have a high claim to authenticity, always provided that it is not characteristic of an activity, interest or emphasis of the earliest Church."[14]

    a. What are Perrin's three principal warrants?
    b. There is the sketch of an argument regarding Jesus' use of the title "Son of Man." Fill in the missing parts in the diagram below:

---

[13]Michael Cook, *The Jesus of Faith* (New York: Paulist Press, 1981), 31–32.
[14]Cook, *The Jesus of Faith,* 32–33.

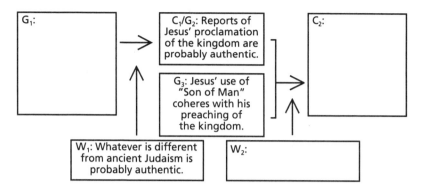

c. In using the criterion of multiple attestation, what potential rebuttal does one always have to guard against?

CHAPTER ELEVEN

Reasoning in Theology

1. Introduction

In biblical studies and especially in history there is now a great deal of agreement about methods of argument, notwithstanding the fact that biblical scholars reach widely different conclusions employing those methods. Theology is a different matter; there may be no other discipline with as *little* agreement about how to proceed as in theology. Volumes have been written about theological methodology, but having read them, the novice may still be at a loss as to how to proceed with the task.

Our coverage of this area, therefore, will be by means of significant examples, along with some brief remarks about historical context.

2. Medieval Theology

There were two main categories of knowledge for medieval scholars: one was *scientia*, which included all that could be derived by deductive reasoning from first principles; the other was *opinio*, or *probable knowledge*. However, this latter category is different from what a modern thinker would expect. For us, probability has to do with the weight of evidence. For medievals (following Aristotle) it had to do with approbation or approval by recognized authorities. (Note that 'probable,' 'approbation,' and 'approval' all derive from the Latin *probare*: to prove or test.)

The consequences of these views of knowledge for theology were, first, that whenever possible, theologians should provide sound deductive arguments for theological conclusions. Preferably they would begin with propositions from scripture, since God is surely the chief authority among all of those with whom scholars have to reckon. But, second, since much of the teaching of the church could not be proved in this way, another ingredient in theological reasoning would have to be a resort to lesser authorities. Much of medieval theology consisted in citing opinions of previous scholars, pro and con, and attempting to reconcile their views.

Thomas Aquinas (to whom we have referred in chapter 8) was a master at reconciling the Christian tradition with the philosophical thought of Aristotle. The typical form of reasoning used in his major doctrinal work, the *Summa Theologiae,* is to state a disputed question, followed by a list of objections (opinions contrary to church teaching in general or to his own theological position). Then the view he will support is stated, often in the words of scripture. There follow Thomas's argument for this view and, finally, rebuttals of the objections. The following passage is an example:

article 8. is man's happiness realized in any created good?

THE EIGHTH POINT: 1. So it would seem. Dionysius says that divine wisdom conjoins the ends and beginnings of prime and secondary creatures, from which we gather that a lower nature at its peak touches a higher at its base. Man reaches his true height in happiness. And since angels are above men in the hierarchy of natures, as we have agreed, it would seem that human happiness consists in somehow reaching to the angels.

2. Further, each thing's final end is realized in its own full development; thus a part is for the sake of the whole, which is its purpose. The whole universe of creatures, called the macrocosm, is compared to man, called the microcosm, as the complete to the incomplete. It is, therefore, as a part integrated within this whole that man realizes his happiness.

3. Again, man is made happy by an object which brings to rest his natural desire. This, however, does not reach out to more good than it can hold. Since he has not the capacity for a good beyond the bounds of all creation, it would seem that he can become happy through some created good, and here he finds his happiness.

ON THE OTHER HAND Augustine says, *As the soul is life for the flesh, so God is the blessed life for man.* And the Psalmist, *Happy the people whose god is the Lord* [Ps. 143:15].

REPLY: For man to rest content with any created good is not possible, for he can be happy only with complete good which satisfies his desire altogether: he would not have reached his ultimate end were there something still remaining to be desired. The object of the will, that is the human appetite, is the Good without reserve. Clearly, then, nothing can satisfy man's will except such goodness, which is found, not in anything created, but in God alone. Everything created is a derivative good. He alone, *who fills with all good things thy desire* [Ps. 102:5], can satisfy our will, and therefore in him alone our happiness lies.

Hence: 1. To say that the heights of human nature rise to the lower flanks of angelic nature is a metaphorical turn of speech. In truth men do not stay there as their utmost limit, but press upward to the universal fount of good, the unrestricted object of bliss for all the blessed, the infinite and complete subsisting good.

2. If the whole itself is not an ultimate but subordinate to a further end, then a person's ultimate end does not lie there but somewhere beyond. The universe of creatures, to which man is compared as part to a whole, is not the ultimate end, but is ordered to God who is the ultimate end. And so man's final destiny is reached with God himself, not within the universe.

3. The phrase, the good of which man is capable, can refer to the good as an intrinsic modification or quality of his being; in this sense a creaturely

good does not exceed his capacity. And thus as a property of derivative being, the goodness of an angel, indeed of the entire universe, is finite and limited. But if it refers to an object, then in this sense creaturely good is less than a man's capacity, for he can reach out to the infinite.[1]

Thomas's first move is to provide a philosophical argument for his claim—one that he takes to be consistent with both scripture and tradition. Somewhat simplified, it goes as follows:

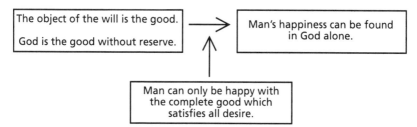

Next, Thomas rebuts in turn each of the contrary arguments. The first one looks like this:

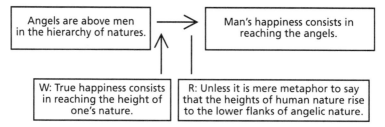

Recall from chapter 8 that Thomas believed that much of the Christian's knowledge of God can be found both in scripture and by the use of reason alone. So he envisioned many theological claims being supported by two different arguments: one grounded in scripture; one in experiential or philosophical truths (the latter often taken on the authority of a philosopher such as Aristotle). This passage is typical of many, though, in using both truths of scripture and principles of reason in the same argument.

3. Reformation Theology

By the time of the Reformation in the sixteenth century it seemed to many that the scriptural grounding of theology had been overshadowed by philosophical argumentation and especially by the influence of Aristotle. So the *sola Scriptura* principle (scripture alone) was meant to reform theology as much as it was to reform the church.

Of course, it is not possible to make arguments *grounded* in scripture without *warrants* of some sort, so *sola Scriptura* can never be followed in an absolute way. Nonetheless, it was possible to shift the emphasis away from

[1]*Summa Theologiae* part 2, first part, question 2, article 8.

philosophy and toward the texts. Consider, for example, John Calvin's (1509–64) argument regarding Christian freedom in his *Institutes of the Christian Religion*.[2]

> We must now discuss Christian freedom. No summary of gospel teaching ought to omit an explanation of this topic. It is a matter of prime necessity, and without a knowledge of it consciences dare undertake almost nothing without faltering; often hesitate and draw back; constantly waver and are afraid. But we have put off a fuller discussion of it to this place (having lightly touched upon it above). For, as soon as Christian freedom is mentioned, either passions boil or wild tumults rise, unless these wanton spirits (who otherwise most wickedly corrupt the best things) are all opposed in time. Partly, on the pretext of this freedom, men shake off all obedience toward God and break into unbridled license; partly, they disdain it, thinking such freedom cancels all moderation, order, and choice of things. What are we, boxed in by such perplexities, to do here? Shall we say goodbye to Christian freedom, thus cutting off occasion for such dangers? But, as we have said, unless this freedom be grasped, neither Christ nor gospel truth is rightly known. Rather, we must take care that so necessary a part of doctrine not be suppressed, yet at the same time that those absurd objections which commonly arise from it be met.
>
> Christian freedom, in my opinion, consists of three parts. The first: that the conscience of believers, while having to seek assurance of their justification before God, should rise above and advance beyond the law, forgetting all law-righteousness. For since, as we have elsewhere shown, the law leaves no one righteous, either we are excluded from all hope of justification or we ought to be freed from it. And in such a way, indeed, that utterly no account is taken of works. For he who thinks that in order to obtain righteousness he ought to bring some trifle of works, is incapable of determining their measure and limit but makes himself debtor to the whole law. Removing, then, mention of the law, and laying aside all consideration of works, we should, when justification is being discussed, embrace God's mercy alone, turn our attention from ourselves, and look only to Christ. For there the question is not how we may become righteous, but how, being unrighteous and unworthy, we may be reckoned righteous. If consciences wish to attain any certainty in this matter, they ought to give no place to the law. Nor can any man rightly infer from this that the law is superfluous for believers, since it does not stop teaching and exhorting and urging them to good, even though before God's judgment-seat it does not have a place in their consciences. For, as these two things are completely different, we must rightly and conscientiously distinguish them. The whole life of Christians ought to be a sort of practice of godliness, because we have been called to sanctification [I Thess. 4:7; cf. Eph. 1:4; I Thess. 4:3]. The function of the law consists in this: by warning men of their duty, to arouse them to pursue holiness and innocence. But where consciences are worried how to make God favorable, what to respond and with what assurance to stand, if called to his judgment—there we are not to reckon what the law requires, but Christ alone, who surpasses all law-perfection, must be set forth for righteousness.
>
> Almost the entire argument of the letter to the Galatians hinges upon this point. For those who teach that Paul in this contends for freedom only from

---

[2]Calvin's *Institutes of the Christian Religion* was first published in 1536 in Basel, Switzerland, and revised and enlarged over the course of Calvin's life. The passage below is from an early version, translated by Ford Lewis Battles (Grand Rapids: Eerdmans, 1975), chap. 6.

ceremonies are absurd interpreters, as can be proved from his proof-passages. Such passages are the following: That Christ "became a curse for us" to "redeem us from the curse of the law" [Gal. 3:13]. Likewise: "Stand fast in the freedom with which Christ has set us free, and do not submit again to the yoke of slavery. Now I, Paul, say . . . that if you become circumcised, Christ will become of no advantage to you. . . . And every man who becomes circumcised is a debtor to the whole law. For you Christ has become of no advantage. Any of you who are justified by the law have fallen away from grace" [Gal. 5:1–4]. These passages certainly contain something loftier than freedom from ceremonies! (176–77).

This piece is typical of much of Calvin's work. First, it begins with a pastoral concern—here, to counter the boiling passion and wild tumults that arise when Christian freedom is mentioned—and sets out to provide a solid theological answer. Second, Calvin generally makes more use of scripture in his arguments than did Thomas Aquinas.

This argument is also typical, some interpreters would say, in that Calvin is attempting to find a middle position between two extremes—here, between the libertines and the scrupulous—but more often between the views he attributed to his opponents: the Catholics and the more radical Anabaptist wing of the Reformation. Just as virtue consists in a mean between two extremes, so truth must be approximated by seeking a way between a defect at one end of the spectrum and an excess at the other.[3] Let us see if this theory about Calvin's philosophy of truth allows us to make sense of the very complex argument quoted above.

We begin by noting that there are two extreme positions reflected here, and that Calvin rebuts both of them. One extreme is the denial of Christian freedom, and there are two arguments in its behalf: one is a rebuttal of the claim that the letter to the Galatians teaches Christian freedom, since it applies only to ceremonial matters. Calvin defeats this rebuttal by calling attention to passages in the letter that are inconsistent with this interpretation.

Calvin's argument against the second extreme is only hinted at in the first paragraph: Christian freedom must be false teaching because it "cancels all moderation, order, and choice of things." Calvin's central claim rebuts this argument and at the same time rebuts the libertine's position. Both of Calvin's opponents are assuming that Christian freedom implies that people are to disregard totally the guidelines for living that the law provides. For the scrupulous this is taken as a *reductio ad absurdum;* for the libertines it is taken as license.

Calvin's rebuttal consists in distinguishing between keeping the law in order to earn one's justification before God and keeping the law as a "sort of practice of godliness." He argues that this must be the proper interpretation of Christian freedom, and notes briefly that it is based on a reading of the whole of Galatians. The following illustrates in a schematic way

---

[3]Donald McKim, "John Calvin: A Theologian for an Age of Limits," in *Readings in Calvin's Theology,* ed. McKim (Grand Rapids: Baker, 1984), 291–310, attributes this view to Ford Lewis Battles, in *Calculus Fidei: Some Ruminations on the Structure of the Theology of John Calvin* (Grand Rapids: Calvin Theological Seminary, 1978).

Calvin's pattern of arguing for a truth lying between two extremes. Note that a single statement regarding the true interpretation of Christian freedom functions as a rebuttal of both erroneous arguments. This rebuttal is grounded in the text of Galatians.

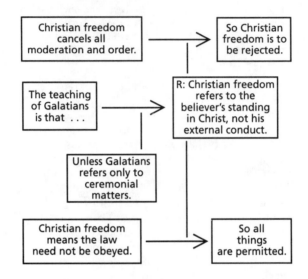

4. The Enlightenment

Philosophers date the beginning of the modern period around 1650. For many years the question of what accounted for the change from medieval to modern thinking was answered by pointing to the rise of modern science. More recently, though, the explanation includes a decisive role for religion. The Reformation had contributed to a great deal of social and political upheaval, culminating in the Thirty Years' War (1618–48). The fighting showed that social, political, and *intellectual* life could no longer be based on the authority of the Christian tradition, for there was no agreement about what that tradition was. The success of modern science suggested that mathematical reasoning combined with human experience could replace the voices of authority from the past.

Consequently, in the period of the Enlightenment (the eighteenth century) there was a great emphasis on the need to reject traditional authority in all realms of life and to work things out again from scratch, using rational argumentation and grounding one's positions either on experience or on rational principles. This movement was bound to have consequences for theology. Theologians might still argue from scripture, but now they would have first to provide a rational argument to legitimate the use of the texts—one could no longer simply assume their divine authority. But better yet, in the minds of many, would be a theology that relied not at all on the authority of scripture. This "natural theology" would argue from universal human experience to theological truths. The religion thus produced would be acceptable to all reasonable folk and religious strife would be forever banished.

4.1. John Locke

Locke (1632–1704) attempted to meet both of the Enlightenment's desiderata for theology. His argument in a book titled *On the Reasonableness of Christianity* (written in 1695) involved the elimination of all but a few central tenets from Christian teaching. He claimed that all one needed to believe in order to be saved was that Jesus was the Messiah, which involved belief in his resurrection, rule, and future return in judgment. Locke claimed that these truths were based directly upon his "attentive and unbiased search" of the scriptures. The main part of the book is a retelling of the life of Jesus, grounded by means of numerous quotations from the gospels, showing that the whole of the story points to and confirms Jesus' Messiahship. This aspect of Locke's work is a hypothetical argument: the hypothesis of Jesus as the Messiah accounts for all the data from the gospel texts.

The requisite argument for the revealed status of the scriptures had been provided five years earlier in Locke's *Essay Concerning Human Understanding*. In a chapter against "enthusiasm" in religion he wrote:

> *Reason* must be our last judge and guide in everything. I do not mean that we must consult reason and examine whether a proposition revealed from God can be made out by natural principles, and if it cannot, that then we may reject it; but consult it we must, and by it examine whether it be a revelation from God or no; and if *reason* finds it to be revealed from God, *reason* then declares for it as much as for any other truth, and makes it one of her dictates. . . .
>
> If this internal light, or any proposition which under that title we take for inspired, be conformable to the principles of reason or to the word of God, which is attested revelation, *reason* warrants it and we may safely receive it for true and be guided by it in our belief and actions. . . . Thus we see the holy men of old, who had *revelations* from God, had something else besides that internal light of assurance in their own minds to testify to them that it was from God. They were not left to their own persuasions alone that those persuasions were from God, but had outward signs to convince them of the author of those revelations. And when they were to convince others, they had a power given them to justify the truth of their commission from heaven, and by visible signs to assert the divine authority of a message they were sent with (Bk. 4, chap. 19).

So theology works as follows for Locke:

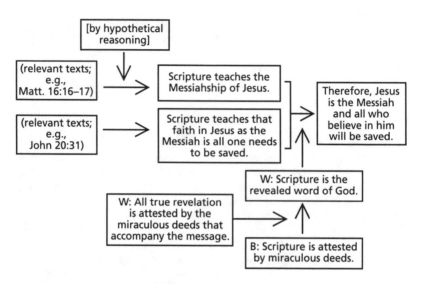

Locke also contributed to the natural theology of his day, which he took to provide additional support for his (minimalist) theology based on revelation. The mainstay of natural theologians was the argument from design, which appeared in various forms. Locke's formulation begins with the existence and powers of human beings:

> I think it is beyond question that *man has a clear perception of his own being:* he knows certainly that he exists and that he is something. . . .
>
> In the next place, man knows, by an intuitive certainty that bare *nothing can no more produce any real being than it can be equal to two right angles.* . . . If, therefore, we know there is some real being, and that nonentity cannot produce any real being, it is an evident demonstration that from eternity there has been something, since what was not from eternity had a beginning, and what had a beginning must be produced by something else.
>
> Next, it is evident that what had its being and beginning from another must also have all that which is in and belongs to its being from another too. All the powers it has must be owing to and received from the same source. This eternal source, then, of all being must also be the source and original of all power: and so *this eternal being must be also the most powerful.*
>
> Again, man finds in himself *perception* and *knowledge.* We have then got one step further, and we are certain now that there is not only some being, but some knowing, intelligent being in the world.
>
> There was a time, then, when there was no knowing being, and when knowledge began to be; or else there has been also *a knowing being from eternity.* If it be said there was a time when no being had any knowledge, when that eternal being was void of all understanding, I reply that then it was impossible there should ever have been any knowledge: it being as impossible that things wholly void of knowledge, and operating blindly and without any perception, should produce a knowing being, as it is impossible that a triangle should make itself three angles bigger than two right ones. For it is as repugnant to the *idea* of senseless matter that it should put into itself sense, perception, and knowledge, as it is repugnant to the *idea* of a triangle that it should put into itself greater angles than two right ones.

Thus, from the consideration of ourselves and what we infallibly find in our own constitutions, our reason leads us to the knowledge of this certain and evident truth: that *there is an eternal, most powerful, and most knowing being,* which whether anyone will please to call *God,* it matters not.[4]

Notice the appeal, on one hand, to experience—here 'experience' of one's own existence and powers—and on the other to reasoning intended to follow the pattern of mathematical (geometric) reasoning. We can sketch this argument as follows:

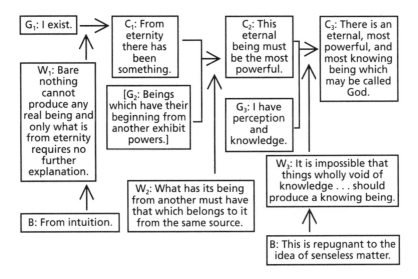

The natural theology of the modern period was relatively short-lived. Later philosophers such as David Hume (1711–76) and Immanuel Kant produced rebuttals for the arguments from design, which many today take to be definitive. Although Kant had more direct influence on the theology of his day, Hume's arguments have better stood the test of time.

4.2. David Hume

Hume set out systematically to destroy all of the arguments for the reasonableness of Christianity that had been developed from Locke's positions. By Hume's day the argument from design focused on the existence and character of the universe, rather than on the person. In typical form it was grounded on the assertion that the universe was like a complex machine or mechanism, and was warranted by the proposition that all complex mechanisms had to have a designer. One of Hume's rebuttals for this argument consisted in pointing out that the hypothesis of an intelligent designer is only one possible explanation of the origin of the world and

[4]John Locke, *An Essay Concerning Human Understanding,* bk. 4, chap. 10, para. 2–6.

depends on our first construing it as a machine or mechanism. If we construe it instead as more analogous to an organism, then it could be produced by propagation. A more important argument for today is that, since we have no experience at all of the origin of universes in general, for all we know it could be the result of a fortuitous arrangement of atoms.[5]

We have seen Hume's argument against knowledge of miracles in Exercise 9. On this basis he claimed that miracles could scarcely serve as an adequate foundation to prop up a doctrine of revelation; so this route for demonstrating the reasonableness of Christianity was also closed.

5. Modern Theology

By the beginning of the nineteenth century it was pretty well agreed (among Protestants, at least) that natural theology was not an option, so theology would have to begin with scripture. However, Locke's view that from "the sole reading of the Scriptures" in "an attentive and unbiased search" one could simply read off the doctrines that are "necessary to be believed," had come to appear hopelessly naive. So the question for theologians was what to *do* with the Bible. What one does with the scriptures in the course of theological argumentation will depend on what one thinks the Bible *is*. We will consider three options: scripture as a record of religious experience (Schleiermacher); scripture as a record of historical facts (Schweitzer); and scripture as a vehicle for God's self-revelation (Barth).

5.1. Scripture and Religious Experience: Friedrich Schleiermacher

For Schleiermacher (1768–1834), the essence of religion is feeling or piety; thought and action are secondary. The central feeling in all religion is an awareness of one's *absolute dependence;* such awareness is tantamount to an awareness of God. For Christians, this feeling takes on a special character due to the influence of Christ, in whom God was fully present—that is, Christ's consciousness of God never dimmed or faded away as it does for the rest of us.

Doctrines are verbal expressions of religious feelings, and the job of the theologian is to make these expressions as precise as possible. Following his own advice, Schleiermacher set out in his systematic theology to clarify the traditional teachings of the church by showing their relations to the religious affections that had given rise to them.[6] In the process he found some doctrines that needed to be redefined or restated, and some that ought to be rejected. For example, in the following passage he argues that there is no basis for the traditional distinction between the doctrines of creation and sustenance.

---

[5]David Hume, *Dialogues Concerning Natural Religion,* probably written in the 1750s but first published posthumously in 1779.

[6]Friedrich Schleiermacher, *The Christian Faith* (Edinburgh: T & T Clark, 1928); translation of *Der christliche Glaube,* first published in 1821–22.

FIRST SECTION

A Description of our Religious Self-Consciousness in so far as the Relation between the World and God is expressed in it.

INTRODUCTION

§ 36. *The original expression of this relation, i.e. that the world exists only in absolute dependence upon God, is divided in Church doctrine into the two propositions— that the world was created by God, and that God sustains the world.* . . .

I. The proposition that the totality of finite being exists only in dependence upon the Infinite is the complete description of that basis of every religious feeling which is here to be set forth. We find ourselves always and only in a continuous existence; our life is always moving along a course; consequently just so far as we regard ourselves as finite being, apart from all other things, our self-consciousness can represent this being only in its continuity. And this in so complete a sense that (the feeling of absolute dependence being so universal an element in our self-consciousness) we may say that in whatever part of the whole or at whatever point of time we may be placed, in every full act of reflection we should recognize ourselves as thus involved in continuity, and should extend the same thought to the whole of finite being. The proposition that God sustains the world, considered in itself, is precisely similar. At least it only seems to have acquired another and lesser content because we have grown accustomed to think of preservation and creation together, and thus a beginning is excluded from the range of the idea of preservation. On the other hand, the proposition, "God has created," considered in itself, lays down absolute dependence, but only for the beginning, with the exclusion of development; and whether the creation is conceived as taking place once for all or in the manner of one part after another, it lays down something which is not immediately given in our self-consciousness. Thus this proposition appears to belong to Dogmatics only so far as creation is complementary to the idea of preservation, with a view of reaching again the idea of unconditional all-inclusive dependence.

2. Thus there is no sufficient reason for retaining this division instead of the original expression which is so natural (*The Christian Faith,* 142–43).

Schematically we can represent this argument as follows:

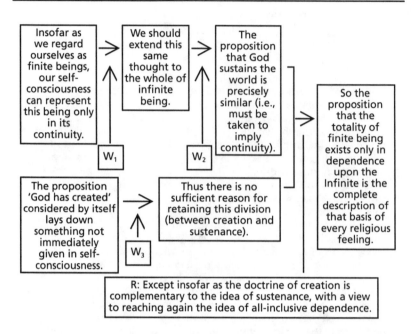

The warrants, which Schleiermacher has not supplied here, can be inferred from earlier passages, where he says:

> All propositions which the system of Christian doctrine has to establish can be regarded either as descriptions of human states, or as conceptions of divine attributes and modes of action, or as utterances regarding the constitution of the world (§30, p. 125).

He goes on to say that there are thus three forms of dogmatic propositions: those of the first (or fundamental) form are descriptions of human states of mind; the second and third forms are descriptions of attributes of God and of qualities of the world. Propositions of the second and third forms are permissible only insofar as they can be developed out of propositions of the first form, "for only on this condition can they be really authenticated as expressions of religious emotion" (§30.2, 126).

In the first branch of Schleiermacher's argument, as represented above, he argues first that our conception of the world's continuity derives from the continuity of our own self-consciousness. The warrant might be stated as follows:

> *W₁:* Propositions asserting qualities of the world are permissible only insofar as they can be developed out of descriptions of human states of mind.

The next step in the argument is to apply the same reasoning to our assertions about the mode of God's action with relation to this world, and the warrant will be similar to the first:

> *W₂:* Descriptions of attributes of God are permissible insofar as they can be developed out of descriptions of human states of mind.

The third warrant is again similar, but more general and stated negatively:

> W_3: Doctrines that are neither descriptions of what is given in immediate self-consciousness nor developed from descriptions of self-consciousness are not permissible.

The backing for these three warrants is Schleiermacher's theory of the nature of religion as essentially a certain form of consciousness (the awareness of absolute dependence) and of the nature of doctrines as *expressions* of those feelings. He has explained and justified these theories in the earlier chapters of the book.

Note that his discussion of possible justification for retaining the doctrine of creation fits in as a rebuttal to his argument: If Christians have come to think of sustenance only as keeping things in existence after creation, then it may be permissible to speak of creation because it is a way of trying to return to the original sense of the continuity of the world in its dependence on God.

So we can conclude that Schleiermacher's theological arguments will have the following general form:

Two things need to be noted: One is that Schleiermacher's approach to theology as so far presented may appear to be entirely independent of scripture and the historical tradition. This appearance is deceptive, however, because, in the first place, the Christian's religious self-consciousness will have been formed by the picture of Jesus presented in the New Testament. In this sense scripture comes in not as grounds for arguments, but one might rather say it works 'causally,' prior to the task of pursuing theological argumentation. Second, how is one to know what Christian doctrines are if one does not look to the New Testament and to the authoritative teachings of one's community? Schleiermacher says:

> §27. All propositions which claim a place in an epitome of Evangelical (Protestant) doctrine must approve themselves both by appeal to Evangelical confessional documents, or in default of these, to the New Testament Scriptures, and by exhibition of their homogeneity with other propositions already recognized (112).

So before a Schleiermacherian argument about the *legitimacy* of a particular doctrine can even get off the ground, we need arguments from within the province of historical theology or church history to inform us *what are* the teachings of our (Catholic or Protestant) tradition.

A second note: We have been speaking of doctrines that pass Schleiermacher's test of experience as "permissible" (his word) or as "legitimate" (my word). The fascinating thing about Schleiermacher's approach to theology (and probably a surprising thing for new students of theology) is that this legitimacy does not entail the truth of the doctrines in any straightforward sense. The doctrines must be *true to* experience, but this does not mean that they are objectively true statements *about* God, the self, or the world. This is not to say that they are untrue, but rather that truth and falsity are not the appropriate standards to apply. Precision of expression is what Schleiermacher aimed for.

Schleiermacher is considered the founder of the Liberal Protestant tradition in theology. His views are still quite influential.

5.2. Scripture and History: Albert Schweitzer

Current theological reasoning cannot be understood without appreciating the impact of historical criticism of the Bible. Criticism has brought about two revolutions in theologians' understanding of the relations among the biblical texts, history, and doctrine: first, a turn to history as a foundation for theology; second, a turn away from history to the "religious meaning" of the texts. For centuries the dominant view was supernaturalistic, and made no distinction between the literal meaning of the text, the history it reported, and the doctrinal truths embodied therein. The assumption, as Hans Frei put it, was that the stories mean literally what they say and their permanent religious significance lies in the report of those supernatural (as well as natural) events.

> All the miracle stories are true, and they form an essential part of the normative doctrine that Jesus is the Messiah, the Son of God incarnate. Again, God shaped the earth, life and man at a specific point beginning temporal history. And similarly, at a specific time soon thereafter the first individual man named Adam and his wife Eve fell from grace in the manner depicted in the story in Genesis, with dire consequences for all their descendants. Because these things happened in this fashion the general doctrine based on them is still true and describes our condition also, unless we are redeemed. This was the Supernaturalists' position.[7]

Beginning in the eighteenth century, critical methods were applied to the Genesis stories and especially to the gospels. The expectation was that the assured results of objective historical investigation would provide a solid ("scientific") foundation for theology. So theological arguments would be set up in two stages—the claims resulting from critical study of the Bible would serve as grounds for theological arguments:

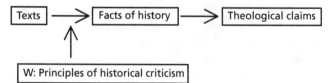

Numerous lives of Jesus were written attempting to reconstruct the "objective history."

[7]Hans Frei, *The Eclipse of Biblical Narrative* (New Haven: Yale University Press, 1974), 119.

However, when critics concluded either that the Jesus of history could not be found behind the doctrinally influenced biblical texts, or else that once found the historical picture of Jesus would undermine traditional church doctrine, a number of approaches to theology were developed that distinguished some special form of *religious* meaning and attempted to establish its independence from all but a minimum of historical fact.

Albert Schweitzer (1875–1965) in *The Quest of the Historical Jesus*[8] summarized and criticized his predecessors in Jesus studies, and put forward his own account of the historical Jesus as thoroughly *eschatological*. That is, Jesus' entire message was the coming Kingdom of God—the end of the world as we know it; his entire ministry was shaped by this expectation and, later, by disappointment when the end did not come as he had predicted.

Schweitzer's grounds for his eschatological interpretation of the life of Jesus are the texts, of course, but more particularly the *discontinuities* in the gospel narratives—the impossibility of making a coherent story out of them on the basis of the more common suppositions about Jesus. So Schweitzer's reasoning is hypothetical. What hypothesis, he asks, can provide a unifying explanation of this set of facts? His answer: only the eschatological hypothesis. For example, Jesus sends the Twelve out on a preaching mission (see Mark 6:7–13). When they return Jesus suddenly drops his teaching and attempts to flee from the crowds. Why?

> This work of preaching the Kingdom was continued until the sending forth of the Twelve; that is to say, at the most for a few weeks. . . . It is certain that Jesus, in the midst of His initial success, left Galilee, journeyed northwards, and only resumed His work as a teacher in Judaea on the way to Jerusalem! Of His "public ministry," therefore, a large section falls out, being canceled by a period of inexplicable concealment; it dwindles to a few weeks of preaching here and there in Galilee and the few days of His sojourn in Jerusalem.
>
> But in that case the public life of Jesus becomes practically unintelligible. The explanation that His cause in Galilee was lost, and that He was obliged to flee, has not the slightest foundation in the text. . . .
>
> If this [eschatological] interpretation of the mystery of the Kingdom of God is correct, Jesus must have expected the coming of the Kingdom at harvest time. And that is just what He did expect. It is for that reason that He sends out His disciples to make known in Israel, as speedily as may be, what is about to happen. . . .
>
> It is equally clear, and here the dogmatic considerations which guided the resolutions of Jesus become still more prominent, that this prediction was not fulfilled. The disciples returned to Him; and the appearing of the Son of Man had not taken place. The actual history disavowed the dogmatic history on which the action of Jesus had been based. . . . That was for Jesus . . . the central event which closed the former period of His activity and gave the coming period a new character. To this extent modern theology is justified when it distinguishes two periods in the Life of Jesus; an earlier, in which He is surrounded by the people, a later in which He is "deserted" by them and travels around with the Twelve only. . . .

[8]Albert Schweitzer, *The Quest of the Historical Jesus,* written in 1906 and published in English by Macmillan, 1950.

The Evangelist, therefore, places the rejection at Nazareth and the mission of the Twelve side by side, simply because he found them in this temporal connexion in the tradition. If he had been working by "association of ideas," he would not have arrived at this order. The want of connexion, the impossibility of applying any natural explanation, is just what is historical, because the course of the history was determined, not by outward events, but by the decisions of Jesus, and these were determined by dogmatic, eschatological considerations (352–53, 358–59).

So the fact to be explained is the sudden alteration of Jesus' behavior after the return of the Twelve; the hypothesis that Jesus had expected the end of the world and was disappointed explains the fact, while previous accounts, such as the desertion by the multitudes, do not stand up to scrutiny.

Schweitzer's conclusions about the relevance of New Testament history to theology are as follows: the 'Jesus' pictured by traditional theology never existed; therefore:

> The historical foundation of Christianity as built up by rationalistic, by liberal, and by modern theology no longer exists; but that does not mean that Christianity has lost its historical foundation. The work which historical theology thought itself bound to carry out, and which fell to pieces just as it was nearing completion, was only the brick facing of the real immovable historical foundation which is independent of any historical confirmation or justification.
>
> Jesus means something to our world because a mighty spiritual force streams forth from Him and flows through our time also. This fact can neither be shaken nor confirmed by any historical discovery. It is the solid foundation of Christianity.
>
> The mistake was to suppose that Jesus could come to mean more to our time by entering into it as a man like ourselves. That is not possible. First because such a Jesus never existed. Secondly because, although historical knowledge can no doubt introduce greater clearness into an existing spiritual life, it cannot call spiritual life into existence (399).

The second revolution is complete: the religious meaning of Jesus is now independent of history except for history's dimmest outlines.

Since Schweitzer's time, mainstream theology (according to Frei, again) has sought to establish some sort of universal religious need, based on an analysis of the human situation, and to show the meaningfulness of Jesus' life and death with regard to that religious need.

> The . . . religious meaningfulness of the narratives is at least in part provided by their answering a universal human condition or need of which we are all at least implicitly aware. . . .
>
> In other words, there is an area of human experience on which the light of the Christian gospel and that of natural, independent insight shine at the same time, illumining it in the same way. The degree to and manner in which the one mode of insight has to be bolstered by the other is a matter of difference among various mediating theologians, and they have invented a wide variety of often very complex ways of stating their views on this subject. But on the substantive point that both modes must be present and correlated they are all agreed. There is no such thing as revelation without someone to

receive it, and receive it, moreover, as a significant answer to or illumination of general life questions.[9]

Within this group of theologians, Frei includes Locke, Schleiermacher, Albrecht Ritschl, Emil Brunner, Rudolf Bultmann, Karl Rahner, Wolfhart Pannenberg, and Jürgen Moltmann. It is surprising that he does not include Paul Tillich and the Niebuhr brothers as well.

5.3. Revelation and the Word of God: Karl Barth

Our final example is Barth (1886–1968), who reacted strongly against attempts to begin theology with anthropology—with human religious experience (Schleiermacher) or with any sort of analysis of the human predicament. The starting point for Barth is the Word of God.

Barth has been such an important figure in recent theology that it would be irresponsible to leave him out of our account. Nonetheless, he is a difficult thinker to include in a book on theological reasoning because argument plays a relatively small role in his works. His style might be called expository rather than logical. A look at typical passages in his *Church Dogmatics*[10] shows him stating a thesis and following it with a long passage unfolding its meaning—but usually not deriving logical consequences from it and, especially, not providing grounds for it of any sort. For example, examine the following passage, where Barth explains his definition of theology.

§ I

THE TASK OF DOGMATICS

As a theological discipline, dogmatics is the scientific test to which the Christian Church puts herself regarding the language about God which is peculiar to her.

I. THE CHURCH, THEOLOGY, SCIENCE

Dogmatics is a theological discipline. But theology is a function of the Church.

The Church confesses God, by the fact that she speaks of God. She does so first of all through her existence in the action of each individual believer. And she does so in the second place through her special action as a community; in proclamation by preaching and administration of the Sacrament, in worship, in instruction, in her mission work within and without the Church, including loving activity among the sick, the weak, and those in jeopardy. Fortunately the Church's reality does not coincide exactly with her action. But her action does coincide with the fact that alike in her existence in believers and in her communal existence as such, she speaks about God. Her action is "theology," alike in the former, broader sense, and in the latter, narrower sense. . . .

But by her very confession of God, the Church also confesses to the humanity and likewise to the responsibility of her action. She is aware of her exposure to fierce temptation in speaking of God, aware also that she has to reckon with God for her speaking. The first, last, and decisive answer to this double compulsion consists in the fact that she finds His grace sufficient,

[9]Frei, *The Eclipse of Biblical Narrative*, 128–29.
[10]Karl Barth, *Church Dogmatics* (Edinburgh: T & T Clark, 1936–39).

whose strength is mighty in the weak. Yet in virtue of her very contentment with that, she recognizes and undertakes, as an active Church, a further human task, the task of criticizing and revising her language about God. This confronts us with the concept of theology in the third, strictest, and proper meaning of the word. . . .

Theology as a science (as distinguished from the "theology" of the simple testimony of faith and life and from the "theology" of public worship) is the Church taking her measure, in view of the temptation and responsibility just mentioned, which attaches to her language. It would be meaningless without justifying grace, which in this case too can alone make good what man as such invariably makes a mess of; yet it may have significance as an act of obedience whereby man in this case too may believe without seeing, that he is doing well for himself. . . .

The Church produces theology in this special and peculiar sense, by subjecting herself to a self-test. She faces herself with the question of truth, i.e. she measures her action, her language about God, against her existence as a Church. Thus theology exists in this special and peculiar sense, because before it and apart from it there is, in the Church, language about God.—Theology follows the language of the Church, so far as, in its question as to the correctness of the Church's procedure therein, it measures it, not by a standard foreign to her, but by her very own source and object. . . .

The question of truth, with which theology is throughout concerned, is the question as to the agreement between the language about God peculiar to the Church and the essence of the Church. The criterion of Christian language, in past and future as well as at the present time, is thus the essence of the Church, which is Jesus Christ, God in His gracious approach to man in revelation and reconciliation. Has Christian language its source in Him? Does it lead to Him? Does it conform to Him? None of these questions can be put without the others, but each in all its force must be put independently. Thus as Biblical theology, theology is the question as to the foundation, as practical theology it is the question as to the aim, as dogmatic theology it is the question as to the content, of the language peculiar to the Church (I/1, 1–3).

I chose this passage as typical of Barth's style of exposition, although he is here speaking about theology rather than doing it, because it helps us understand the lack of argument in his dogmatics. Notice that we can detect an assumption about the task of theology that is similar to Schleiermacher's: the role of theology is to examine critically the language of the church—to determine what is a *legitimate* part of its teaching. But here the source is not human experience (as it was for Schleiermacher) but the Word of God, God's self-revelation in Jesus. Scripture (and preaching) witness to this revelation, but again, scripture itself does not play the part we might expect, providing straightforward grounds for theological claims. Rather, God acts through the church's reading of the word to reveal himself to the church. It is this revelation that is normative for theology.

So what are the grounds for theological arguments? Well, there are none of the sorts of grounds we might have come to expect: no Schleiermacherian religious experience; no philosophical arguments. Previous formulations of church doctrine are to be taken seriously, but today's theology cannot simply be based on the past. Hendrikus Berkhof says of Barth's understanding of theology:

The content of faith does not permit itself to be grounded by the human intellect but only to be unfolded by reflection. Theological thought, insofar as this is possible, brings out *a posteriori* the *ratio*, the inner coherence, of revelation.[11]

For a complementary view of Barth's theology, I turn to a book by David Kelsey. Kelsey offers a schematization of a "macro-argument" that he takes to represent a family of arguments found in Barth's discussion of the perfections of God.[12] In other words, the following argument represents an overview of a large part of Barth's thought, even though it is not found in this condensed form in any particular passage.[13]

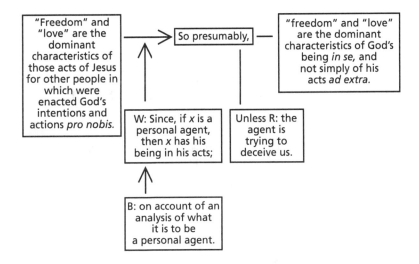

The grounding here is a statement about Jesus Christ, who, in Barth's words, is "God in his gracious approach to man in revelation and reconciliation." The claim is about the language with which the church is to speak of God, namely in terms of God's "freedom" and "love." The warrant comes from philosophical analysis of the relations between an agent's being and actions.

So, looked at 'from a distance,' Barth's theology can be seen to fall into the structure of an argument. From 'up close,' that is, in a page-by-page analysis, one sees the fine-structure of this thought, which includes a few brief arguments, but much more that is explication and expansion of each major point.

[11]Hendrikus Berkhof, *Two Hundred Years of Theology*, trans. John Vriend (Grand Rapids: Eerdmans, 1989), 206.

[12]In Barth, *Church Dogmatics* II/1.

[13]David Kelsey, *The Uses of Scripture in Recent Theology* (Philadelphia: Fortress, 1975), 133. I strongly recommend this book for supplementary reading.

6. Conclusion

Our survey of theologians and of typical arguments found in their work is consistent with a conclusion of Kelsey's own survey of theological argument, namely that there is no special theological way to argue. Theological positions are clusters of loosely connected arguments that use grounds, warrants, and backing from a vast array of sources.

In responding to a commonly expressed charge that theologies go wrong by choosing the wrong starting point, Kelsey offers a contrasting picture of the structure of theology:

> The "position" taken as a whole would then be more aptly discussed in quasi-aesthetic terms as the expression of a particular vision of the basic character or "essence" of Christian faith and not in logical terms as though it were one large argument. An aesthetic entity, after all, unlike an argument, doesn't logically "begin" at any one point except in the trivial sense in which a play "begins" with its first word, and a sonata begins with its first note. . . . The point of suggesting that theological systems be taken on analogy with a sculpture by Calder rather than on analogy with a train or a plant is not to deny that different sorts of questions and different sorts of intellectual inquiry do tend to dominate different theological "systems," nor to deny that this difference helps give each system its peculiar characteristics. . . . Tillich's interest in ontological questions has a lot to do with the differences between his theology and Barth's. . . . The point is, rather, that it will be more illuminating if, instead of asking where it "begins," we analyze a theological "position" by asking (a) what *roles* are played in the structure of the whole position by its discussion of each of the several theological *loci* [i.e., Christ, God, church, etc.], and (b) by asking what *roles* are played in the arguments found in each of those discussions by various kinds of intellectual inquiry such as historical research (including biblical scholarship), phenomenology of religious experience, metaphysical schemes, etc., asking what they do, i.e., what are they *used* for within the "system" as a whole.[14]

Consequently (and this is the main point of Kelsey's book), to say that scripture is authoritative for theology is to say very little until one examines exactly how scripture is used by particular theologians. As we have seen above, it can be used in a surprising variety of ways. How scripture is to be used in theology will be determined by "a decision a theologian must make about what is the subject matter of theology. And that is determined, not by the results of historical-critical biblical study, but by the way in which he [or she] tries to catch up what Christianity is basically all about in a single, synoptic, imaginative judgment" (159). In the next chapter we shall see if we can find a place for such a judgment.

---

[14]Kelsey, *The Uses of Scripture in Recent Theology*, 137–38.

EXERCISE ELEVEN

Study the passages below and answer the questions that follow.

1. This is a typical passage from Schleiermacher's theology, in which he is assessing two traditional doctrines.

   > §69. *We are conscious of sin partly as having its source in ourselves, partly as having its source outside our own being.*
   >   . . . It is this twofold relation, found universally though in varying proportions in all consciousness of sin, that forms the essential and ultimate ground for the fact that the explication of the Christian consciousness of sin in the teaching of the Church falls into two doctrines of "original sin" and "actual sin."[15]

   a. Write a typical Schleiermacherian claim that could be supported using grounds from this passage.
   b. Supply a warrant for the argument.

2. This passage by Barth is about the nature of Jesus' resurrection—distinguishing it from more ordinary events.

   > (1) The happening on the third day which followed that of Golgotha is the act of God with the same seriousness, but it is unequivocally marked off from the first happening [Jesus' death] by the fact that it does not have in the very least this component of human willing and activity. Not merely in purpose and ordination, but in its fulfilment, too, it is exclusively the act of God. . . . Like creation, it takes place as a sovereign act of God, and only in this way.
   >   We do not come to this conclusion merely because of its specific content, the coming to life of a man who was actually and in truth dead and buried.
   >   (2) It is, of course, true that even in this respect it breaks through this context; it is not the kind of event which can be the result of human will and activity or can be made clear or intelligible as such. (3) An event which continues the being of man after death cannot be the result of the will and activity either of the man himself or of other men. (4) To be dead means not to be. (5) Those who are not, cannot will and do, nor can they possibly be objects of the willing and doing of others. [Resurrection from the dead] is not one possibility of this kind with others. Where it takes place, God and God alone is at work. To raise . . . the dead, to give life . . . to the dead, is, like the creative summoning into being of non-being, a matter wholly and exclusively for God alone, quite outside the sphere of any possible co-operating factors (Heb. 11:19; 2 Cor. 1:9; Rom. 4:17). And this is primarily and particularly the case in the resurrection of Jesus Christ.[16]

   a. Considering only the numbered statements, which is Barth's claim?
   b. If we take 3 as the warrant for Barth's argument, write a statement that he must be *assuming* as the grounds.
   c. Which statements serve as backing for 3?

[15]Schleiermacher, *The Christian Faith*, 279, 281.
[16]Barth, *Church Dogmatics*, IV/1, 300–301.

3. Here Calvin is presenting part of a larger argument against "works righteousness."

> (1) Next, even if it were possible for us to have some wholly pure and righteous works, yet, as the prophet says, one sin is enough to wipe out and extinguish every memory of that previous righteousness [Ezek. 18:24]. (2) James agrees with him: "Whoever," he says, "fails in one point, has become guilty of all" [James 2:10]. (3) Now since this mortal life is never pure or devoid of sin, (4) whatever righteousness we might attain [Prov. 24:16; 1 John 1:8], when it is corrupted, oppressed and destroyed by the sins that follow, could not come into God's sight or be reckoned to us as righteousness.[17]

   a. In which statement is the claim to be found?
   b. Which statement contains the grounds?
   c. There are two similar statements that contain warrants for the argument. Which are they?
   d. What is the backing for the warrants?

4. Locke is writing here about the so-called messianic secret. There has been much discussion about whether Jesus intended to conceal the fact that he was the Messiah.

> (1) Nay, so far was he from publicly owning himself to be the Messiah that he forbid the doing of it: Mark 8:27–30. . . .
>
> (2) This concealment of himself will seem strange in one who was to bring light into the world, and was to suffer death for the testimony of truth. (3) This reservedness will be thought to look as if he had a mind to conceal himself and not to be known to the world for the Messiah, nor to be believed on as such. (4) But we shall be of another mind, and conclude this proceeding of his according to divine wisdom and suited to a fuller manifestation and evidence of his being the Messiah, when we consider that (5) he was to fill out the time foretold of his ministry; and after a life illustrious in miracles and good words, attended with humility, meekness, patience, and sufferings, and every way conformable to the prophecies of him, and should be led as sheep to the slaughter, and with all quiet and submission be brought to the cross, though there were no guilt or fault found in him. (6) This could not have been if, as soon as he appeared in public and began to preach, he had presently confessed himself to have been the Messiah, the king that owned that kingdom he published to be at hand. For the Sanhedrin would then have laid hold on it to have got him into their power, and thereby to have taken away his life—at least they would have disturbed his ministry, and hindered the work he was about. (7) That this made him cautious, and avoid, as much as he could, the occasions of provoking them and falling into their hands is plain from John 7:1, "After these things Jesus walked in Galilee," out of the way of the chief priests and rulers, "for he would not walk in Jewry, because the Jews sought to kill him."[18]

   a. On the basis of what was said in this chapter about Locke, what role does this passage play in his overall argument?

[17]Calvin, *Institutes*, 32.
[18]Locke, *The Reasonableness of Christianity*, para. 61–62.

b. What is the evidence in this passage against Locke's overall claim?

c. Which statement contains the claim Locke is making in *this* passage?

d. Which statements contain grounds for the claim in this passage? (Note: no warrants are stated.)

5. This argument by Thomas is closely related to the one at the beginning of this chapter. It pertains to a major point of his theology, that the end or *telos* of human life is the beatific vision.

article 8. is man's happiness the vision of God's very essence?

THE EIGHTH POINT: I. It seems not. For Dionysius teaches that the height of understanding is for man to be conjoined to God as the wholly unknown. Could anything be further from seeing an essence? So then at its peak of happiness the mind does not see God by His essence.

II. Moreover, the higher a nature the higher its perfection. Seeing the divine essence is proper to the divine mind. The human mind stands below this, and at full height does not break through to such a vision.

ON THE OTHER HAND we are promised, *When He shall appear, we shall be like Him and see Him as He is* (1 Jn. 3:2).

REPLY: (1) There can be no complete and final happiness for us save in the vision of God. The evidence? Consider first, that (2) man is not perfectly happy so long as something remains for him to desire and seek; and secondly, that (3) a power's full development comes only from its shaping object. (4) Now we agree with the *De Anima* [Aristotle], (5) the object of the mind is *what really is*, that is the essence of a thing. And so the mind's expansion into perfection is proportionate to its possession of what really is.

(6) If, then, the essence of an effect is known through which, however, the essence of its cause cannot be known, namely what it really is, then quite simply the mind does not reach to the cause, though it may be able to gather from the effect that a cause is really there. (7) Accordingly when a man knows an effect and also that it has a cause, then the desire still stirs in him to know also what the cause really is. (8) This is part of his constitution, and full of wonder, which, as noticed at the opening of the *Metaphysics* [Aristotle, again], sets us out to explore. (9) For instance, on seeing a solar eclipse, we reflect that there must be a cause for it, yet because this is not known we start to wonder and so go on to investigate, nor shall we rest until we come to see the cause for what it really is.

(10) Well then, were the human mind, from knowing what the created effects about us were, to have reached the position of knowing no more about God than that he exists, then (11) not yet would it have come to the point of perfection by knowing the first cause unreservedly, and a natural desire to find it would remain. (12) Not yet would a man be in perfect bliss. (13) Complete happiness requires the mind to come through to the essence itself of the first cause. (14) And so it will have its fulfilment by union with God as its object, for we have already explained that in this alone our happiness lies.

Hence: I. Dionysius is referring to the knowledge we have as pilgrims to happiness.

II. We have already noted that there are two sides to an end. One is the thing itself which is desired, and we have stated that is one and the same for lower and higher natures, indeed for all things. The other is the actual reaching of it, and in this respect ends are diverse for lower and higher natures according to their various relationships to that one thing. So therefore God's happiness in comprehending His essence is higher than the happiness of men and angels, who see but do not comprehend him.[19]

a. What is the claim for which Thomas argues here?
b. What is the function in the argument of each of the *two* sets of passages marked with Roman numerals?
c. Using numbered statements from Thomas's argument, fill in appropriate warrants and backing in the argument below:

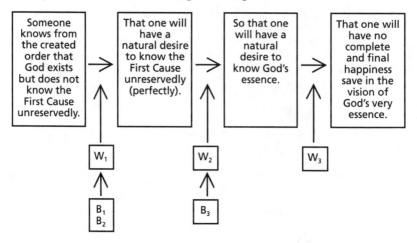

6. Rudolf Bultmann, an early twentieth-century theologian and New Testament scholar, created a great stir with his program of demythologization of the New Testament. Both passages below are from a defense of this method.

> The whole conception of the world which is presupposed in the preaching of Jesus as in the New Testament generally is mythological; i.e., the conception of the world as being structured in three stories, heaven, earth and hell; the conception of the intervention of supernatural powers in the course of events; and the conception of miracles, . . . This conception of the world we call mythological because it is different from the conception of the world which has been formed and developed by science. . . . In this modern conception of the world the cause-and-effect nexus is fundamental. . . .
> Then the question inevitably arises: is it possible that Jesus' preaching of the Kingdom of God still has any importance for modern men . . . ?
> We must ask whether the eschatological preaching and the mythological sayings as a whole contain a still deeper meaning which is concealed under the cover of mythology. If that is so, let us abandon the mythological conceptions precisely because we want to retain their deeper meaning. This method of interpretation of the New Testament which tries to recover

[19]Thomas Aquinas, *Summa Theologiae*, part 2, first part, question 3, article 8.

the deeper meaning behind the mythological conceptions I call *de-my-thologizing*—an unsatisfactory word, to be sure. Its aim is not to eliminate the mythological statements but to interpret them. It is a method of hermeneutics.[20]

a. What does this passage suggest theological claims will be about?
b. What is the primary source of grounds for Bultmann's theological claims, as far as one can tell from this passage?

Bultmann continues:

We can understand the problem best when we remember that *de-mytholo-gizing is an hermeneutic method,* that is, a method of interpretation, of exegesis. . . .

Reflection on hermeneutics . . . makes it clear that interpretation . . . is always based on principles and conceptions which guide exegesis as presuppositions, although interpreters are often not aware of this fact. . . .

But then the question arises, which conceptions are right and adequate? Which presuppositions are right and adequate? . . .

It can be said that [exegetical] method is nothing other than a kind of questioning, a way of putting questions [to the text]. . . .

You obtain your conceptions from your own physical life. The resulting or corresponding presupposition of exegesis is that you do have a relation to the subject-matter . . . about which you interrogate a given text.

. . . If it is true that the right questions are concerned with the possibilities of understanding human existence, then it is necessary to discover the adequate conceptions by which such understanding is to be expressed. To discover these conceptions is the task of philosophy. . . .

Our question is simply which philosophy today offers the most adequate perspective and conceptions for understanding human existence. Here it seems to me that we should learn from existentialist philosophy, because in this philosophical school human existence is directly the object of attention. . . .

Thus it follows that existentialist philosophy can offer adequate conceptions for the interpretation of the Bible, since the interpretation of the Bible is concerned with the understanding of existence.[21]

c. This passage shows that for Bultmann theological method has to do with interpretation or "translation." What is translated, and from what kind of language or concepts?
d. To what part of an argument is the question of presuppositions in hermeneutics relevant?
e. So the question how to determine that these presuppositions are the correct ones has to do with what part of a theological argument?
f. Into what sort of language or concepts should the Christian message be translated?
g. So what *two* roles does existentialist philosophy play in Bultmann's theology?

[20]Rudolf Bultmann, *Jesus Christ and Mythology* (New York: Scribner's, 1958), 15–18.
[21]Bultmann, *Jesus Christ and Mythology*, 45–57 *passim*.

PART THREE

The Rationality of Religion

CHAPTER TWELVE

Relating the Theological Disciplines

1. The Standard Model

How is one to relate the assorted disciplines making up the theological curriculum? This question has stirred lively debate for almost as long as there have been schools of theology. Let us see what contribution we can make to this discussion by thinking about the *arguments* we find in the relevant disciplines.

The most common view today of the relations among the five disciplines examined here is the following: the results of biblical studies and historical studies *support* systematic theology, while the results of systematic theology are *applied* in Christian ethics, preaching (and practical theology). In our language: claims from biblical and historical studies provide grounds for theological claims; theological claims provide grounds for ethical claims. (The relation between a theological claim and its appearance in a sermon cannot be so neatly summarized.) Schematically, the model can be represented as follows:

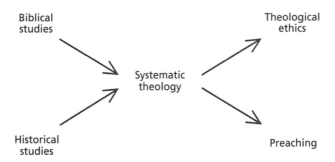

Biblical studies

Historical studies

Systematic theology

Theological ethics

Preaching

This model evolved from its origin in the Protestant Reformation and the fourfold division of studies seen then as necessary to prepare pastors and teachers for their ministries. The fundamental task was study of the Bible, but the need for some way of arranging biblical teaching into a coherent presentation led to the incorporation of "dogmatic" or "systematic" theology into the curriculum. In the early days, church history and history of doctrine often focused on the vindication of the Protestant movement against Catholic claims, but the most basic task was to measure historical developments against the biblical norm. The fourth major topic of study (in addition to the biblical, dogmatic, and historical) was the pastoral office itself, and here, too, scripture was taken as normative for a conception of the ministry.

This model of the relation of theological disciplines can be represented as follows. Notice that ethics was not a distinct discipline in the older Reformation model.[1]

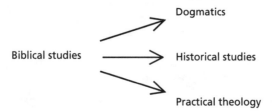

Friedrich Schleiermacher was largely responsible for moving theology into the central, mediating position it now holds in the "standard model."

Let us take the standard model as a rough starting point for our discussion, and see what elaborations, qualifications, and corrections might need to be made.

2. Systematic Theology, Biblical Studies, and History

We ended chapter 11 with David Kelsey's suggestion that we *not* look for a fixed starting point for theology, as though it were one large, continuous argument. A theology is rather a cluster of loosely connected arguments using a variety of grounds and warrants. What, then, could be meant by the term *'systematic* theology'? Let us consider what sorts of connections there are (or could be) among the theological doctrines and the arguments pertaining to each. Different theologians connect the doctrines differently, so the following will be examples of the sorts of connections for which a theologian *might* argue.

The standard *loci* (areas, positions) around or within which theologians and church bodies formulate doctrinal claims include the following: doctrine of God, Christology, doctrine of the Holy Spirit (pneumatology), doctrines of sin, salvation, and atonement, doctrine of creation, doctrine

---

[1]See Charles Wood, *Vision and Discernment: An Orientation in Theological Study* (Atlanta: Scholars Press, 1985), chap. 1, for a more detailed history of these changes. The exercise at the end of this chapter includes Wood's own view of the theological curriculum, as well as a proposal by Bernard Lonergan, one of the most influential recent Catholic theologians. The excerpt from John Howard Yoder represents current anabaptist thinking in that it exemplifies the central role this tradition gives to theological ethics.

of the church and of its signs and sacraments, and, finally, the doctrine of last things (eschatology).

Within the locus of Christology, for example, a doctrine of the two natures of Christ may be related to two lower-level theses regarding the full humanity of Christ and the divinity of Christ. The two-natures doctrine can be seen as a hypothesis formed to reconcile these two, apparently contradictory, statements about Christ. The attribution of divinity to Christ (and also to the Holy Spirit) calls for still another explanatory hypothesis: the doctrine of the Trinity can be seen as a theory to reconcile Christological and pneumatological positions with a monotheistic conception of God.

It is common to make connections between Christology and the doctrine of the atonement (i.e., the doctrine that explains how the work of Christ reconciles humankind with God). For example, Anselm (1033–1109) argued that only a God-man could reconcile sinful humans with God since only God could make adequate satisfaction for sin, and only one who was truly human could make satisfaction *for us.*

The doctrine of the Spirit has often been linked with the doctrine of the church as the source of the church's efficacy or identity.

The doctrine of creation must always account for the observable evil in God's good creation. Often this is done by means of the doctrine of sin: free human choice is the explanation for what has gone wrong with an all-good creation.

These examples suggest that while theology may be systematic in the sense of being interconnected, it is not systematic in the sense that we can make the connections by means of a single linear argument. If we try to sketch the relations of the doctrines we get a picture something like the following:

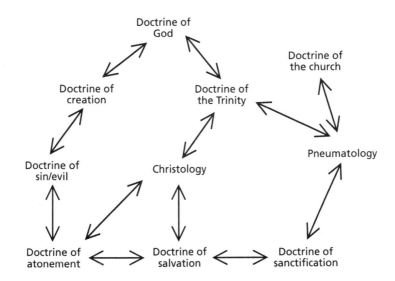

2.1. Foundationalism

What we have just seen of the web-like structure of systematic theology relates to a hot debate in epistemology: What is the 'shape' of our system of knowledge? How do the parts relate to one another? For several centuries it has been assumed that the system must be shaped like a building with a foundation.

The main structure of our belief system must rest on a set of beliefs that are 'foundational' in the sense that they are self-supporting—that is, obviously true and therefore not in need of justification of any sort. We have noted earlier that we can often call the grounds of an argument into question, requiring that the proposer of the argument add more basic grounds to support them. The foundationalist point is that such questioning has to stop somewhere or the whole argument can never get started. And, furthermore, those special starting grounds must not only be grounds that we simply *do* not question but, rather, grounds that no one *could* (reasonably) call into question.

Philosophers have proposed different kinds of beliefs to fulfill the foundational function. For René Descartes (1596–1650) it was clear and distinct intuitions—that is, ideas he found in his mind and was unable to doubt, such as the fact that he was thinking. Our Anglo-American empiricist tradition has taken the immediate deliverances of sense experience to be foundational for all other knowledge.

Once the ground of all grounds (the foundation) is given, the construction can proceed, but in one direction only—up. So the standard picture of knowledge is a building with the foundation on the bottom and one or more 'stories' built upon it. In philosophy of science this has been called the "layer-cake" model of science.

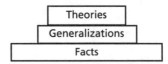

Foundationalist theories of knowledge have had a profound effect on modern theology. If the theological positions (doctrines) are layers in the cake or stories in the building, what constitutes the foundation? There are two plausible answers here: scripture or experience.

If scripture has to play the role of foundation, then it must have the indubitable, unquestionable character of Descartes' clear and distinct ideas. The motivation for an inerrantist account of scripture is obvious.

If experience is to serve as a foundation, it must have an indubitable character similar to that of our immediate perceptions; so experiences of miracles will not serve—they are all too questionable. A better sort of experience is something like Friedrich Schleiermacher's sense of absolute dependence—a self-authenticating, immediate awareness such that one who has it is unable to deny it.

2.2. Quine's Holism

W. V. O. Quine made an important contribution to the theory of knowledge by suggesting a different 'picture' of how the system works. He described his new "holist" model as follows:

> The totality of our so-called knowledge or beliefs, from the most casual matters of geography and history to the profoundest laws of atomic physics or even of pure mathematics and logic, is a man-made fabric which impinges on experience only along the edges. Or, to change the figure, total science is like a field of force whose boundary conditions are experience. A conflict with experience at the periphery occasions readjustments in the interior of the field. . . . Reevaluation of some statements entails reevaluation of others, because of their logical interconnections. . . . But the total field is so underdetermined by its boundary conditions, experience, that there is much latitude of choice as to what statements to reevaluate in the light of any single contrary experience. No particular experiences are linked with any particular statements in the interior of the field, except indirectly through considerations of equilibrium affecting the field as a whole. . . .
>
> For vividness I have been speaking in terms of varying distances from a sensory periphery. Let me try now to clarify this notion without metaphor. Certain statements, though about physical objects and not sense experience, seem peculiarly germane to sense experience—and in a selective way: some statements to some experiences, others to others. Such statements, especially germane to sense experiences, I picture as near the periphery. But in this relation of "germaneness" I envisage nothing more than a loose association reflecting the relative likelihood, in practice, of our choosing one statement rather than another for revision in the event of recalcitrant experience. For example, we can imagine recalcitrant experiences to which we would surely be inclined to accommodate our system by reevaluating just the statement that there are brick houses on Elm Street, together with related statements on the same topic. . . . A recalcitrant experience can, I have urged, be accommodated by any of various alternative reevaluations in various alternative quarters of the total system; but in the cases which we are now imagining, our natural tendency to disturb the total system as little as possible would lead us to focus our revisions upon these specific statements concerning brick houses. . . . These statements are felt, therefore, to have a sharper empirical reference than highly theoretical statements of physics or logic or ontology. The latter statements may be thought of as relatively centrally located within the total network.[2]

We have already seen that the theoretical content of theology is more web-like than it is like a building towering straight up from its foundation. However, if theology is to fit Quine's model, we must ask what are the beliefs closest to the edge of the web, and what are the "boundary conditions" that correspond to sensory experience in his model of empirical knowledge. Two possibilities come naturally to mind: experience (though perhaps of a different sort than for science or everyday knowledge) and the scriptural texts. So beliefs closest to the periphery are *descriptions* of biblical texts and *descriptions* of experience.

[2]W. V. O. Quine, "Two Dogmas of Empiricism," in *From a Logical Point of View* (Cambridge: Harvard University Press, 1953), 43–44.

2.2.1. Experience

To see the role of experience in a web of theological beliefs, consider Schleiermacher's account. Here the experience in question would be the sense of absolute dependence. The beliefs most directly influenced by that experience are descriptions of the forms it takes for Christians. Theological beliefs fill the interior regions.

But somewhere in the web, also, are Schleiermacher's warrants, which explain why it is legitimate to draw conclusions about theology from descriptions of *that* kind of experience. Schleiermacher's warrants depend in turn upon his view of the nature of religion and of theology. So part of Schleiermacher's theology could be represented as below, where *E*s stand for grounds that are descriptions of experience, *T*s are theological claims, and *B* is his theory of the nature of religion and theology, which backs his warrants.

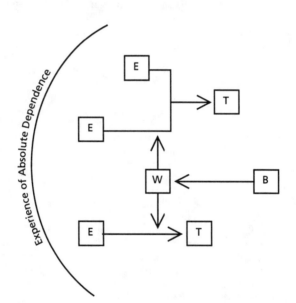

Notice that the kind of warrants one uses in theology determines the *kind* of grounds that are relevant. To see this, consider the very different kinds of experience a Pentecostal theologian might use to support a claim. For example, the theory that the Holy Spirit operates by means of a specific set of gifts could be supported by reports of what Pentecostal Christians experience by way of such "gifts of the Spirit." The experience of speaking in tongues or prophesying is quite different from the experience of one's absolute dependence upon God.

So we find here another of the ways that Quine's holist model better describes theological knowledge than does the foundationalist model. We can insert into our web controlling beliefs (warrants and backing) that explain *which* beliefs to take as grounds and *how* to argue from them to theological claims. There is no place to put these elements in the foundationalist picture.

Another feature of theological knowledge that makes fitting the foundationalist model difficult is that, according to the foundationalist, one always has to start with the foundation, and the direction of argument can only go one way—from grounds to theory. We see from our Schleiermacherian example that reasoning also goes from the very central, highly theoretical beliefs (Schleiermacher's theory of religion) toward the edges. In a sense, grounds are partially determined by theory as well as the other way around. In the following pictures the arrows represent the directions of argument assumed by the two different models of knowledge:

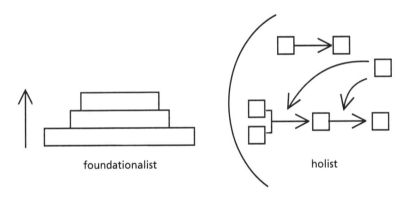

foundationalist   holist

2.2.2. Scripture

We find the same sort of 'semi-circular' reasoning when we think about the use of scriptural facts as grounds for theology. Consider, for example, the very different uses made of the texts by John Locke and Albert Schweitzer (see chapter 11). For Locke one can argue directly from what the text says to theological claims. For example, the texts say that faith in Jesus is what is required to be saved; therefore, what is required to be saved is faith in Jesus. Arguments of this sort are warranted by the statement that scripture is the revealed word of God. This warrant is backed by theoretical beliefs about how God acts—in particular about how God has chosen to make himself known. Such an approach to scripture presupposes a supernaturalist worldview.

This is in sharp contrast to the presuppositions of Schweitzer and many theologians of his day, who rejected any sort of supernaturalism. For them, the texts yield knowledge about history, which in turn supports theological claims. The warrants that take one from statements about the texts to statements about history presuppose a nonmiraculous view of reality, one that is governed by strict natural laws. The decision to base theological claims on historical grounds presupposes a different view from Locke's about how God acts—namely through the processes of human history rather than by miraculous intervention.

So, again, we see that highly theoretical beliefs (ones far from the edges of the web) react back on the reasoning we do at the edges in two ways: (1) selectively determining the sorts of things we will attend to in the texts (say, Jesus' moral teaching rather than the miracle accounts), and (2) determining the sorts of warrants one will use in constructing arguments from those grounds to theological conclusions. Kelsey says that the *way* scripture is brought to bear to ground theological claims depends on a "single, synoptic judgment" by which the theologian attempts to catch up what Christianity is all about. So the picture might look like this, where Ss are statements about the texts, Ts are theological claims, and J stands for the judgment of what Christianity is all about:

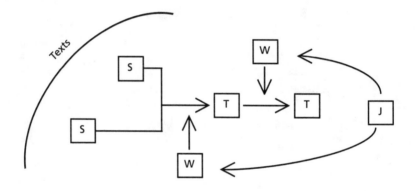

Many theologians refuse to choose between a theology grounded in experience (of whatever sort) and one grounded in scripture, claiming that theological formulations are rightly subject to controls of both sorts. Exactly how these two sorts of grounds are to be coordinated is not always clear. Notice that I have drawn two fragments of a web of theological beliefs, one grounded in scripture, one in experience, and have not yet tried to put the pictures together. Let us save that task until after we have considered the role of historical studies. For the present, let us just note that when we think of theological claims it would be helpful if we could draw our arguments in such a way as to indicate that grounding in experience (G_e) is a different sort of grounding than that from scripture (G_s); it seems to come 'from a different direction.'[3]

---

[3]The independence of scripture and experience as grounds for theology can be overstated, however, since it turns out that our experience sometimes plays a role in interpreting scripture and often our experience is shaped by scripture and described in its terms.

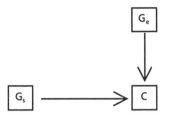

2.3. The Historical Dimension

Quine borrows an image from Otto Neurath: with regard to our system of beliefs we are like people on a ship; we can repair and change the ship bit by bit, plank by plank. The ship stays afloat only because at each alteration we keep the bulk of it intact.[4] So the main business of scholars is not to build ships from scratch, but rather to effect repairs of the one we are on—repairing our common network of beliefs by removing inconsistencies and adding bits here and there. When inconsistencies arise, however, they can be repaired in any number of ways. The point of Neurath's image is that conservatism is nearly always the best policy: keep as much of the original structure intact as possible.

Theology is often contrasted with science in that theology is said to be conservative, while science is not. If Quine and Neurath are correct, though, the difference can only be one of degree; if science, too, were not largely conservative it would have 'sunk' a long time ago. So theologians cannot be faulted for seeking, insofar as possible, to retain old conceptions and formulations. The claim that a theological theory ought to be accepted because it always has been is not, in general, unreasonable.

Thus we discover another constraint on theological theorizing: conservatism or continuity with the past. Putting this in terms of reasoning and arguments, we can say that the *presumption* in any dispute will always be with the inherited formulation; the *burden of proof* falls on the one who argues for change. And so we have discovered one role of history in the theological curriculum: it informs us about past formulations of the tradition.

It is time to summarize: Systematic theology is a web of beliefs in which each doctrinal claim must be supported by a cluster of arguments. The arguments form the links between one claim and another and between each claim and its respective grounds. Theological formulations are governed by the requirement of *consistency:* they must be consistent with one another (and insofar as they are, they are mutually supporting); they must be tied to grounds from at least one of two sources (scripture and experience); and in the process of seeking the best solution to these several demands, the theologian must seek to deviate as little as possible from previous formulations (the requirement of continuity).

[4]See W. V. O. Quine, *Word and Object* (Cambridge: MIT Press, 1960), 3–4.

Notice that theologians from different denominations will make different uses of history. Some denominations regard "tradition" positively and accord great weight to certain formulations therein—to pronouncements of ecumenical councils or Vatican councils; to the writings of reformers or of canonized theologians. Others attempt insofar as possible to return to the scriptures alone.

So scripture can be thought of in two ways. If we consider the texts as something existing in the present we may think of them as on a par with experience in providing grounds for theology. However, a more reasonable way to look at the texts may be as records of the earliest formulations of the tradition, which were themselves written from within the constraints of the experiences of those days. If so, we can picture the Christian tradition, developing over the centuries, not as a two-dimensional web, but rather as a three-dimensional series of webs, where the earliest webs are what we now call scripture, where later webs constitute what we call "tradition" or historical theology, and where the most recent is constructive or systematic theology. The boundary of each web in the series is the experience of Christians in those days. So both scripture (S) and current experience (E) bear directly on current theological formulation (T); past experience bears indirectly through its effects on earlier formulations, represented by H in the figure on the facing page.

This diagram is an oversimplification, of course, because it fails to show the diversity within the tradition: different and irreconcilable sources; a spaghetti-like tangle of diverging and converging denominational traditions; theological disagreements and disputes.[5] The diagram does have the advantage, though, of allowing us to represent pictorially the relations among contemporary theology, history, scripture, and experience. So we now have a model of the relations among biblical studies, history, and theology quite different in appearance from the standard model with which we began. Nonetheless, it is still fair to say, as did the proposers of the standard model, that some of the claims made by biblical and historical scholars function as grounds for theological claims.

However, the new diagram still fails to indicate the complexity of the arguments that take us from scriptural or historical texts to present formulations. Nor does it reflect the 'semi-circular' reasoning discussed above—the way current worldview and related theological presuppositions influence the selection of the kinds of grounds and warrants that are used, not only by theologians but by historians and biblical scholars as well.

It has often been said that theology is subject to four controls: scripture, tradition, experience, and reason. Notice that *reason* is of a different

---

[5]Alasdair MacIntyre has said that a tradition is an ongoing *argument*—an argument about how to interpret and apply its formative texts. And here the word 'argument' bears both senses of reasoning to a conclusion and disputing with others.

Notice that 'tradition' is being used in two different ways here. We are using it to refer to the whole stream of thought, beginning with the oldest texts of the Bible up through the most recent theological proposals. However, it has been common to use the word in a more restricted sense to refer to authoritative formulations from the past, written after the close of the New Testament period. To avoid confusion I indicate the more restrictive use by putting the word in double quotation marks.

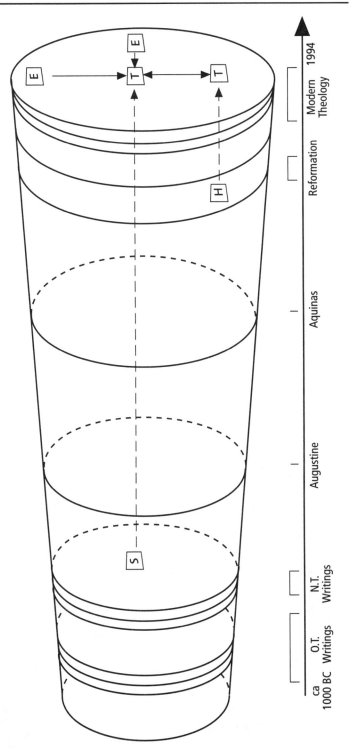

category (a different kind of thing) from the other three. It *is* represented in the diagram, though, by means of the lines—the lines of argument connecting the *T*s with one another and with their several sorts of grounds.

3. Theological Ethics

We have already made a number of alterations in the standard model of the relations among the disciplines making up the theological curriculum. We will want to make more drastic changes as we consider the relations between theology and ethics. The standard model assumes that theological ethics is a consequence of (application of) systematic theology, and this is certainly not an unreasonable supposition. We can construct a number of ethical arguments that are grounded or warranted by theological claims. For example:

1. The God of the Bible is a God who defends and liberates oppressed peoples. Therefore, the faithful Christian will work for liberation of the oppressed. (Here a statement about the character of God serves as grounds for an ethical claim.)

2. Jesus Christ taught his disciples to love their enemies. Because Christ is the Divine Son of God his teaching is authoritative. Therefore, love of enemies is a moral duty. (Here the divinity of Christ serves as backing for the warrant which states that Christ's teaching is morally binding.)

3. Jesus taught love of enemies, which implies a refusal to take up arms. But one cannot draw one's ethics from Jesus alone; one also has to consider the implications of God's other acts, such as creation. If you derive your value system from creation you will defend the state, which is an institution of creation. (Here the doctrine of creation is used as part of the rebuttal of an argument for Christian pacifism.)

An interesting fact about at least two of these arguments is that, historically, the ethical understanding preceded the theological formulation. In Latin America, Christians found themselves drawn into the struggle for liberation, *then* (drawing upon Marxist analyses) developed liberation theologies and related them to the biblical texts. Similarly, Jesus' disciples called him the Lord of their lives long before any theoretical account of his divinity had been worked out.

Historical sequences such as these may figure in the positions of a number of thinkers who believe that in general ethics *precedes* doctrine. That is, Christianity is first a way of life; its doctrinal formulations arise secondarily to explain and justify the practices of the Christian church, including its morality. George Tyrrell provides a clear example of a theologian who reverses the order of ethics and theology in this way. Tyrrell was an important contributor to the Catholic modernist movement at the beginning of the twentieth century. He claimed that the system of Christian thought begins with an experiential sense of right and wrong that gradually shapes a code of behavior and a devotional life. Religious belief grows up to account for religious life by providing an imagined view of spiritual realities that are beyond our experience. Theology, he says, must be reminded that "like science, its hypotheses, theories and explanations must square with facts—the facts here being the Christian religion as lived by its consistent professors."[6]

The clue to settling the disagreement over the relation between theology and ethics is to note Tyrrell's suggestion that the form of reasoning from ethical precepts to theological doctrines is *hypothetical;* a doctrinal claim is supported by the fact that it explains or justifies the moral precept. But recall that a hypothesis is said to explain a fact when the fact *follows reasonably* from the hypothesis. So we can reconstruct the reasoning of liberation theologians as follows: First, from experience in Christian base communities, some participants come to the conclusion that it is their Christian calling to support the struggles of the oppressed. To explain why this is so they begin to reconsider the character of God and form a hypothesis regarding God's intentions for human life. Then (in accord with the demands of hypothetical reasoning) they look for further confirmation of their hypothesis and find that the scriptures, read in this new light, provide startling confirmation. Furthermore, pursuit of the liberationist agenda provides additional experiential confirmation.

This (oversimplified) reconstruction of the origin of liberation theology fits Tyrrell's model wherein ethics is temporally first in the argument, but it also fits the standard model in that the ethical precepts follow (logically) from the doctrinal positions—otherwise the hypothetical reasoning involved would be invalid. And once the doctrine is established, further ethical consequence can be drawn from it.

These examples suggest that theology and ethics are not as readily separable as the standard model suggested, and that arguments from one to the other can generally go in both directions. We may want to represent the interrelations here (as we did above) by means of a holist web, where ethical claims and theological claims are intermingled—perhaps with ethical claims nearer the periphery to indicate that they are often more closely associated with experience than are doctrinal claims.

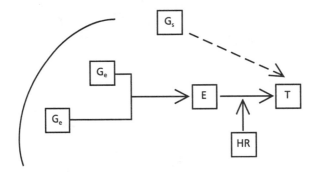

[6]George Tyrrell, *Through Scylla and Charybdis* (London: Longmans, Green & Co., 1907), 104.

Here experiential grounds support an ethical claim, which in turn supports (by hypothetical reasoning) a theological claim. The theological claim is, in addition, grounded scripturally.

4. Homiletics

In the previous sections we have seen the standard model of the theological curriculum amplified and corrected, in great part due to recognition that arguments are often two-way streets; or to return to our metaphor, in the Christian web of beliefs, the spider can crawl backwards as well as forwards along the strands connecting one belief with another. Will we find the same back-and-forth relations between theology and preaching?

Anyone who has visited a variety of churches will have noted a great variety in styles of preaching—not just differences in delivery, but (apparent) differences in understandings of what a sermon is, what it is intended to do, how it is related to biblical texts, and how it is related to theology. We have discussed several of these issues in chapter 7. Let us begin here with the relation between systematic theology and the preaching task.

Some might object immediately that there need not be any such relation. The object of a sermon is to declare the word of scripture, preferably without interference from theology. We have already noted, though, that theological (and other 'worldview-ish') presuppositions affect one's use of scripture. These effects can be either conscious and deliberate or unconscious. Likewise, history will inevitably influence one's preaching of a text. For example, no one after Luther can preach from Paul's Letter to the Romans without reacting positively or negatively to Luther's interpretation.

If we revert to our three-dimensional model of the web of Christian beliefs it becomes clear that no matter what aspect of the faith a preacher intends to communicate, it will necessarily be interconnected with contemporary theological and ethical positions, and with formulations from the past, both scriptural and others. These multifarious connections ought to be celebrated, since it is the very interconnectedness of each belief with others, with experience, and with the past that gives rational credibility to the whole.

What, now, about the relations between theology and the preached word? Is it a one-way relation of applying and communicating for public consumption the conclusions reached by theologians? I offer as a countersuggestion the views of one theologian. Paul Jewett writes the following by way of justification for including sermons as an integral part of his systematic theology:

> Finally, a word concerning the decision to include sermons in a book of systematic theology. When studying with Emil Brunner, then professor of dogmatics at the University of Zurich, I was surprised to discover that he also held professorial rank in the department of preaching. As I became acquainted with his thought, I came to understand why this was so. The church's commission, Brunner argued, is the proclamation of the message which the apostles preached, as that message is preserved in Scripture. Dogmatic theology, therefore, arises out of the preaching of the church. . . . Dogmatics is, by definition,

the self-reflection of the church on the content and meaning of the message proclaimed in the gospel. This being the case, the discipline of dogmatics is not an end in itself. Its purpose is rather to clarify the message that the church proclaims. . . .

Convinced by Brunner's argument . . . I have long since concluded that theology done in such a way that it cannot be preached is like the salt of which our Lord speaks: having lost its savor, it is really good for nothing. Theology, in a word, is authenticated by the fact that it is preachable.[7]

So the question "Will it preach?" suggests yet another criterion for the evaluation of a theological proposal. And we have found yet another two-way street between theological disciplines.[8]

The theological task is one with no fixed starting point. Each of the disciplines considered here (and others besides) contributes to all the others. Each in one way or another makes use of or presupposes the results of the others. We are reminded of Neurath's image of the ship that must be repaired plank by plank while we are afloat at sea.

EXERCISE TWELVE

Read the passages and answer the questions.

1. This passage by John Howard Yoder, a Mennonite historian, theologian, and ethicist, is from a book on Christian pacifism.

   [T]his text [John 1:1–18], like a few others elsewhere in the New Testament, says two apparently contradictory things.

   It says first that what has come among us in the word and work of Jesus is far more than the word and work of a man, since what it brings us has the dignity of preexistence, of having shared in the divine work of creation. That the world is created, or that God is Creator, was not a new idea and was not significant information to a Jewish Christian reader when this passage said it. But that that which comes to us in Jesus is no different from the truth and the power of creation is a new claim. It is in fact a claim which, in a systematic way, most theologies to our day do not really believe.

   Most theologies distinguish in some deep way between creation and redemption. For example, according to Martin Luther in classical Protestantism, or Emil Brunner or H. Richard Niebuhr in recent times, creation and redemption have two different sets of ethical implications. If you derive your value system from creation, you will, for instance, defend the state, which is an institution of creation. If you derive your guidance from redemption alone, then the teachings and the example of Jesus can be normative for you, which may lead to nonresistance. But you only have the right to draw nonresistant conclusions from the teachings of Jesus if you admit that the realm of creation is governed by other laws and other

---

[7]Paul Jewett, *God, Creation, and Revelation: A Neo-Evangelical Theology* (Grand Rapids: Eerdmans, 1990), xviii–xix.

[8]See the section on Ludwig Wittgenstein (chap. 13, sec. 2.2.2), for a comparable view of the intimate relation between theology and the "first-order" language of preaching.

authorities. In other words, Jesus speaks for God all right, as did the prophets before him, but God also has other distinct channels through which he has said other distinct things, which we may perceive by using other modes of hearing God, such as the reasonable analysis of the Word that is in creation.

It is thus not simply a speculative difference, but a very concrete one, when the apostolic generation responsible for this text and its parallels insisted that what is known in Jesus is precisely the same, in authority and in meaning, as what underlies creation. When he says "there was nothing of what came to be that did not come to be through him," John is not propounding a new theory about creation. He is simply repeating the Genesis report, which shows God creating by his Word. But from that report he draws a negation. God has not revealed himself otherwise. He has not revealed a different purpose or character through creation than what we now encounter through Jesus.[9]

a. The sketch below is a simplified version of the overall argument Yoder is defending in the essay from which this excerpt is taken. What claim, unstated here, must he be arguing for?

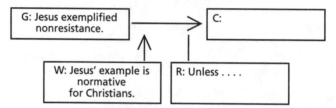

b. To which of the disciplines we have studied (homiletics, ethics, history, biblical studies, theology) does this claim belong?
c. Summarize the rebuttal (in the third paragraph) that Yoder is attempting to defeat in this excerpt.
d. Upon which of the disciplines we have studied does this rebuttal primarily depend?
e. So what role does Yoder's discussion of John 1:1–18 play in his *overall* argument?
f. What *historical* fact does Yoder use to ground his interpretation of the real significance of John 1:1–18?
g. If G in the sketch above were challenged, what sort of grounds would he have to add?
h. To which discipline would this extension of Yoder's argument belong?

2. This passage is a summary of Bernard Lonergan's proposal for understanding the components of the theological curriculum. He uses different names for disciplines and subdisciplines, and your main task is to match his "functional specialties" with the disciplines we have studied. Lonergan was one of the most influential Catholic theologians of the twentieth century.

[9]John Howard Yoder, *He Came Preaching Peace* (Scottdale, Pa.: Herald Press, 1985), 81–82.

In this section we propose to describe briefly eight functional specialties in theology, namely, research, interpretation, history, dialectic, foundations, doctrines, systematics, and communications. . . .

(1) Research makes available the data relevant to theological investigation. It is either general or special. Special research is concerned with assembling the data relevant to some particular question or problem, such as the doctrine of Mr. X on the question of Y. Such special research operates all the more rapidly and effectively the more familiar it is with the tools made available by general research. General research locates, excavates, and maps ancient cities. It fills museums and reproduces or copies inscriptions, symbols, pictures, statues. It deciphers unknown scripts and languages. It collects and catalogues manuscripts, and prepares critical editions of texts. It composes indices, tables, repertories, encyclopedias. . . .

(2) While research makes available what was written, interpretation understands what was meant. It grasps that meaning in its proper historical context, in accord with its proper mode and level of thought and expression, in the light of the circumstances and intention of the writer. Its product is the commentary or monograph. . .

(3) History is basic, special, or general.

Basic history tells where (places, territories) and when (dates, periods) who (persons, peoples) did what (public life, external acts) to enjoy what success, suffer what reverses, exert what influence. . . .

Special histories tell of movements whether cultural (language, art, literature, religion), institutional (family, mores, society, education, state, law, church, sect, economy, technology), or doctrinal (mathematics, natural science, human science, philosophy, history, theology).

General history is, perhaps, just an ideal. It would be basic history illuminated and completed by the special histories.

History, as a functional specialty within theology, is concerned in different degrees and manners with basic, special, and general history. In the main it has to presuppose basic history. Its substantial concern is the doctrinal history of Christian theology with its antecedents and consequents in the cultural and institutional histories of the Christian religion and the Christian churches and sects. Finally, it cannot remain aloof from general history, for it is only within the full view that can be grasped the differences between the Christian churches and sects, the relations between different religions, and the role of Christianity in world history. . . .

(4) Our fourth functional specialty is dialectic. . . . Dialectic has to do with the concrete, the dynamic, and the contradictory, and so it finds abundant materials in the history of Christian movements. For all movements are at once concrete and dynamic, while Christian movements have been marked with external and internal conflict, whether one considers Christianity as a whole or even this or that larger church or communion.

The materials of dialectic, then, are primarily the conflicts centering in Christian movements. But to these must be added the secondary conflicts in historical accounts and theological interpretations of the movements. . . .

(5) As conversion is basic to Christian living, so an objectification of conversion provides theology with its foundations. . . .

Inasmuch as conversion itself is made thematic and explicitly objectified, there emerges the fifth functional specialty, foundations. . . . Foundations presents, not doctrines, but the horizon within which the meaning of doctrines can be apprehended. Just as in religious living "a man who is unspiritual refuses what belongs to the Spirit of God; it is folly to him; he cannot grasp it" (1 Cor. 2:14), so in theological reflection on religious living there have to be distinguished the horizons within which religious doctrines can or cannot be apprehended; and this distinction is foundational. . . .

(6) Doctrines express judgments of fact and judgments of value. They are concerned, then, with the affirmations and negations not only of dogmatic theology but also of moral, ascetical, mystical, pastoral, and any similar branch.

Such doctrines stand within the horizon of foundations. They have their precise definition from dialectic, their positive wealth of clarification and development from history, their grounds in the interpretation of the data proper to theology.

(7) The facts and values affirmed in doctrines give rise to further questions. For doctrinal expression may be figurative or symbolic. It may be descriptive and based ultimately on the meaning of words rather than on an understanding of realities. It may, if pressed, quickly become vague and indefinite. It may seem, when examined, to be involved in inconsistency or fallacy.

The functional specialty, systematics, attempts to meet these issues. It is concerned to work out appropriate systems of conceptualization, to remove apparent inconsistencies, to move towards some grasp of spiritual matters both from their own inner coherence and from the analogies offered by more familiar human experience.

(8) Communications is concerned with theology in its external relations. These are of three kinds. There are interdisciplinary relations with art, language, literature, and other religions, with the natural and the human sciences, with philosophy and history. Further, there are the transpositions that theological thought has to develop if religion is to retain its identity and yet at the same time find access into the minds and hearts of men of all cultures and classes. Finally, there are the adaptations needed to make full and proper use of the diverse media of communication that are available at any place and time.[10]

a. Lonergan's functional specialty called "research" could provide grounds most directly for which two of the disciplines we have studied (ethics, history, biblical studies, homiletics, theology)?
b. Interpretation would involve making claims that belong to which two disciplines?
c. To which one of our five disciplines does dialectic most closely correspond?
d. List the two functional specialties that most clearly belong to theology, as 'theology' is used in this book.
e. In which functional specialty does ethics first appear?
f. To which functional specialty does homiletics belong?
g. There is an obvious place for scripture and "tradition" in Lonergan's understanding of the theological disciplines. What about Christian experience? Where among the functional specialties is it most clearly brought to bear?
h. Does Lonergan's view of the relation of theology to ethics fit better with what we have called the standard model, or with the view developed in this chapter?

---

[10]Bernard Lonergan, *Method in Theology* (New York: Crossroad, 1972), 127–33.

3. Charles Wood is also writing about the theological curriculum. In this passage he is attempting to define theology in such a way as to shed light on the relations among the theological disciplines. Like Lonergan, he is developing some new terminology.

> The comprehensive aim of Christian theological inquiry is to test Christian witness by the criteria which pertain to its validity precisely as Christian witness. . . . To develop this understanding of the plurality and unity of theology, it is necessary to turn to [the] elucidation of the concept of Christian witness . . . and to show how the dimensions of theological inquiry correspond to its features. . . .
>
> Trading on the ambiguity created by the fact that ['witness'] possesses a normative as well as an empirical sense, one may state the central question of theology: To what extent is Christian witness Christian witness? . . .
>
> One of the illuminating formal features of the concept of Christian witness is that such witness is witness to Jesus Christ. It is not simply a matter of stating one's own convictions, but also one of representing the authentic Christian message in doing so. . . . The extent to which what is offered as Christian witness really is *Christian* witness, i.e., really does represent what it is intended to represent, . . . is the first of our three principal theological questions.
>
> The second principal question is provoked by the fact that, although Christians engaged in witness are not *simply* stating their convictions, they are stating their convictions. To bear witness is to represent something as the truth. . . . The critical theological question which corresponds to this feature of its object is, naturally enough: Is this witness really true? What claims to truth does it make or imply, and how are those claims to be judged? This is the central question of a second dimension of theological inquiry.
>
> The third principal question corresponds to a third feature of the concept. . . . Witness is not merely "expression" for its own sake, but rather an attempt to convey a message. . . . Its fitness to the context in which it is enacted must also be examined. . . . An act which conveys one message in one setting may be taken quite differently in another. There is a kind of fidelity to "tradition," an adherence to old forms and to the memory of old situations, which amounts to betrayal. . . .
>
> The critical question theology has to raise in response to this feature of Christian witness is: Is this witness fittingly enacted?
>
> The discipline which takes shape around the first of our principal questions may be called *historical theology*. . . . Historical theology is so named in this account because it is the use of the resources and methods of historical study to pursue the theological question of the "Christianness," i.e., the faithfulness to what is normatively Christian, of Christian witness. . . . It asks by what criteria the "Christianness" of something might be judged, and it asks how such criteria might be applied in various sorts of cases, and it proceeds then to make appropriate judgments and proposals. . . .
>
> The second of our principal theological questions, that of the truth of Christian witness, is the focus of a second discipline, which may be called *philosophical theology*. . . . The philosophical study of any human activity aims at exhibiting the "logic" of that activity, that is, at uncovering the principles relevant to its understanding and criticism. . . . Philosophical study typically involves coming to terms with the pertinent body of discourse so as to clarify the conditions of meaningful and appropriate thought

and speech. . . . A philosophical study of Christian witness . . . thus aims to discover and display the sorts of meaning the discourse and activity of Christian witness involve, including the sorts of claims to truth which that witness may make. . . . It uses the resources of philosophical inquiry to pursue the critical theological question: Is this witness true? . . .

The question of the fitting enactment of Christian witness is the leading question of a third basic theological discipline, which may be called by the conventional name of *practical theology*. . . . The chief justification for the name . . . must be this: it calls attention to the fact that Christian witness is a practice. . . . Practical theology . . . . asks by what standards this practice is to be judged, and it proceeds to make the relevant judgments concerning past, present, or prospective instances of it. . . .

Systematic theology is the name we might give to a fourth major theological discipline, which is constituted by the effort to integrate these three basic inquiries in a comprehensive and constructive fashion. As was noted earlier, in many accounts of the structure of theology, systematic theology is essentially assigned the task given in the present scheme to philosophical theology; further, it is situated strategically between the historical and the practical disciplines, in a mediating role. It receives the results of historical investigation; reflects upon their content, testing, refining, and ordering it in some appropriate fashion; and transmits the product to the practical field for implementation. . . .

A problematic feature of such an understanding, however, is that it tends to suggest—even if it does not assert outright—that the flow of traffic among these disciplines is one-way. . . . For this reason, as well as for the sake of a clearer recognition of the distinctive task of philosophical theology, it is better to avoid the convention of regarding systematic theology as the "middle discipline" and try to show how it is a complex mode of reflection involving all three dimensions of theology. . . .

Systematic theology is "systematic" in three senses. First, it integrates the three inquiries already outlined, bringing the resources and insights of each to bear upon each of the others, and coordinating them as aspects of a single inquiry into the validity of Christian witness. Secondly, it is comprehensive in its scope: it deals with the Christian witness in its entirety, and gives attention to its consistency and integrity. Thirdly, it is constructive as well as critical: it attempts to give a positive, coherent answer to the question of what constitutes valid Christian witness. . . .

A fifth major theological discipline must be included in this account, since the question of its relationship to the foregoing disciplines is frequently raised. . . . Christian *moral theology,* or theological ethics, may be defined as a critical inquiry into the validity of Christian witness concerning human conduct.[11]

a. What, according to Wood, do theologians make claims about in general?
b. This excerpt does not mention biblical studies. Into which of Wood's disciplines would it best fit?
c. What do you suppose Wood has in mind as grounds for historical theology?

---

[11]Charles Wood, *Vision and Discernment* (Atlanta: Scholars Press, 1985), 37–54 *passim.*

d. We noted in earlier chapters that one of the main ingredients in becoming proficient in a discipline is learning the warrants that are assumed and used in it, and that much intellectual discussion aims at disputing or backing warrants. There are two places where Wood alludes to the choosing and judging of warrants in the theological disciplines he envisions. Identify them.
e. Is Wood's account of the integration of the theological disciplines closer to the standard model or to the account given in this chapter?
f. Where does he describe the standard model?
g. Is Wood a foundationalist or a holist?
h. What is your evidence for this judgment?

CHAPTER THIRTEEN

Philosophy of Religion

1. Philosophy and Religion

While there are interesting things to be said about the relations between philosophy and the other religions, we shall concentrate here, as we have throughout, on Christianity. "What has Jerusalem to do with Athens, the church with the academy?"—Tertullian's tart question sets the theme of this section.

It is no simple matter to give an account of the relations between Christianity and philosophy, since this relation depends upon at least three variables:

1. Christianity's intellectual self-understanding has evolved through the centuries, and with it Christian scholars' views of the relevance of philosophy to their work. We have seen a small part of this evolution in chapter 11, on theology. There we began with argumentative Aquinas, for whom theological method consisted in reconciling the authorities—the biblical authors, Aristotle, and everyone else in between. We ended with Karl Barth, who sought to avoid all philosophical systems, and whose style of writing might better be described as persuasive elaboration of the tradition than as formal argument. And if these changes are not enough, a number of new conceptions of theological method appear on the horizon, with varying relations to recent philosophical developments.

2. Another factor of which we must take account is the fact that there have been, in every age, different views of the appropriate relation of Christianity to culture in general—and thus toward philosophy. H. Richard Niebuhr identified five "ideal types"[1] that serve as a classification system for theologians, apologists, and religious movements throughout Christian history.[2] The two extreme positions he called the "Christ of culture" type and the "Christ against culture" type. The first of these represents a thorough accommodation of Christian teaching to the ideas and values of

---

[1]That is, *pure* positions, which actual individuals or groups manifest in varying degrees.
[2]H. Richard Niebuhr, *Christ and Culture* (New York: Harper and Row, 1951).

the day; the second represents the attempt to reject the surrounding culture altogether. Pertinent examples of the "Christ of culture" type were those in the first few centuries of Christianity who translated its teachings into gnostic categories. Gnosticism was a set of religious and philosophical speculations common throughout the Greco-Roman world at that time. Its central features included a dualistic view of matter and spirit; the belief that salvation consisted in the escape of the human spirit from its imprisonment in the evil world of matter; this deliverance was to be accomplished by means of secret knowledge (*gnosis*) brought by a messenger from the kingdom of light. The possibilities for accommodating Christian teaching to this system are obvious.

Tertullian (c. 160–220), quoted above, is an apt representative of the "Christ against culture" type. With regard to philosophy, he said, "Away with all attempts to produce a mottled Christianity of Stoic, Platonic and dialectic composition. We want no curious disputation after possessing Jesus Christ. . . . With our faith we desire no further belief."[3]

Between these two extremes Niebuhr finds three types: "Christ above culture" is well represented by Thomas Aquinas's synthesis of Christian theology and Aristotelian philosophy, in which revelation crowns and completes what can be known by reason.

Martin Luther represents the "Christ and culture in paradox" type. Such thinkers may be called dualists, but it is not a simple dualism of church against the world; rather, it is the holy God in contrast to all of sinful humanity. The church is the community of reconciled sinners; yet the world is not beyond God's plans and control—and thus Christians must participate in the life of culture on its own terms. This resulted, according to Niebuhr, in Luther's paradoxical view of philosophy: "Though philosophy offered no road to faith, yet the faithful . . . could take the philosophic road to such goals as were attainable by that way. In a person 'regenerate and enlightened by the Holy Spirit through the Word' the natural wisdom of man 'is a fair and glorious instrument and work of God.'"[4]

Niebuhr's own preferred type is "Christ the transformer of culture." He classifies Augustine as most nearly of this type. Augustine, with his radical doctrine of sin, taught that all human culture, including the products of human intellect, were corrupted. Yet, unlike the dualists, he believed that the life of the mind could be transformed by God's revelation. The life of reason apart from conversion is what the wisdom of God reveals as folly, but it can be reoriented by being given a new first principle—by beginning with faith in God rather than with confidence in itself.

To *some* extent, different Christian denominations exhibit tendencies toward these types in their attitudes toward philosophy. For example, Catholics tend to follow Thomas; Lutherans, Luther; and Calvinist or Reformed churches, Augustine.

3. The third factor accounting for the complexity of the relations between Christian thought and philosophy is the series of changes that have

---

[3]Tertullian, *Prescription Against Heretics*, vii; *Apology*, xlvi. Quoted by Niebuhr in *Christ and Culture*, 54.
[4]Niebuhr, *Christ and Culture*, 174.

occurred in philosophy's own self-understanding through the centuries. In fact, there are two related kinds of changes. The first is in views about what concerns are central to philosophy. In the ancient and medieval periods, a branch of philosophy called *metaphysics* was most prominent. 'Metaphysics' can be defined as the attempt to answer, in the most general terms, the question: What is there? At the beginning of the modern period, *epistemology* (or theory of knowledge) supplanted metaphysics as philosophy's central concern. It seeks to answer the questions: Is knowledge possible? and How is it possible? Around the middle of the twentieth century (arguably the end of the modern period.[5]) *philosophy of language* has become the most prominent branch of philosophy. This discipline seeks to understand how language works—how it relates to the world—and to answer philosophical questions by an analysis of the language in which we express them.

This is not to say that ancient philosophers had nothing to say about knowledge and language, or that modern philosophers make no contributions to metaphysics—it is only to recognize that in each of these periods, one branch of philosophy or another was seen as most important, most interesting, and as the *key* to all the others.

The second kind of change in the history of philosophy is an even more basic change in views of the very nature of the enterprise. In the ancient and medieval periods, philosophy was regarded primarily as a *body of knowledge*. In fact, philosophy was, in effect, the systematizing of the knowledge of those ages: In the ancient period there was as yet no distinction between philosophy and what we now call natural theology (that is, theology based on reason alone—apart from revelation). In both the ancient and medieval periods there was no distinction between philosophy and science. So philosophy was the attempt to systematize all existing knowledge about everything. Notice how appropriate it is that metaphysics be regarded as central to philosophy thus understood: it is the science of everything, the science of 'being' itself.

However, beginning with the modern period (with René Descartes in the early 1600s), and culminating with the analytic philosophers in the mid-1900s, philosophy came to be regarded primarily as a *method*. We see in Descartes' *Discourse on Method* (1637) a concern to find the right manner of reasoning by which the claims of theology and the new sciences, as well as ethics and political thought, could be evaluated.

Philosophers after Descartes still, in some cases, produced *systems* of thought. However, by the time of the analytic philosophers (e.g., Ludwig Wittgenstein and Gilbert Ryle) philosophy was defined by its method: its job was the analysis of the concepts (language) of other bodies of knowledge; it had no special content of its own. Thus there had come to be philosophy *of* science, philosophy *of* history, philosophy *of* law, philosophy *of* mathematics, and others. In the early modern period, the analysis of these bodies of knowledge focused primarily on their methods of rea-

---

[5]See Nancey Murphy and James William McClendon, Jr., "Distinguishing Modern and Postmodern Theologies," *Modern Theology* 5 (April 1989): 145–68.

soning; in the analytic period, on their language. Notice the correlation with the rise and fall of epistemology as the center of philosophical interest. By this time metaphysics had nearly disappeared, except for the analysis of the linguistic categories needed to describe reality in the most basic terms.

We may now be moving away from this extreme position on the methodological character of philosophy, but it is hard to imagine that philosophy will ever again be seen as a body of knowledge alongside of or in competition with other bodies of knowledge such as the sciences.

Notice how the change to philosophy as method has changed the question of the relation between Christianity and philosophy, between "faith and reason." In the early years of the church, and even in Thomas's day, philosophy provided a worldview that might compete with the Christian worldview—Aristotle's Prime Mover versus the God of the Bible; or Plato's body-soul dualism versus a more holistic Christian anthropology. But now the choice for Christians between reason and faith amounts to a choice between a faith held *with good reason* versus faith seen as a blind leap—a nonrational or even irrational commitment.

And so, with the focus of philosophy having turned to method, whether it be methods of reasoning (of justifying belief), or methods for the analysis of language, we do better to speak not of philosophy *and* religion, but rather of philosophy *of* religion and *philosophical* theology. To the first of these we now turn; we will then take up the second in section 3.

2. Philosophy of Religion

By now it should be clear why the term 'philosophy of religion' first appears in the modern period, despite the fact that philosophical speculation about things religious goes back to the beginning of Western philosophy: its invention coincides with the view of philosophy as a second-order discipline that studies the claims and language of other (first-order) disciplines.

Philosophers of religion concern themselves with a varied set of problems: the existence and nature of God, the problem of evil, free will and determinism, the nature of the human person (e.g., the soul and its relation to the body, personal immortality), miracles, the nature of religious experience, the possibility of revelation, the problem of religious pluralism.

The perceptive reader may have noticed that all of these topics are treated by theologians as well. It is time to admit that the distinction between philosophy of religion and philosophical theology is not a sharp one.[6] It is sometimes said that the difference lies in the fact that whereas philosophical theology presupposes Christian convictions, philosophy of religion

---

[6]Many of the topics treated by philosophers of religion (and philosophical theologians) fall within the province of the apologist as well. Again, lines cannot be drawn sharply. If apologetics is the defense of Christian belief undertaken from the standpoint of the outsider, it will aim to support views held by theologians, but may well *use* the (supposedly) neutral philosophical categories of the day. We take up apologetics in the final chapter.

intends to examine religion from a neutral, objective standpoint. To some extent this is a useful distinction; it is common for philosophical theologians to assume various elements of the Christian tradition in their discussions. However, the modern hope that such matters could be dealt with 'from the point of view of eternity' has turned out to be a false one. It is now widely recognized that all thought is historically conditioned and presupposes basic assumptions about reality (for example, that the existence of the universe is—or is not—self-explanatory). Thus it may be more accurate to distinguish the two disciplines according to their traditions and communities of reference—theological versus philosophical. The differences, in fact, are as often rhetorical as substantive; they employ different styles of discourse, and because they address different audiences they can make different assumptions. Thus Alvin Plantinga, who argues that belief in God is a proper starting point for *philosophy,* will never be mistaken for a theologian, and David Tracy, who questions whether philosophical *theology* ought to be done from a standpoint of faith, will never be mistaken for a philosopher.

2.1. Arguments for the Existence of God

Our concern in this volume is with methods of reasoning. The various philosophical methods can best be seen by taking a historical survey of various approaches to a single topic. Because arguments for the existence of God have had such a prominent place in philosophy of religion, both before and after formal recognition of the discipline, this will be our topic.

It is customary in discussing these arguments to classify them into three types: Ontological arguments are those that are based on the *concept* or *idea* of God, and claim that a being of this sort could not fail to exist. (It is called "ontological" because ontology is the science of being.) Cosmological arguments are based upon some general feature of the universe (the cosmos). For example, the *contingency* of the universe is said to require that there be a *necessary* being, which is God. Teleological arguments are those based on evidence of intelligent design or purpose in the universe. However, there is no sharp distinction among these three categories. A better classification system is simply to distinguish between *a priori* arguments, which do not depend on any experience of the world, and *a posteriori* arguments, which do.

2.1.1. Anselm's Ontological Argument

Anselm (c. 1033–1109), a Benedictine monk and archbishop of Canterbury, is well known for contributions to both theology and philosophy. The following is part of his argument for the existence of God:

> Well then, Lord, You who give understanding to faith, grant that I may understand, as much as You see fit, that You exist as we believe You to exist, and that You are what we believe You to be. Now we believe that You are something than which nothing greater can be thought. Or can it be that a thing of such

a nature does not exist, since "the Fool has said in his heart, there is no God" [Psalm 14:1; 53:1]? But surely, when this same Fool hears what I am speaking about, namely, "something-than-which-nothing-greater-can-be-thought," he understands what he hears, and what he understands is in his mind, even if he does not understand that it actually exists. For it is one thing for an object to exist in the mind, and another thing to understand that an object actually exists. Thus, when a painter plans beforehand what he is going to execute, he has [the picture] in his mind, but he does not yet think that it actually exists because he has not yet executed it. However, when he has actually painted it, then he both has it in his mind and understands that it exists because he has now made it. Even the Fool, then, is forced to agree that something-than-which-nothing-greater-can-be-thought exists in the mind, since he understands this when he hears it, and whatever is understood is in the mind. And surely that-than-which-a-greater-cannot-be-thought cannot exist in the mind alone. For if it exists solely in the mind even, it can be thought to exist in reality also, which is greater. If then that-than-which-a-greater-cannot-be-thought exists in the mind alone, this same that-than-which-a-greater-*cannot*-be-thought is that-than-which-a-greater-*can*-be-thought. But this is obviously impossible. Therefore there is absolutely no doubt that something-than-which-nothing-greater-can-be-thought exists both in the mind and in reality. [7]

This argument depends on the idea that objects of thought can exist in the mind alone or in both the mind and reality. The example illustrating and supporting this is the instance of the painting. This idea functions as a warrant in Anselm's argument. In the schema below, we let t stand for "that-than-which-a-greater-cannot-be-thought."

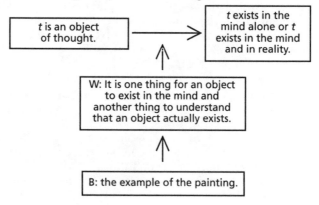

From this point, Anselm uses the method called *reductio ad absurdum* to eliminate one of the two possible modes of existence for t. He assumes that t exists only in the mind and then shows that this option leads to a contradiction. In the following argument he is assuming a warrant to the effect that something that exists in reality is greater than that which exists in the mind alone.

[7]*Proslogion*, chap. 2.

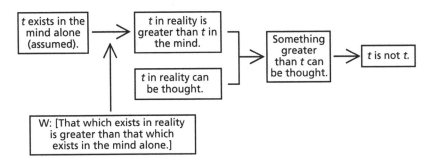

The penultimate claim, expanded, reads, "something greater than that-than-which-a-greater-cannot-be-thought can be thought."

Having thus eliminated the option that *t* exists in the mind alone, Anselm must conclude that *t* exists both in the mind and in reality. Since God is by definition that-than-which-a-greater-cannot-be-thought, God exists in reality as well as in the fool's mind. Notice the strong qualifier Anselm uses: "there is absolutely no doubt that . . . "

Volumes have been written about this argument. Most readers (modern readers, at least) have the sense that, despite Anselm's confidence, it involves a mistake somewhere. Laying it out in our Toulminian form helps locate the trouble: it appears to be in the assumed warrant, "that which exists in reality is greater than that which exists in the mind alone." Modern readers would probably not say that this statement is false, but rather that it does not make sense. We have no appropriate scale for comparing thoughts and real things and judging one *greater* than the other. The reason Anselm could do this and we cannot is that *metaphysics* has changed. Our concepts of reality and goodness and a great number of other related concepts have changed since Anselm's day, making it impossible to use metaphysical language in the same way as he did.

2.1.2. Thomas's Cosmological and Teleological Arguments

Thomas was not impressed by Anselm's ontological argument, and produced a set of five proofs, three of which are forms of the cosmological argument; the fifth is a form of the teleological argument. The following are his third and fifth "ways":

> The third way is taken from possibility and necessity, and runs thus. We find in nature things that are possible to be and not to be, since they are found to be generated, and to be corrupted, and consequently, it is possible for them to be and not to be. But it is impossible for these always to exist, for that which can not-be at some time is not. Therefore, if everything can not-be, then at one time there was nothing in existence, because that which does not exist begins to exist only through something already existing. Therefore, if at one time nothing was in existence, it would have been impossible for anything to have begun to exist; and thus even now nothing would be in existence—which is absurd. Therefore, not all beings are merely possible, but there must exist something the existence of which is necessary. But every necessary being

either has its necessity caused by another, or not. Now it is impossible to go on to infinity in necessary things which have their necessity caused by another, as has been already proved. . . . Therefore we cannot but admit the existence of some being having of itself its own necessity, and not receiving it from another but rather causing in others their necessity. This all men speak of as God.

Modern commentators on this argument would point out that the sentence "Necessarily something exists" is *not* equivalent to "There exists a necessary being." That is, 'necessarily' is properly a qualifier for a claim, not a predicate or characteristic of a being.

The fifth way is taken from the governance of the world. We see that things which lack knowledge, such as natural bodies, act for an end, and this is evident from their acting always, or nearly always, in the same way, so as to obtain the best result. Hence it is plain that they achieve their end, not fortuitously, but designedly. Now whatever lacks knowledge cannot move towards an end, unless it be directed by some being endowed with knowledge and intelligence; as the arrow is directed by the archer. Therefore some intelligent being exists by whom all natural things are directed to their end; and this being we call God.[8]

An interesting factor in this argument is that in presupposing, as he did, the Aristotelian worldview, Thomas would have seen the world suffused with purpose to a far greater extent that we can today. For example, according to Aristotle, even the fall of a heavy object exhibits purpose— the earthy substance is *seeking* its natural place at the center of the universe. Much of the history of the birth of modern science is the history of the gradual replacement of purposive accounts of natural phenomena by mechanistic accounts, first in the physical sciences and later in biology.

We will not pause here to evaluate these arguments further, but will press on to compare them to examples from modern philosophy.

2.1.3. Descartes

Despite the fact that Descartes is considered to be the first modern philosopher, his arguments for the existence of God are not radically different from those of his medieval predecessors. In his ontological argument (in *Meditations*) he begins with the fact that he has ideas in his mind that "have their own true and immutable natures." For example, the idea of a triangle involves its having three angles that together are equal to two right angles, and it is not possible for him to conceive otherwise. He then turns his attention to the idea of God:

It is certain that I find in my mind the idea of God, of a supremely perfect Being . . . ; and I recognize that an eternal existence belongs to his nature no less clearly and distinctly than I recognize that all I can demonstrate about some figure or number actually belongs to the nature of that figure or number . . . .

[8]*Summa Theologiae*, part 1, question 2, article 3.

> From the fact alone that I cannot conceive of God except as existing, it follows that existence is inseparable from him, and consequently that he does, in truth, exist. (meditation v)

This version makes it explicit that God's existence is taken to be a perfection or predicate of God. It also exemplifies one of Descartes' methodological principles stated in his *Discourse on Method:*

> The first [rule] was to accept nothing as true which I did not clearly recognize to be so: that is to say, carefully to avoid precipitation and prejudice in judgments, and to accept in them nothing more than what was presented to my mind so clearly and distinctly that I could have no occasion to doubt it. (discourse ii)

Recall (from chapter 12) that Descartes was the first *foundationalist*—setting out to reconstruct all knowledge on sure foundations. Here he states that the criterion he will use for selecting beliefs to be used as grounds for rebuilding his system is to count as certainly true any that he "clearly and distinctly" cannot conceive to be false.

Descartes has another argument that begins, as does the ontological argument, with the fact that he has an idea of God as a wholly perfect being, but then he goes on to argue that God must exist as the *cause* of this idea, since "it is obvious, according to the light of nature, that there must be at least as much reality in the total efficient cause as in its effect" (meditation iii).

Here we find a metaphysical principle that Descartes was unable to doubt, but one that modern thinkers can doubt several times before breakfast—another example of the way changes in metaphysics, or the general worldview, change the status of particular assertions. This, again, is a principle that a modern thinker would not judge false, but rather as nonsensical—as a misuse of the terms employed.

2.1.4. Modern Teleological Arguments

When we come to modern arguments from design, we find a style of argument that departs from the medieval pattern. Two important features shared by all the medieval arguments (including Descartes') are that they are intended as strict *proofs* (that is, deductive arguments) and that they trade heavily, as we have seen, on *metaphysical* principles. Modern design arguments, such as William Paley's (see "A Brief History of Apologetics" in chapter 14, sec. 1.1), take empirical features of the world as evidence for God's existence, and are free of obvious metaphysical presuppositions. The following excerpt from David Hume's *Dialogues concerning Natural Religion* presents, first, a classic example of the argument, followed in the second paragraph by an ironic expression of modern skepticism regarding medieval demonstrations:

> CLEANTHES: . . . Look round the world: contemplate the whole and every part of it: You will find it to be nothing but one great machine, subdivided into an infinite number of lesser machines, and even their most minute parts,

are adjusted to each other with an accuracy, which ravishes into admiration all men, who have ever contemplated them. The curious adapting of means to ends, throughout all nature, resembles exactly, though it much exceeds, the productions of human contrivance; of human designs, thought, wisdom, and intelligence. Since therefore the effects resemble each other, we are led to infer, by all the rules of analogy, that the causes also resemble; and that the Author of Nature is somewhat similar to the mind of man; though possessed of much larger faculties, proportioned to the grandeur of the work, which he has executed. By this argument *a posteriori*, and by this argument alone, do we prove at once the existence of a Deity, and his similarity to human mind and intelligence.

I shall be so free, CLEANTHES, said DEMEA, as to tell you, that from the beginning I could not approve of your conclusion concerning the similarity of the Deity to men; still less can I approve of the mediums, by which, you endeavour to establish it. What! No demonstration of the Being of a God! No abstract arguments! No proofs *a priori!* Are these, which have hitherto been so much insisted on by philosophers, all fallacy, all sophism? Can we reach no farther in this subject than experience and probability? (pt. ii)

Despite the fact that Cleanthes describes his argument as a proof, it is clear both from Demea's objections and from the fact that it is an argument from analogy that it is *not* meant to be taken as a deductive proof of the existence of God. In this regard it is interesting to compare it to Thomas's fifth way. Thomas's argument employs a universal warrant that "whatever lacks knowledge cannot move towards an end, unless it be directed by some being endowed with knowledge and intelligence." The mention of the arrow directed by the archer is an illustration, not a bit of evidence for the warrant. In other words, Thomas believed that one could know, on the basis of reason, that *all* purpose must be the result of intelligence. Hume's modern character recognizes the empirical nature (and therefore the fallibility) of such a judgment, and thus treats God's agency as based merely on analogy with instances with which we are familiar. In short, these modern philosophers of religion obey the maxim that "a wise man proportions his belief to the evidence."

2.1.5. Kant's Critiques

Hume's attacks on theistic arguments (see discussion on Hume in chapter 11, sec. 4.2) gave aid and comfort to the skeptical, but it was Immanuel Kant's critique of all three types of argument that had the most powerful impact on Christianity—so much so that to this day many Protestants reject all attempts at natural theology and steer clear of philosophy. Kant is also of interest here because his work represents one of the most decisive shifts in the history of philosophy's self-understanding. His "critical" method approaches philosophical problems by means of an analysis of the powers and limitations of human reason.

Kant began his philosophical career as a rationalist metaphysician in the tradition of Descartes, but he was "awakened from [his] dogmatic slumbers" by reading Hume's skeptical attacks on Cartesian certitude.

Kant's later work can be summed up as the attempt to achieve three goals: (1) to save Newtonian science from Hume's skepticism; (2) to save human freedom from (deterministic) Newtonian science; and (3) to save religion from both Newtonian determinism and Humean skepticism. To accomplish the first of these goals, Kant distinguished between the *content* of our experience (e.g., colors or noises) and the *form* of experience. Its form consists in the fact that the sensations are perceived as belonging to individual objects, extended in space and time, and in causal relations to one another. The forms of experience, he argued, are imposed on it by the human mind. Arithmetic, geometry, and Newtonian science are about the forms of experience only, not the content. Thus, so long as the structures of the mind were unchanging (and Kant never imagined otherwise), these three branches of knowledge were safe from revision or refutation. However, this assurance came at a cost: Things-as-they-appear-to-us, that is, the world of 'en-formed' experience, he called "phenomena." Things-as-they-are-in-themselves he called "noumena." We can only know phenomena, never noumena. We cannot even say that there are noumenal objects that cause our phenomenal experiences, since object-hood (substance) and causality are phenomenal categories only and cannot legitimately be applied to noumena or to relations between noumena and phenomena.

Kant produced a revolution in philosophy by applying this theory of knowledge to metaphysical speculation and argument. We can see the consequences by returning to our pursuit of the various arguments for the existence of God. Kant thought of the teleological arguments as least important of the three types, but his critique is nonetheless important since many, even today, put great stock in arguments of this sort. God, if there is one, must be a noumenon, since God is not a possible object of human sensory experience. And thus any argument for God's existence based on a supposed *causal* relation between God and the phenomenal world is invalid, for reasons just explained. In his *Critique of Pure Reason* he wrote that we violate the limits of human knowledge by attempting to extend the causal relation beyond experience.

> Now I maintain that all attempts to employ reason in theology in any merely speculative manner are altogether fruitless and by their very nature null and void, and that the principles of its employment in the study of nature do not lead to any theology whatsoever. . . . All synthetic principles of reason allow only of an immanent employment; and in order to have knowledge of a supreme being we should have to put them to a transcendent use, for which our understanding is in no way fitted. If the empirically valid law of causality is to lead to the original being, the latter must belong to the chain of objects of experience, and in that case it would, like all appearances, be itself again conditioned (chap. 3, sec. 7).

Kant claimed that the cosmological argument depends implicitly on an ontological argument. His reasoning here is obscure, but I believe his point can be made as follows: Suppose we can argue to the necessary existence of some *x* by showing that its existence is a *necessary condition* for the existence of all that we know to exist. How, then, to identify this *x* with the highest reality, namely God? Only by means of a concept that characterizes God as the one and only necessary (necessarily existing) being. But if we can make this step we could just as well have begun with the concept of God as necessarily existing, as does Descartes' ontological argument.

Kant then criticized the ontological argument—a criticism taken by most to be devastating. All such arguments treat existence as a *predicate*. But to say that God exists is not to add information about God (to predicate existence of the subject, God, who might otherwise have lacked it); rather it is to say that the concept *God* (however defined) has an instance—it is *instantiated*. And so the argument is simply confused.

I claimed at the beginning of this section that one of Kant's major goals was to save religion from Hume and Newton. The reader may be thinking at this point that with friends like Kant, religion needs no enemies. Nonetheless, he saw his work as a service to true religion. Traditional religion, he believed, had nothing to do with speculative theology and metaphysics, but rather with the moral life. In his *Critique of Pure Reason* he was denying knowledge of God (knowledge in the strict sense of the word) to make room for faith. His positive approach was to argue that God's existence (as well as human freedom and immortality) are necessary postulates for making sense of the *moral* world.

Kant's influence on Protestant theology can scarcely be overstated. He had, it seemed, closed the door to all natural theology: God could not be known by the operations of pure reason or on the basis of evidence from experience. But at the same time he set a precedent for Friedrich Schleiermacher and all of Schleiermacher's liberal followers in regarding religion as an entirely separate category of human experience from that of scientific knowledge. Kant identified religion with the moral sphere; Schleiermacher argued that in fact it belonged to a sphere all its own, equally distinct from morality. But in one way or another, a gulf was fixed between religion and our ordinary knowledge of the world.

Kant is credited, too, with a total reorientation of philosophical method. His "Copernican revolution" meant that all philosophical questions needed to be approached not directly but by means of an analysis of how human knowledge is possible. In Kant's case, he began with the study of scientific knowledge; from this he drew conclusions about what must be the case in order to make scientific knowledge possible. This method of reasoning, beginning with experience of some sort, and asking about its necessary conditions, he called "transcendental deduction." His conclusions about the 'division of labor' between the human mind and the external world in accounting for sensory experience was then used as a tool to criticize other disciplines—other putative bodies of knowledge—most notably, theology and metaphysics.

While the particulars of Kant's theory of knowledge have been supplanted (and while philosophy has undergone yet another revolution) there remains the recognition that putative knowledge cannot be taken at face value as a simple awareness of reality: we must always take into account the contribution we, the knowers, make to the knowing process. Thus, all human knowledge is *human* knowledge, and we can never know what it would be like to know things as they are in themselves, apart from those human contributions.

2.2. The Linguistic Turn

Kant's arguments for the impossibility of metaphysical and theological knowledge were taken more seriously by liberal theologians than by philosophers. By the early twentieth century metaphysics was going strong, especially on the European continent. In part as a reaction against this, a short-lived (1925 to c. 1938) but important philosophical movement arose in Vienna. "Logical positivism" was the quintessential modern philosophical position. The members of the "Vienna Circle" sought, with Descartes, the indubitable foundations of knowledge; but following Locke and Hume, they turned to immediate sensory knowledge to fill the bill. They had the advantage over early modern empiricists of greater logical rigor, thanks to developments in the mean time in the discipline of formal logic.

2.2.1. A. J. Ayer

The views of the logical positivists were promoted in the English-speaking world by A. J. Ayer. Ayer's *Language, Truth, and Logic* heralded the beginning of a new era in philosophy of religion: a shift in focus from the *truth* of religious claims—the epistemological question—to the *meaningfulness* of religious discourse—a question germane to the philosophy of language.[9]

The logical positivists had proposed the verificationist theory of meaning: the meaning of any statement is to be found in its method of verification. Any statement that could not be verified by any conceivable empirical observations was counted not as false but as meaningless. This criterion was intended as an account of the meaning of scientific statements, but also as a criterion to rule out all metaphysical discourse.

Ayer's account of meaning was slightly more flexible. He recognized three classes of statements: First, there are the statements of logic and mathematics—combinations of symbols whose truth is guaranteed by definitions of the symbols (e.g., $a = a$). Second, there are factual assertions of science and common sense—these statements count as meaningful insofar as some sense experience is relevant for showing them true or false. Third, there are utterances that express attitudes and emotions, but have no factual meaning. In this last category Ayer classed aesthetic and ethical judgments, metaphysics, and theology:

> Our own analysis has shown that the phenomena of moral experience cannot fairly be used to support any rationalist or metaphysical doctrine whatsoever. In particular, they cannot, as Kant hoped, be used to establish the existence of a transcendent God.
> This mention of God brings us to the question of the possibility of religious knowledge. We shall see that this possibility has already been ruled out

[9]A. J. Ayer, *Language, Truth and Logic* (1936; New York: Dover Publications, 1952).

by our treatment of metaphysics. But, as this is a point of considerable interest, we may be permitted to discuss it at some length. (114)

Ayer's "lengthy" treatment is just under four pages, an excerpt of which follows:

> It is now generally admitted, at any rate by philosophers, that the existence of a being having the attributes which define the god of any non-animistic religion cannot be demonstratively proved. To see that this is so, we have only to ask ourselves what are the premises from which the existence of such a god could be deduced. If the conclusion that a god exists is to be demonstratively certain, then these premises must be certain; for, as the conclusion of a deductive argument is already contained in the premises, any uncertainty there may be about the truth of the premises is necessarily shared by it. But we know that no empirical proposition can ever be anything more than probable. It is only *a priori* propositions that are logically certain. But we cannot deduce the existence of a god from an *a priori* proposition. For we know that the reason why *a priori* propositions are certain is that they are tautologies. And from a set of tautologies nothing but a further tautology can be validly deduced. It follows that there is no possibility of demonstrating the existence of a god.
>
> What is not so generally recognised is that there can be no way of proving that the existence of a god, such as the God of Christianity, is even probable. Yet this also is easily shown. For if the existence of such a god were probable, then the proposition that he existed would be an empirical hypothesis. And in that case it would be possible to deduce from it, and other empirical hypotheses, certain experiential propositions which were not deducible from those other hypotheses alone. But in fact this is not possible. It is sometimes claimed, indeed, that the existence of a certain sort of regularity in nature constitutes sufficient evidence for the existence of a god. But if the sentence "god exists" entails no more than that certain types of phenomena occur in certain sequences, then to assert the existence of a god will be simply equivalent to asserting that there is the requisite regularity in nature; and no religious man would admit that this was all he intended to assert in asserting the existence of a god. He would say that in talking about God, he was talking about a transcendent being who might be known through certain empirical manifestations, but certainly could not be defined in terms of those manifestations. But in that case the term "god" is a metaphysical term. And if "god" is a metaphysical term, then it cannot be even probable that a god exists. For to say that "God exists" is to make a metaphysical utterance which cannot be either true or false. . . .
>
> It is important not to confuse this view of religious assertions with the view that is adopted by atheists, or agnostics. For it is characteristic of an agnostic to hold that the existence of a god is a possibility in which there is no good reason either to believe or disbelieve; and it is characteristic of an atheist to hold that it is at least probable that no god exists. And our view that all utterances about the nature of God are nonsensical, so far from being identical with, or even lending any support to, either of these familiar contentions, is actually incompatible with them (114–15).

One might expect that those who wished to take issue with Ayer's quick dismissal of religion would begin by challenging his claim that no empirical consequences follow from the hypothesis of God's existence (and we shall take this up below). However, philosophy of religion took a different turn—preferring to examine religious language and to attempt to describe the sense in which it is in fact meaningful. Two factors probably account for this turn. The first is that religious language *is* interestingly different from ordinary language about the world. The second is that the most exciting philosophical developments in the 1940s and '50s happened to be in philosophy of language. During these years, J. L. Austin and Ludwig Wittgenstein, at Oxford and Cambridge respectively, produced nothing short of a revolution in philosophers' understanding of language. We mentioned Austin above (chapter 10, sec. 8). In the following sections we survey Wittgenstein's contributions to philosophy of language, and the appropriation of his later work for philosophy of religion.

2.2.2. Ludwig Wittgenstein

Wittgenstein is surely the most interesting character in the history of the philosophy of language. His early book, the *Tractatus Logico-Philosophicus* (1921) is a classic representation of the modern approach to language. It had long been assumed that words derived their meaning from the *objects* in the world to which they refer; thus 'horse' gets its meaning from the relevant class of critters. This is a problematic view, however, since many words have no referent; to what, for example, do 'and' and 'on' refer, not to mention 'justice' and 'unicorn' and 'atonement'? Wittgenstein's solution was to take whole sentences as units and to account for their meaning on the basis of the facts or states of affairs that they describe. So, for instance, the sentence 'That grey horse belongs to Nancy's son' describes a state of affairs, and gets its meaning from that fact.

Notice how short a step it is from this understanding of language to the verification theory of meaning. If there is no conceivable state of affairs for a sentence to describe, how can it mean anything?

Notice, also, that the state of affairs this sentence describes is complex. It refers to three individuals: a grey horse, a son, and Nancy. In mentioning these three we have already given a sentence-worth of information about each: of the first that it *is* a horse and that it is grey; of the second and third, that they bear the relationship to one another of son to mother. And all of this before getting around to the real business of the sentence, to assert the relation of ownership of the horse by the son. Bertrand Russell developed a symbolic notation to analyze such sentences—to show their true "logical form." He would represent our sentence as follows:

$$\exists x\, \exists y\, [(Hx \& Gx) \& (ySn) \& (xBy)]$$

which reads: There exists an x and there exists a y such that x is a horse and x is grey, and y is the son of Nancy, and x belongs to y.

However, to say that x is a horse is already a fairly complex assertion, since the concept *horse* is itself complex. How should it be analyzed? The recognition of the complexity of even the simplest sentences in ordinary language led Wittgenstein to assume that there must be more basic units of language (of an artificial language—not ordinary English or German). Perfectly simple sentences ought to describe the most basic facts of which the world is composed. To know how to describe such facts is to solve the problem of the basis (foundation) of knowledge, and one can now see how philosophy of language came to be seen as the key to epistemological problems.

Having published his *Tractatus,* Wittgenstein retired from philosophy— there was nothing more to be said. However, after discussions with members of the Vienna Circle, he came to realize that the problems of philosophy had not all been solved, and eventually repudiated his early approach to philosophy of language. It is Wittgenstein's later work that has most influenced philosophers of religion.[10]

While Wittgenstein maintained an interest in religion throughout his life, in the period represented by the *Tractatus* he agreed with the positivists that nothing meaningful could be said about God. However, in his later work he rejected the view that language describing empirical facts was the only (or even the most basic) kind of language. In place of a single theory about the nature of language, he began to investigate and appreciate the assorted things we *do* with language—the various "language games" in which we engage. Describing the physical world is one language game, but other equally legitimate ones include telling stories, guessing riddles, giving and obeying orders, confessing one's faith, and praying. This position left the door open for philosophers of religion to investigate the uses of religious and theological language on their own terms.

Before turning to applications of Wittgenstein's later work in philosophy of religion, it is important to appreciate the revolution in the understanding of the nature of philosophy that Wittgenstein's later work represents. Many philosophical problems, he believed, were the result of misunderstandings created by taking the "surface grammar" of language at face value, or of extracting an expression from the language game in which it normally functions and thus finding ourselves puzzled by it. So, for example, consider the following three sentences:

> This horse has long legs.
> This horse has a fast trot.
> This woman has a quick mind.

It makes sense to ask *where* the horse's legs are, but not to ask where its fast trot is. If we did so, we would have been fooled by the surface similarities between the first two sentences. The typical ways we speak about the mental *attributes* of people and of their intelligent *behavior* have led philosophers, in a similar way, to ask unnecessary and unanswerable ques-

---

[10]I have argued that Wittgenstein's later work is so radically different from his earlier views as to place him among the philosophers who have moved beyond the boundaries of modern ways of thinking. Other 'postmodern' philosophers mentioned in this volume include Imre Lakatos, Alasdair MacIntyre, and J. L. Austin. See Murphy and McClendon, "Distinguishing Modern and Postmodern Theologies."

tions about an entity referred to by the word 'mind,' such as where it is and how it interacts with the body. Philosophy as linguistic analysis or 'therapy' does not seek to answer such questions, but rather to show us both why the questions are illegitimate and why we are tempted to ask them anyway.

Wittgenstein's early work provides an example of the shift from Kant's concern with the limits of knowledge to a concern with the limits of meaningful language. In Wittgenstein's later work we see a shift from the attempt to establish the limits of language on the basis of an abstract theory of language to an attempt to catalogue and understand the functioning of the variety of forms of meaningful discourse. It involves the recognition that, in most cases, ordinary language aptly employs and reflects the human race's knowledge of reality. But the relation between language and the world cannot be studied from a standpoint outside of or 'above' ordinary language. The possibilities and limits of reasoning and of linguistic expression are to be found in the structures and rules of the language itself—more particularly, in the rules of the various language games in which we participate. The proper role for the philosopher is to study and explicate the 'grammar' (the rules for appropriate use) of these various kinds of language within their own proper "forms of life."

Wittgenstein's philosophy is *linguistic,* both in the sense that his primary concern is with language and how it functions, and that the method of approaching these and other philosophical questions is by means of the study of the language in which they arise.

Philosophers of religion have used Wittgenstein's conclusions about the variety of language games, each acceptable within its own form of life, to argue that religious language needs no special justification or defense in terms of some other kind of language or reasoning. In particular, one need not show that religious language meets the same criteria for meaningfulness as does scientific language.

Perhaps the most interesting development in Wittgensteinian philosophy of religion is the view of theology that has been developed from Wittgenstein's cryptic remark that "theology is grammar." Paul Holmer, for example, claims that the language of faith (praying, preaching, confessing) is the basic language of the Christian form of life. Theology is a second-order discipline that studies in a systematic way the proper uses of religious expressions.

> Theology answers the question—what is Christianity? But it tells us the answer by giving us the order and priorities, the structure and morphology, of the Christian faith. It does this by placing the big words, like *man, God, Jesus, world,* in such a sequence and context that their use becomes ruled for us.[11]

Holmer's position has been adopted and elaborated recently by philosophical theologian George Lindbeck, who develops the ancient idea that doctrines are "rules of faith." The Chalcedonian doctrine of the two natures of Christ, for example, does not so much *describe* Christ as tell speakers of the language of Christianity what may not rightly be said of him: for

---

[11]Paul Holmer, *The Grammar of Faith* (San Francisco: Harper and Row, 1978), 20.

instance, it may not be said that the divine and human natures are *confused* or *changed* in Christ's person. Lindbeck proposes this view of doctrine as part of a program to move beyond the modern stand-off between liberal and conservative approaches to theology.[12]

How does all of this relate to our original topic of arguments for the existence of God? Wittgensteinian philosophers of religion (and philosophical theologians) would first point out that within Christian discourse (or religious discourse in general) the statement 'God exists' has no natural role to play. Christians speak of, pray to, preach about God; but the question of God's existence never arises. It is simply presupposed, and legitimately so if the entire Christian form of life is a legitimate form of human existence. If philosophers outside of the faith can find no meaningful way to prove God's existence, that is not surprising. The attempt is philosophically illegitimate.

So, while the Wittgensteinian approach has marked a vast improvement over earlier views, such as Ayer's, of the nature and function of religious language, there continue to be justifiable worries that this approach leads to a "fideist" view of religion—that no legitimate criticism of a particular religion's discourse is possible from outside.[13] Unless and until this concern is answered to critics' satisfaction, it is worthwhile to investigate alternative understandings of religious language and reasoning.

2.3. A New Design Argument?

We mentioned above that a reasonable response to Ayer might be to question his claim that no empirical consequences follow from the hypothesis of the existence of God. Recent developments in scientific cosmology have, in fact, called this contention into question; these discoveries might contribute to a new argument from design. Since the 1950s cosmologists and other scientists have been amassing measurements and calculations suggesting that the universe is "fine-tuned" to support intelligent life. There is a small set of basic numbers that account for the general features of the universe such as its rate of expansion, temperature, degree of homogeneity, and chemical composition. These numbers include the strengths of the four basic forces (gravity, electromagnetism, and the strong and weak nuclear forces), its mass (i.e., the total amount of 'stuff' in it), and a few others. Calculations show that if any of these numbers had been much different from what it is, the general features of the universe would be vastly different—different in ways that would make life impossible.

All of these calculations assume the general outlines of the Big Bang theory of the origin of the universe. The universe is now expanding and cooling; projecting these changes back in time we come to a point around

---

[12]See George Lindbeck, *The Nature of Doctrine* (Philadelphia: Westminster, 1984).
[13]D. Z. Phillips is the philosopher most often accused of drawing this conclusion, although he himself denies the charge. See "Religious Belief and Philosophical Inquiry," in *Faith and Philosophical Inquiry* (London: Routledge and Kegan Paul, 1970), 62–76.

20 billion years ago when the universe would have been unimaginably hot and dense. Its behavior from that point on resembles the effects of a terrific explosion. Now, working our way forward from that point, the universe would first have been composed of a 'matter-energy soup' since matter, as we know it, could not have formed under the earliest conditions. The first matter to form would have been particles of the lightest gases: hydrogen and helium. Stars would have formed when gravitational attraction condensed clouds of gas with enough centripetal force to produce nuclear burning.

As stars go through their life span, heavier elements are 'cooked' in their nuclear furnaces. At a particular point in the life of a star it explodes, distributing the heavier elements as dust in the surrounding region. Our planet, and indeed our bodies, are composed of this dust. Current estimates suggest that this process takes around 10 billion years.

Thus, for life to exist in the universe, the universe must be at least 10 billion years old. Here we can see one of the needs for fine-tuning. The mass of the universe and the strength of the gravitational constant need to be carefully balanced. Two forces are operative on expansion speed of the universe—the outward force of the initial explosion, and gravity, which tends to pull it all back together. Gravitational pull is related to the amount of matter in the universe. If the universe were more massive than it is, or if the force of gravity itself were stronger, the universe would have first slowed its expansion and then collapsed in on itself before life had a chance to develop. Alternatively, if the universe had been smaller or the force of gravity weaker, it would have spread out and cooled off too quickly for stars to form and, again, it would have remained lifeless.

In some cases, numerical estimates of requirements such as these have been made. Carbon is one of the basic elements needed for life and many of the calculations have to do with necessary conditions for its formation and distribution. If the nuclear strong force were 1 percent weaker or stronger, carbon would not form within the stellar ovens. In fact, it has been calculated that the strong force had to be within 0.8 and 1.2 times its actual strength for there to be any elements at all with atomic weights greater than 4. Also, if electromagnetism had been stronger, stars would not explode and the heavier elements needed for life would not be available.

The nuclear weak force's very weakness makes our sun burn gently for billions of years instead of blowing up like a bomb. Had this force been appreciably stronger, stars of this sort would be impossible. But if it were much weaker the universe would be composed entirely of helium.

Here are some remarkable numbers: Electrons and protons have equal but opposite charges. It has been estimated that a charge difference of more than one part in 10 billion would mean that there could be no macroscopic objects; that is, there could be no solid bodies weighing more than about a gram.

The ratio of the strengths of electromagnetism to gravity appears to be crucial. Changes in either force by 1 part in 10 to the fortieth power (ten followed by forty zeros) would spell catastrophe for stars like our sun.

The ratio between gravity and the nuclear weak force may have to be adjusted as accurately as one part in 10 to the hundredth power to avoid either a swift collapse of the universe or an explosion.

Cosmologists began noting these remarkable coincidences in the 1950s. By now several books have appeared with page after page of such conclusions.[14] What are we to make of these results?

Some scientists, philosophers, and theologians conclude that such dramatic 'fine-tuning' cries out for explanation. One possible answer is to postulate a Master Tuner, in which case we have a new sort of design argument.

However, there are other possible explanations, suggesting that the fine-tuning is only apparent. Three of the competitors are:

1. Pure chance
2. Mathematical (logical) necessity
3. Many universes

One suggestion is that, while it is amazing that the universe should have turned out to be life-supporting, this is just a matter of chance and there is nothing more to be said. This claim can be taken in either of two ways: It might be taken as a statement about the limits of knowledge—prediction that the null hypothesis will ever be our lot. However, it may be better to take the chance hypothesis as a sort of metaphysical claim that chance is somehow the ultimate principle behind reality. In either case, we have a metascientific claim, and one that is difficult to imagine confirming independently, since neither seems to fit into a network of other claims or to be empirically testable.

Another suggestion is that it will someday be shown that only one set of numbers can be used to solve the equations comprising the basic laws of nature. If so, this would in a sense provide a scientific explanation for the fine-tuning of the individual constants, masses, and other quantities. It provides no ultimate explanation, however, because we still can wonder at the coincidence that the only possible universe is also life-supporting, and at the fact that this one-and-only possibility is instantiated—the old question why there is something rather than nothing.

A natural move to explain (explain away?) the wonder at finding the universe finely tuned for life is to propose that it is but one of vastly many universes—all different—and that we naturally find ourselves in the one (or one of the ones) that, by random variation, happened to be suitable for life. One or another of these many-universes explanations looks to be the most promising for straightforward scientific status. The crucial issue in evaluating these competitors has to do with whether any independent evidence for additional universes can be provided. At present, it seems that the many-universes hypotheses are *ad hoc:* they explain the appearance of fine-tuning but play no further role in our system of knowledge—they have no other connections within the web of beliefs. In this regard

---

[14]Two prominent books are J. Barrow and F. Tipler, *The Anthropic Cosmological Principle* (Oxford: Oxford University Press, 1986); and John Leslie, *Universes* (London: Routledge, 1989). The figures above are from Leslie.

(other things being equal), they are at a disadvantage when compared with the design hypothesis.

If these competing hypotheses (and the other more exotic ones I have not mentioned) could be eliminated, the apparent fine-tuning of the universe would provide rather striking grounds for a theistic hypothesis. The most that can be said so far is that the Christian hypothesis of creation has independent confirmation (from history, religious experience, and other arguments, perhaps) while the competitors are either unconfirmable in principle or as yet unconfirmed. So at present this appears to be a fruitful topic to pursue for those interested in design arguments. Notice, though, that the results will not be in the form of a short and simple argument like Thomas's fifth way. Rather, they will involve judicious evaluation of all the competing hypotheses, and will never provide more than probability for God's existence—as is the case with all hypothetical arguments. In a way, though, such an argument takes us back to a more medieval outlook, in that no sharp distinction is drawn between science and theology, making arguments from one to the other illegitimate. So the argument will also have to include a response to modern objections to this sort of commingling of science and theology.

3. Philosophical Theology

The term 'philosophical theology' is another newcomer to the intellectual scene. As suggested above, it is sometimes used to refer to theologians' work on the topics assigned to philosophy of religion, but it has other uses as well. Perhaps it is most accurate to say that there are several disciplines that bear this name. I suggest the following four categories of intellectual pursuits, despite the fact that they are neither mutually exclusive (some cases may fit into more than one category) nor exhaustive (some works in philosophical theology may not fit neatly into any of the categories): (1) theological foundations; (2) explication of Christian doctrine by means of philosophical concepts; (3) investigation of philosophical problems that arise from theological claims; and (4) inquiry at the interface between theology and other disciplines.

3.1. Theological Foundations

This is the part of systematic or doctrinal theology that deals with questions of theological method: the sorts of grounds that are appropriate (for example, scripture, religious experience, "tradition"), and the appropriate form of theological arguments. The assorted theological methods presented in chapter 11 illustrate a variety of positions on theological foundations; the view of the proper relations among the theological disciplines proposed in chapter 12 is intended as a contribution to this subject. So it is already apparent that there are a wide variety of approaches. The variety is due in part to ecclesiastical differences, for example, the Protestant emphasis on scripture alone versus the Catholic emphasis on the teaching authority of the church.[15] However, it may be clear from chapter 11 that an even greater amount of the variation can be accounted for on the basis of philosophical changes; for example, from the epistemology of authority assumed by Thomas to the modern emphasis on 'foundations' and evidence.

A more recent development in theological foundations is a response to the change from foundationalist to holist epistemology (see chapter 12). "Postliberal" theologians claim that foundationalist epistemology led their modern predecessors to misconstrue the nature of theological reasoning, in particular by leading them to seek an *indubitable* starting point for theology. One option, as we have seen, was to begin with scripture, but this placed a greater burden on the doctrine of revelation than it could rightly bear—inerrantist accounts of scriptural truth being the most extreme example.[16]

George Lindbeck, Ronald Thiemann, and others argue that the consequence of accepting a nonfoundational view of knowledge is an "intratextual" approach to theology, where the coherence of the network of belief *and practice* (a Wittgensteinian emphasis) is the primary criterion for justification.[17] A second consequence will surely be a thorough rethinking of this part of philosophical theology. And of course the very name 'theological foundations' will have to change if nonfoundationalist theologians have their way.

3.2. Explication of Doctrines Using Philosophical Concepts

Within this category it is necessary to distinguish two varieties. One is the systematic presentation of Christian theology within the context of a philosophical worldview. Thomas's synthesis of Christianity with Aristotelian cosmology is one example, but recent existentialist theology, such as that of Paul Tillich, is another. The second variety aims more at analysis than synthesis, and uses philosophical concepts as tools to examine and explain individual theological doctrines. An example is the application of relative identity logic to the doctrine of the Trinity. Relative identity logic is a set of formalisms designed to answer the question whether it is possible for a to be identical with b when we consider a and b under one concept (a is the same *river* as b) but not under another concept (a is not the same *body of water* as b).

Differences between these two varieties of philosophical theology reflect the change described earlier in this chapter from a view of philosophy as a body of knowledge to philosophy as method. Philosophical theology of the systematic sort generally presupposes the older and grander

---

[15]Note that Catholic theologians more often call this part of theology "fundamental theology." See Gerald O'Collins, "Fundamental Theology," in *Dictionary of Christian Theology,* ed. Alan Richardson (Philadelphia: Westminster, 1969).

[16]See Ronald Thiemann, *Revelation and Theology* (Notre Dame: University of Notre Dame Press, 1985).

[17]See Lindbeck, *The Nature of Doctrine;* and William Placher, *Unapologetic Theology* (Louisville: Westminster/John Knox, 1989).

view of philosophy, while the second sort presupposes the view of philosophy as conceptual clarification.

3.3. Philosophical Problems Arising from Theological Claims

This is the branch or subdivision of philosophical theology whose interests overlap with those of philosophy of religion.

A growing awareness of the *tradition-dependent* character of all discourse may be the most significant recent development in this sort of philosophical theology. It has led, for example, to a change in the tone of theological discussions of world religions. It has led to a blurring of distinctions between discussions of theological method (category 1) and essays on the rationality of Christian belief—in a pluralist world one cannot talk about theological method without thinking how one's theological formulations will stand up to scrutiny in other communities. Even discussions of the problem of evil tend to take account of the fact that there is no universal view of what constitutes blessedness or suffering.

It is not possible to survey developments in individual topics here; one illustration will have to suffice. The problem of God's action in the world has long been understood as a question of how to reconcile the Christian view of God as the cause of all that happens with a scientific or commonsense view that events have natural causes. The problem became especially acute in the modern period, when it was thought that events were determined by a system of natural laws: How could God have continuing intercourse with the world without violating the very laws that were established by divine decree at creation?

Two things have happened to alter discussion on this issue. One is that science itself has called causal determinism into question.[18] The second shift is a new philosophical perspective on the problem. Whereas it was originally seen as a metaphysical problem—how to reconcile two kinds of causation—it is now very often treated as a problem in philosophy of action. Here inquiry begins with the question of what we mean in attributing action to an agent—what are the necessary conditions for saying that *x* performed action *a?* Then it is possible to ask whether or how God's reported acts meet these conditions; for example, is there an analogy between a human agent acting by means of bodily movements and God acting by means of events within the universe at large?

3.4. The Interface between Theology and Other Disciplines

As has been made clear above, philosophical theology shares concerns with various branches of philosophy—most notably with philosophy of religion, but also with epistemology, ethics, philosophy of language, philosophy of action. Theology shares concerns with a number of other disciplines as well: anthropology and the other human sciences, history, and

---

[18]See, for example, Arthur Peacocke, *Theology for a Scientific Age* (1990; Minneapolis: Fortress, 1994).

even with the natural sciences. To call investigations of the relations between theology and these other disciplines philosophical theology requires some explanation. In general, whenever one steps back from a discipline and considers its very nature and the relations of that discipline to another, one is engaging in a philosophical task—philosophy *of* science, or philosophy *of* history. However, to do so in light of a Christian view of knowledge, history, and so on, makes it a theological task as well. For example, we have seen that Wolfhart Pannenberg criticizes the standard views of historiography (theories about how to justify historical knowledge) as being too anthropocentric (rather than theocentric) and as being systematically biased against recognizing claims about the unique acts of God in history.[19] Thus, he engages in the debate about the nature of historical research (a question for the philosophy of history), and he does so from a theological standpoint. Hence, it is reasonable to describe his work on this topic as philosophical theology.

The most striking development within this category of philosophical theology is an increased interest in the relations between theology and the natural sciences. Conservative Christians, especially since Darwin, have been concerned about the relations between theology and science. Liberal Christians, following Kant's lead, have not only been inclined to see no relations between theology and science, but have positively asserted that no relation is possible. However, since the 1970s works on theology and the natural sciences by theologians with liberal roots have been appearing in ever greater number.[20] These attempts to relate theology positively to the natural sciences reflect changes in views of the nature of theology, of theological method, and of theological language; they therefore relate closely to topics in other categories of philosophical theology. Furthermore, the content of science (as well as other disciplines) is sometimes seen to have an important bearing on problems in philosophical theology; for example, the change from deterministic to relativistic physics may have some bearing on the problem of God's action in the world.

4. Conclusion

The intellectual world is not as tidy as it was in the modern period. Once-sharp distinctions between disciplines have been blurred—for example, between philosophy of religion and philosophical theology. Neat little arguments can no longer be evaluated out of context—we saw that Anselm's ontological argument presupposed metaphysical truths; Thomas's teleological argument traded heavily upon seeing natural processes through Aristotelian eyes. We have come, gradually, over the past 200 years, to recognize the historical conditioning of all human thought—there are ar-

[19]See Wolfhart Pannenberg, *Theology and the Philosophy of Science* (Philadelphia: Westminster, 1976); and also Pannenberg's argument for the historicity of Jesus' resurrection in chapter 9, section 7, above.
[20]Ian Barbour's *Issues in Science and Religion* (New York: Harper and Row, 1966), and *Myths, Models, and Paradigms* (New York: Harper and Row, 1974), have been two of the most influential.

guments that worked in their own day and age that must now be seen as elementary logical errors.

What then? Is nothing certain? Is all knowledge merely relative, and thus not worth counting as knowledge at all? This is the central question for our time and place in intellectual history. We look at a few replies in the final chapter.

EXERCISE THIRTEEN

1. The following is Thomas's "first way."

WHETHER GOD EXISTS

We proceed thus to the Third Article:—

Objection 1. It seems that God does not exist; because if one of two contraries be infinite, the other would be altogether destroyed. But the name *God* means that He is infinite goodness. If, therefore, God existed, there would be no evil discoverable; but there is evil in the world. Therefore God does not exist. . . .

On the contrary, it is said in the person of God: *I am Who I am (Exod. iii. 14).*

I answer that, The existence of God can be proved in five ways.

The first and more manifest way is the argument from motion. It is certain, and evident to our senses, that in the world some things are in motion. Now whatever is moved is moved by another, for nothing can be moved except it is in potentiality to that towards which it is moved; whereas a thing moves inasmuch as it is in act. For motion is nothing else than the reduction of something from potentiality to actuality. Thus that which is actually hot, as fire, makes wood, which is potentially hot, to be actually hot, and thereby moves and changes it. Now it is not possible that the same thing should be at once in actuality and potentiality in the same respect, but only in different respects. For what is actually hot cannot simultaneously be potentially hot; but it is simultaneously potentially cold. It is therefore impossible that in the same respect and in the same way a thing should be both mover and moved, i.e., that it should move itself. Therefore, whatever is moved must needs be moved by another. If that by which it is moved by itself moves, then this also must needs be moved by another, and that by another again. But this cannot go on to infinity, because then there would be no first mover, and, consequently, no other mover, seeing that subsequent movers move only inasmuch as they are moved by the first mover; as the staff moves only because it is moved by the hand. Therefore it is necessary to arrive at a first mover, moved by no other; and this everyone understands to be God.[21]

a. Diagram the argument in Objection 1. Note: the backing is the interesting part.

b. Is Thomas's first way an *a priori* or an *a posteriori* argument? What sentence makes it so?

c. What function does "Whatever is moved is moved by another" serve in Thomas's first way?

[21]Thomas Aquinas, *Summa Theologiae,* part 1, question 2, article 3.

    d. What part in the argument does the business about potentiality play?
    e. Part of Thomas's argument involves showing that the assumption of an infinite regress of movers leads to a contradiction. What is the name of this kind of argument?
    f. What criticism would Kant make of this argument?

2. Here is Kant's argument for the existence of God.

> I assume that there really are pure moral laws which determine completely *a priori* . . . what is and is not to be done. . . .
>
> Since reason commands that such actions should take place, it must be possible for them to take place. Consequently, a special kind of systematic unity, namely the moral, must likewise be possible. . . .
>
> The idea of a moral world has, therefore, objective reality. . . .
>
> Morality, by itself, constitutes a system. Happiness, however, does not do so, save in so far as it is distributed in exact proportion to morality. But this is possible only in the intelligible world under a wise Author and Ruler. Such a Ruler, together with life in such a world, which we must regard as a future world, reason finds itself constrained to assume; otherwise it would have to regard the moral laws as empty figments of the brain, since without this postulate the necessary consequence which it itself connects with these laws could not follow. Hence also everyone regards the moral laws as *commands;* and this the moral laws could not be if they did not connect *a priori* suitable consequences with their rules, and thus carry with them *promises* and *threats.* But this again they could not do, if they did not reside in a necessary being, as the supreme good, which alone can make such a purposive unity possible. . . .
>
> If we consider from the point of view of moral unity, as a necessary law of the world, what the cause must be that can alone give to this law its appropriate effect, and so for us obligatory force, we conclude that there must be one sole supreme will, which comprehends all these laws in itself. For how, under different wills, should we find complete unity of ends. This Divine Being must be omnipotent, in order that the whole of nature and its relation to morality in the world may be subject to his will; omniscient, that He may know our innermost sentiments and their moral worth; omnipresent, that He may be immediately at hand for the satisfying of every need which the highest good demands; eternal, that this harmony of nature and freedom may never fail, etc.[22]

    a. What is the name of Kant's method of reasoning that begins with experience and argues to the necessary conditions for such experience?
    b. With what kind of experience does Kant begin here?
    c. In a word, what is the necessary condition for this experience?

Write grounds and warrants to fill in d–j in the following argument using statements (or summaries of statements) from the preceding passage.

---

[22]Immanuel Kant, *Critique of Pure Reason,* trans. Norman Kemp Smith (London: Macmillan, 1958), 636–42 *passim.*

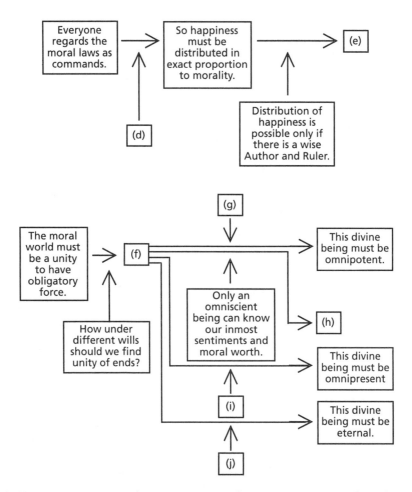

3. Note: no orienting information is given here since it is your job to determine from the context the approach D. M. MacKinnon is taking.

> To many contemporary philosophers it seems that claims to survive death must be described as nonsense statements, and that the philosopher's job is to lay bare their nonsensical character, and uncover the violations of syntactical propriety they contain. Of course, we do talk regularly of people surviving catastrophes and *escaping* death. We may even in certain unusual circumstances be justified in speaking of dead men as not really dead: in cases of catalepsy, and so on. But death itself is not something we can significantly speak of surviving. If we say we survive death, we do not know what we are saying. For we cannot stretch our lines of connection with ordinary usage far enough to establish the sense of it. The words are combined in a way that, if we attend to them closely, defies the possibility of our attaching sense to them. . . .

> Christian theology, which did so much to transform men's attitude to the after-life, speaks less of immortality than of resurrection, less of personal survival than of the life of the world to come. It speaks less of assur-

ance that something will survive as of hope that "all manner of thing will be well." To develop this theme properly belongs not to philosophy but to theology, and above all to Christology, the pivot and centre of characteristically Christian theology. Indeed sometimes the man who is at all trained in this theology must be impatient of discussions of immortality, which studiously refrain from referring to the *event* of the death and resurrection of Christ.[23]

a. If we take Ayer, Russell, and the early Wittgenstein to represent one school of thought regarding religious language, and the later Wittgenstein and Holmer to represent a second, to which school do the "contemporary philosophers" of the first paragraph belong?
b. Why?
c. MacKinnon's reply (in the second paragraph) places him within which of these two schools of philosophers?

4. Richard Grigg is influenced by Paul Tillich, whom we mentioned briefly above (sec. 3.2). Tillich's theology was much influenced by existentialism, a popular philosophical movement just after World War II.

The word "theology" derives from the Greek *theos,* which means god, and *logos,* which means word or reason. . . . Thus, our investigation begins with an analysis of the *theos* and *logos* of the special sort of theology we seek. What is to be understood, first of all, by the word *theos* or "god"? . . .

The principle we shall attempt to follow is this: *theos* ought to be defined as precisely as possible given the proviso that the resultant notion of *theos* must be consistent with the diverse notions of ultimate reality found in the various world religions. Thus, the meaning of "god" or *theos* cannot be specified so precisely that it is at odds with the Jewish or Christian God, the Muslim Allah, the Buddhist Nirvana, the Taoist Tao, or the Hindu Brahman. . . . The following definition of *theos* seems consistent with a good many of the world religions and yet has a definite and significant content: *theos* is that infinite dimension of reality that can deliver human beings from certain fundamental threats that result from the fact that human being is finite being. . . .

Furthermore, we can add specificity to our proposed notion of *theos* by indicating precisely which sorts of threats are involved in human finitude. Paul Tillich provides a useful analysis of these threats in . . . his claim that the fundamental threats we encounter because of our finitude are presented to human consciousness as anxiety. Anxiety is a state of mind that is to be distinguished from fear. Fear always has a definite object: I am afraid of some particular danger, such as a vicious dog. . . . By contrast, anxiety has no definite object, yet it makes us conscious of a real threat. Or, to put it another way, anxiety does have an object, but that object is nothingness. Anxiety is a mood that makes us aware of a threat to our very essence as human beings; it alerts us to the threat of nonbeing, the threat that our being may be undermined or eroded. . . .

What about *logos?* If the word *logos* means reason or word, then its being attached to *theos* suggests that theology involves thinking about and speaking about the infinite. Indeed, the particular species of theology we

[23]D. M. MacKinnon, "Death," in *New Essays in Philosophical Theology,* ed. A. Flew and A. MacIntyre (London: SCM Press, 1955), 261, 265–66.

are seeking to define is theology as a disciplined way of thinking that merits a place among the contemporary academic disciplines.

Theology as such a way of thinking can be defined by a tripartite formula: the theologian (1) must provide a clear account (2) of precisely what he or she knows about the infinite (3) and of just how he or she knows it.

The theologian must employ a frame of reference that is not his or hers alone, but one that is available to other people as well. . . . In fact, we must go so far as to say that giving an account and being accountable means employing a frame of reference that is not limited even to a particular group of people, but employing one that is, at least in principle, available to all intelligent persons. . . . Thus theology has to do not with something peculiar to the experience of a particular individual or a particular group, but with human being as such, with what we might call "human nature." . . .

The three parts of our *logos* formula are all contained, at least in germ, in a single word, . . . *correlation*. . . .

One can find theologians writing today who . . . make explicit reference to the principle of correlation. For example, David Tracy, in his attempt to recommend a method for a specifically Christian theology, says that "the two principal sources for theology are Christian texts and common human experience and language." He goes on to explain that "the theological task will involve a critical correlation of the results of the investigations of the two sources of theology."[24]

a. To which discipline (philosophy of religion or philosophical theology) does this passage as a whole belong?
b. Grigg's proposal regarding the method of correlation involves what two sources of grounds for theology?
c. Which of these two sources of grounds appears to be the more important for Grigg?
d. This proposal belongs to which category within philosophical theology?
e. Would Grigg and Tracy recognize as grounds for theological arguments descriptions of experiences such as conversion experiences or gifts of the Spirit? Why or why not?
f. The second and third paragraphs provide an example of which category within philosophical theology?
g. Look back at the section on Wittgenstein's *later* work, and then write a Wittgensteinian critique of Grigg's sentence: "Or, to put it another way, anxiety does have an object, but that object is nothingness."

5. Kai Nielsen is one of the best-known proponents of philosophical atheism.

> (1) God is my Creator to whom everything is owed
>
> and
>
> (2) God is the God of mercy of whose forgiveness I stand in need
>
> are paradigms of the above mentioned use of religious discourse; they presumably are fact-stating uses of discourse, though this is not all they are, and they are closely linked with other uses of religious discourse. . . .

[24]Richard Grigg, *Theology as a Way of Thinking* (Atlanta: Scholars Press, 1990), 1–13 *passim*.

We must not examine religious utterances—especially those which appear to have a statement-making function—in isolation, but we should examine them on location as part of that complex activity we call "religion." . . .

When a religious man utters (1) or (2)—our paradigm religious utterances quoted above—there is the presumption that the speaker understands "God" and knows or believes in the reality of what is being talked about. The acceptance of the truth of (1) and (2) is partially definitive of what it is to be a Jew or Christian. In asserting (1) and (2), the religious man *presupposes* that there is a God and that this God has a certain character. . . .

The most crucial question we can ask about Judaism, Christianity, and Islam is whether these religious presuppositions are justified.

It might be felt that I have already too much ignored context. In live religious discourse, it is sometimes maintained, questions about the existence of God or the coherence of the concept of God do not arise. It is only by ignoring the context of religious talk that I can even make them seem like real questions.

There are multiple confusions involved in this objection. First, believers characteristically have doubts; even the man in "the circle of faith" is threatened with disbelief. Tormenting religious doubts arise in the religious life itself and they are often engendered by some first-order uses of God-talk. . . . Most atheists and agnostics were once believers . . . and they have a participant's understanding of these forms of life. . . . Context or not, it is this traditional and central question [whether there is a God] that we need to face in asking fundamental questions about the Judeo-Christian tradition. . . .

I shall argue that both the agnostic and the believer are mistaken. Careful reflection on the use of "God" in the stream of Jewish and Christian life is enough to justify an atheism which asserts that the concept of God is so incoherent that there could not possibly be a referent for the word "God."[25]

a. Where in the progression from Kant, to Ayer, to the early Wittgenstein, to the later Wittgenstein does Nielsen stand?
b. How can you tell?
c. What claim of his immediate predecessors does Nielsen rebut?
d. How does he rebut it?
e. In what respect does Nielsen's position resemble Ayer's?

---

[25]Kai Nielsen, *Philosophy and Atheism* (Buffalo: Prometheus Books, 1985), 77–82 *passim*.

CHAPTER FOURTEEN

Apologetics and Religious Pluralism

1. Apologetics

While Christian apologetics is as old as Christianity itself, it has been somewhat out of fashion during the past generation, and few seminaries now offer courses in the subject. However, it may be enjoying a rebirth, signaled by the appearance of books with titles such as *An Apology for Apologetics,* and *Unapologetic Theology.*[1]

Apologetics may be defined as the defense of the Christian faith. However, in so defining it we take caution from B. B. Warfield's claim that "nearly every writer has a definition of his own, and describes the task of the discipline in a fashion more or less peculiar to himself; and there is scarcely a corner of the theological encyclopedia into which it has not been thrust."[2] With this diversity of views on the nature of apologetics it is perhaps best to begin with a survey of some of the forms apologetic discourse has taken through the centuries.

We will then take up the problem of religious pluralism, one of the most pressing of apologetic concerns in our era. In these days, when Christians are aware of the existence *and value* of the other world religions, can they make claims that their religion alone is true? It may be fair to say that a general approach to apologetics in seminaries has been eclipsed by attention to this one problem.

In the final section of the chapter we shall see what light is shed on apologetic problems by the recent developments in theory of knowledge discussed in chapter 12.

---

[1]Paul J. Griffiths, *An Apology for Apologetics* (New York: Orbis, 1991); William Placher, *Unapologetic Theology* (Louisville: Westminster/John Knox, 1989).

[2]B. B. Warfield, "Apologetics," *The New Schaff-Herzog Encyclopedia of Religious Knowledge,* ed. Samuel MacAuley Jackson (New York: Funk and Wagnalls, 1908), 1: 233. By the way, Warfield says that apologetics is not the defense of Christianity, but rather the establishment of the grounds of the possibility of theology—a task we have assigned to philosophical theology!

1.1. A Brief History of Apologetics

The first Christians needed to address two skeptical audiences. First, they needed to convince their fellow Jews that Jesus, despite appearances to the contrary, was the long-awaited Messiah. Their central strategy was to search the Jewish scriptures for material that could be seen to point to Jesus. In Acts, Luke describes Peter doing just this as he addresses the crowds on Pentecost. The objection Peter must answer arises from Jesus' crucifixion. How could someone who had been executed as a criminal be the Messiah? Peter's answer to this rebuttal is to claim that Jesus had to be handed over to death in order that David's prophecy of the Messiah's resurrection might be fulfilled (see Acts 2:22–31).

Perhaps the more difficult apologetic task was to find a way to interpret Jesus as Messiah to a Greek audience. There were two obstacles: The first was certain of the presuppositions of Greek philosophy. For example, resurrection was a ridiculous idea to a Greek, since bodily existence was seen as the primary hindrance to reaching full spiritual potential. A second obstacle was the polytheism of the Greco-Roman world. We find a classic example of apologetics in Paul's speech to the Athenians, where he takes their polytheistic worship as a starting point:

> Then Paul stood in front of the Aeropagus and said, "Athenians, I see how extremely religious you are in every way. For as I went through the city and looked carefully at the objects of your worship, I found among them an altar with the inscription, 'To an unknown god.' What therefore you worship as unknown, this I proclaim to you. The God who made the world and everything in it, he who is Lord of heaven and earth, does not live in shrines made by human hands, nor is he served by human hands, as though he needed anything, since he himself gives to all mortals life and breath and all things" (Acts 17:22–25).

Notice that just as apologists to the Jews took a preexisting category of thought—the concept of *Messiah*—and showed that Jesus fit it (at least with some reinterpretation); so, too, Paul takes a preexisting idea—the unknown god—and argues that the Christian God is the one who fits it. But Paul also reinterprets this category: the shrine would have been to a god conceived in a radically different manner from the God of the Jews and Christians. We see illustrated here an important fact about apologetics. It often takes up the language and concepts of the critic, but in the process subtly changes them to suit its own purposes.

When historians speak of *the* apologists they are referring to a series of Christian writers of the second through the fourth centuries: Tertullian, Justin Martyr, Irenaeus, Origen, and others. The emphasis in the second century was on defense of Christian behavior, but from the third century onward the concerns were more of a doctrinal nature—thus, for example, the anti-Gnostic writings of Irenaeus.

After Christianity became the official religion of the Roman Empire (in the fourth century) it became less important to provide a *general* defense, and attention turned to specific problems within Christian thought. One notable example is the problem of evil, which can be formulated as follows: if God is all-good then he would want to eliminate evil; if God is all-powerful then he should be able to eliminate evil; yet there is evil.

Augustine's answer to this (apparent) inconsistency in Christian thought continues to be important today. Augustine was preoccupied throughout his life with the question of the source of evil. Other popular systems of thought provided their own answers. The Manichaeans postulated two deities, one good, one evil, and explained the prevalence of evil by claiming that the good deity was weak and passive. Augustine saw that a Christian needed to deny the dualism of Manichaeism and stand up for the power and sovereignty of the one, all-good God.

Another way of accounting for evil was that of the Neoplatonist philosophers, who taught that the world was not the *creation* of God, but rather that it was an *emanation*—an overflowing—from God. Just as light gets dimmer farther from its source, reality is less good as it is farther from its source in God. Matter, for the Neoplatonists, was so far from God that it was totally devoid of goodness. Hence moral evil could be accounted for as a consequence of corruption by material reality.

Augustine found many aspects of Neoplatonic thought to be compatible with Christianity and useful for its defense. He accepted the Neoplatonist view of gradations of reality: angels were higher than humans, humans higher than animals, and so forth. But all that God had made was good. In fact, the best cosmos God could create was one with all possible levels of reality filled. Evil only appears when intelligent creatures choose to leave their proper place in that divinely ordained order—and so Augustine interpreted the Genesis story of the first sin as that of the first couple striving to be like God. This sin and its effects, rather than the gradations in reality themselves, are the true source of evil in the cosmos.

So what we see in Augustine's apology is the amplification of Christian teaching about sin, making use of (while reinterpreting) categories from Neoplatonic thought, in order to answer a pressing question of his day. Notice that there is no fixed line between apologetics and theology; much of Augustine's apologetic work (for example, his doctrine of original sin) became a standard part of orthodox theology and has great influence even today.

Augustine stands at the turning point between two eras. The ancient world was passing away at the hands of invaders from the north. As Christianity spread throughout Europe during the medieval period, the need for defense against rival systems of thought (philosophies and pagan religions) gradually diminished. However, there were still rival religions—Judaism within, and Islam to the east and south. The most notable apologetic work of the Middle Ages was Thomas Aquinas's *Summa Contra Gentiles,* aimed primarily at the teachings of the Muslims.

When the Christian consensus of the Middle Ages began to disintegrate in the modern period, the greatest threat came not from competing religions, but from rationalism. Philosophers such as David Hume questioned the rationality of Christian belief. Apologists such as William Paley provided arguments for theism, only to be criticized by a new generation of skeptics.

Two things should be noted about modern apologetics. First, we see a return to arguments designed to defend Christianity as a whole (in contrast to the repair of inconsistencies within the system). Second is the influence of foundationalist epistemology (see chapter 12).

Apologetic arguments from Locke through Paley followed a common strategy—to establish a foundation consisting of a few propositions, and then to support the whole of Christian theology thereupon. The arguments go something like this:

> God's existence is known by means of argument(s) from design.
> If God exists, he should be expected to have revealed himself to humankind.
> The miracles (and prophecies) associated with scripture show them to be the expected revelation.
> Therefore, whatever scripture says (teaches) can be accepted as true on the basis of God's testimony.

In chapter 12 we represented the foundationalist view of *science* as a layer cake:

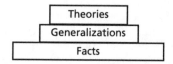

We might represent the modern approach to apologetics as follows, where an argument from design serves as one leg of the foundation and the argument from miracles as the other. Together these support the claim that the scriptures are the revealed word of God, and this, in turn, supports the claims of Christian theologians.

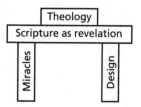

(See chapter 11 for Locke's version of this argument and for Hume's rebuttals.) Paley, writing after Locke and Hume, still understood apologetics in this manner, despite Hume's criticisms. In *A View of the Evidences of Christianity,*[3] he sought to answer Hume's rebuttal of the argument from miracles. Hume had claimed that testimony to the occurrence of a miracle is inherently suspect, since by definition it goes against established experience. Hume claimed, further, that there was no good reason to accept the testimony of the witnesses on the basis of their character. Paley conceded Hume's first point but argued for the reliability of the witnesses on the

---

[3]William Paley, *A View of the Evidences of Christianity,* 2 vols. (London, 1794).

basis of the fact that they were willing to stand by their reports despite risks to comfort, happiness, and even life.

Paley is most noted for his *Natural Theology; or Evidences of the Existence and Attributes of the Deity, Collected from the Appearances of Nature.*[4] Here, in an often quoted passage, he argues that if he found a stone on the heath and were asked how it came to be there he might answer that

> for any thing I knew to the contrary, it had lain there forever; nor would it perhaps be very easy to show the absurdity of this answer. But suppose I had found a watch upon the ground, and it should be enquired how the watch happened to be in that place, I should hardly think of the answer which I had before given, that, for anything I knew, the watch might have always been there. Yet why should not this answer serve for the watch, as well as for the stone?

Paley answers

> For this reason, and for no other, viz. that when we come to inspect the watch, we perceive (what we could not discover in the stone) that its several parts are framed and put together for a purpose.[5]

The universe, Paley claims, is like a watch. For his evidence he turns mainly to anatomy for examples of parts adapted to their functions. His conclusion is that there must be a divine mind, whose goodness is shown by the fact that we have been created with the capacity for pleasure. And such an intelligent, benevolent creator must be expected to reveal himself to his creatures.

It is unfortunate that while Paley elaborated one of the most engaging of modern statements of the design argument he did not provide a reply to Hume's prior rebuttal of any argument that relies on construing the universe as analogous to a mechanism.

2. The Plurality of Religions

At the present time, in the waning of the modern period, naturalistic understandings of the universe based on science still provide lively competitors for the Christian worldview, but the apologetic problem that has taken precedence is that of Christianity's place in a world with many venerable religious traditions. More precisely, there are two related apologetic problems here: one has to do with claims about knowledge or truth, and the other with claims about salvation.

The problem of *salvation* is a problem of consistency. Many Christians take passages such as the following to show that there is no salvation for those who do not know and explicitly accept Christ: "I am the way, and the truth, and the life. No one comes to the Father except through me" (John 14:6). But if this is the case, it is clear that only a small part of the

---

[4]William Paley, *Natural Theology; or Evidences of the Existence and Attributes of the Deity, Collected from the Appearances of Nature* (London, 1802).

[5]Quoted by Elmer Sprague, in "William Paley," *Encyclopedia of Philosophy,* ed. Paul Edwards (New York: Macmillan, 1967), 6:20.

human race can be saved. There were many generations before the coming of Christ; even today, after centuries of missionary activity and with remarkable capabilities for worldwide communication, there are countless people who have either inadequate knowledge or no knowledge at all of the Christian gospel. Surely, some argue, the eternal loss of so many is incompatible with the goodness of the God whom Christians preach. The difficulties are exacerbated if one adds the view that those who are not saved suffer eternal torment in Hell.

The pluralist problem with regard to *truth* can be expressed as follows: The assorted religions make contradictory claims about the divine, about humankind, the next life, and so forth. Obviously, they cannot all be true. Why should it be assumed that Christianity alone is true and all the others false?

Note that while the problems of truth and salvation can be distinguished in this way, responses to one issue usually involve the other as well. So for purposes of exposition we will consider them together. We shall examine the positions of two scholars here: Karl Barth and John Hick. While their views are not as far apart as one could imagine, they well represent the diversity in this area.

2.1. John Hick

Hick argues that the infinite Reality is unknowable *as it is in itself*. We can only speak of it as experienced from within our own cultural ways of knowing and being. Thus, only formal ('empty') concepts such as *the infinite Reality* or *the Transcendent* can be applied literally to God. All of the rest of our religious language is best understood as mythological. Hick defines mythic truth as follows: "A statement or set of statements about X is mythologically true if it is not literally true but nevertheless tends to evoke an appropriate dispositional attitude to X." Since myths do not *correspond* in any way to the reality to which they refer, the usual rules regarding logical consistency and contradiction do not apply: "Myths, functioning in their separate mythic spaces, do not clash with one another."[6] Thus there is no need to select one of the many religions as true and reject all others.

In addition, Hick maintains that all of the major religions are salvific. He understands salvation as transformation of the person from an absorbing self-concern to a new centering in the Real. This transformation is readily observable by its moral fruits—growth toward an ethical ideal common to all the great traditions. With salvation so understood, it is a simple step to argue from the observed transformation of devotees of the various religions to the conclusion that those religions are all paths to salvation.

So, to sum up, Hick solves the problem of truth by explaining religious knowledge in such a way that apparently contradictory claims can all be true; Christianity is true (in the mythic sense of 'true'), but not the only truth. The conflict between God's goodness and "exclusivist" views of salvation is eliminated by recognizing the other world religions as compa-

[6]John Hick, *An Interpretation of Religion* (New Haven: Yale University Press, 1989), 348, 15.

rable paths to salvation. All that remains, then, is to explain (or explain away) the Christian teachings that make it appear that Christ is the only way to salvation. Doctrines regarding the status of Christ (for example, that he is the only incarnation of the second person of the Trinity) can be *mythologically* true if they evoke appropriate religious attitudes toward God and neighbor. But, Hick warns, taking such doctrines to be *literally* true can lead Christians to feel uniquely privileged and therefore free to patronize and exploit the non-Christian majority of the human race.

2.2. Karl Barth

Barth deals with the problem of other religions by making the sharpest possible distinction between God's action and human activity, with regard to both salvation and revelation. The world religions are not salvific; they are human attempts at self-justification and thus fall under the judgment of God. But Christianity, too, is a human religion—it is not a path to salvation. Rather, salvation comes through God's grace alone.

> Religion is unbelief. It is a concern, indeed, we must say that it is the one great concern, of godless man. . . . From the standpoint of revelation religion is clearly seen to be a human attempt to anticipate what God in His revelation wills to do and does do. It is the attempted replacement of the divine work by a human manufacture. The divine reality offered and manifested to us in revelation is replaced by a concept of God arbitrarily and willfully evolved by man.[7]

Commentators have pointed out that Barth's doctrine of salvation entails universalism—the view that all people will be saved. However, Barth apparently never stated this conclusion. In any event, he was not "exclusivist" in the sense of denying the possibility of salvation outside the Christian church. Thus his views are not the most sharply opposed to Hick's that one could imagine.

As the above quotation suggests, Barth responds to the problem of truth by distinguishing between revelation and religion. Revelation is God's doing, God's self-disclosure, but religion, including Christianity, is human contrivance. Barth makes uniqueness claims for God's revelation in Christ, but not for Christianity. Recall that the problem here is the competing truth claims of the variety of religious traditions, and the apparent presumptuousness of asserting that one among the many, Christianity, is *the* truth. Barth solves the problem (at least formally) because, while the Christian religion has many competitors, God's revelatory act in Jesus Christ is taken to be unique.

It is important to note that neither Barth nor Hick has set out to address the problem of the plurality of religions as a Christian *apologist*. Hick's work belongs to the category of philosophy of religion. However, he argues for a *religious* interpretation of religions to displace the social-scientific theories that understand religion as a purely human phenomenon.

---

[7]Karl Barth, *Church Dogmatics* I/2, trans. G. T. Thomason and H. Knight (Edinburgh: T & T Clark, 1956), 299–300.

On this account we might say that he is writing an apology for religion in general, albeit that many believers would object that he has done so by making an unacceptable reduction in the status of *all* religious truth claims.

Barth's intention is best described as the provision of a theology of religions. A non-Christian might respond to his argument by pointing out that for all that he distinguishes between Christianity and God's revelation in Christ, he is still having to assume the truth of *Christian* scripture to make that distinction. And so the apologetic challenge arises afresh: Why assume without argument that *this,* among all of the world's possibilities, is true? Barth would reply that it is not up to him to justify the word of God, only to proclaim it. God alone justifies.

No easy answers or reconciliation of opposing positions can be presented here. A definitive answer may yet be found, and if so it may be aided by recent work in theory of knowledge. We turn now to see what these developments might offer to the contemporary apologist.

3. Contemporary Apologetics

Perhaps one reason for the decline in interest in apologetics during the past generation was recognition of the extent to which the evidence one can provide for a system of thought is conditioned by that system. Paley saw human eyes and rabbit spines as machine-like because he had already construed them as the product of intelligent design. Skeptics, such as Hume, failed to see them in this light. Barth saw other religions as sinful attempts at self-justification because of his background belief in God's revelation in Christ. To others, such as Hick, this position appears parochial.

At this point it may appear impossible to settle such disputes. Still, in some fields of thought (science, especially) it is now recognized that while the evidence for any broad framework (Newtonian versus Einsteinian worldviews, for instance) *is* theory-laden—that is, partially determined by the presuppositions of that very system—this does not entail that there can be no rational adjudication among competing systems of thought.

If there is to be a rebirth of apologetics, it is likely that it will take into account the *holist* view of knowledge (see chapter 12); it will begin by attempting to show the coherence and consistency of the Christian web of beliefs; but, finally, it will have to answer the question how we are to choose among two or more equally coherent and consistent webs.

Consistency requires that there be no beliefs that contradict one another, or whose direct consequences contradict some other belief in the web. For example, we noted above that the following set of beliefs has been taken by many to be inconsistent:

> God is all-good.
> God is all-powerful.
> There is evil in the world.

Augustine and all of the others who have written on the problem of evil have been engaged in an important aspect of apologetics—that of establishing the consistency of the Christian web of beliefs.

Coherence requires that the web of beliefs be tightly interconnected. A pressing apologetic problem for Christians of our era is that Christian beliefs are almost entirely disconnected from scientific beliefs about the physical world. Most of us actually operate with two distinct webs, where experience of the physical world plays no role in supporting theological beliefs, and Christian theology has no bearing on scientific theory. Whenever scholars make progress in linking theological beliefs to the rest of our knowledge they are contributing to the apologetic task.[8]

The demand for coherence includes the requirement to show that theoretical beliefs at the interior of the web are tied to beliefs based on experience. So we can say that a third aspect of apologetics is to show how Christian beliefs relate to experience. Good preachers do this when they interpret the listeners' experience in light of biblical texts.

So, to sum up, the first steps in apologetics have to do with Christians' own network of beliefs: demonstrating that it is consistent, coherent, and adequate to experience.

The most pressing question, however, is this: What if it turns out that more than one web of beliefs fulfills these three criteria equally well?[9] A variety of answers have been proposed.

3.1. The Relativist Answer

There is no rational way to choose, so all webs are equally *un*justified, and we really have no access to the truth.

3.2. Hick's Pluralist Answer

First, the choice between a religious and a naturalistic worldview is underdetermined by the evidence, and thus it is not irrational to adhere to either. Second, the great world religions may all be equally true when regarded as mythic systems.

3.3. Pragmatic Approaches

There are at least two varieties here: George Lindbeck points out that several religions may be intrasystematically true, meaning that their beliefs and practices are coherent and consistent. In order to count as ontologically true, a religion must in addition possess categorial adequacy, meaning that

---

[8]There are now far too many books and articles on the relations between theology and science to mention here. Two of my favorites are Arthur Peacocke, *Creation and the World of Science* (Oxford: Clarendon Press, 1979)—a bold approach to an evolutionary Christian worldview; and Nicholas Wolterstorff, *Religion within the Bounds of Religion*, 2d ed. (Grand Rapids: Eerdmans, 1984)—the best account I have found of how Christian belief can and ought to influence the development of scientific theories.

[9]Note that no system of natural knowledge fulfills all of these criteria perfectly. We always have some inconsistencies and a great deal of incoherence in our networks of belief.

it provides the language or category system that best conforms its adherents to the Ultimately Real.[10] Note the close affinity with Hick's approach when we consider that Hick's criterion for assessing mythological truth is whether it engenders suitable attitudes toward the Real.

A more straightforwardly pragmatic approach can be derived from the thought of Rudolf Carnap. Carnap made a distinction between internal and external questions. For example, we have a framework (worldview, conceptual scheme) that includes the concept of a *material object*. We can ask internal questions about various material objects, such as "Is a unicorn a material object?"—that is, "Do unicorns exist?" But if we ask instead if material objects exist (as philosophers are wont to do) we are asking an external question—a question about the framework itself. We might mean to ask whether we should continue to speak in terms of material objects, or whether sense-data language would be better. In short, it is a question whether we should keep *material object* as one of our central philosophical categories. The answer to an external question cannot be based simply on the facts of the matter, as can the question about unicorns; it is rather, for Carnap, a pragmatic question.

This distinction may become clearer if we apply it to a category that we can more easily imagine doing without. "Is John possessed by a demon?" is an internal question, which assumes that it makes sense to speak of demons and that we would know one if we met one. "Is there really any such thing as a demon?" is an external question, and asks, in effect, if we can legitimately include the category *demon* in our conceptual scheme.

Applied to the apologetic task we might say that the debate between Christianity as a comprehensive framework and its many religious and secular competitors can best be seen not as a matter of individual facts, but as whether the Christian category system (*God* and the *Spirit* and *sin* and *salvation*) is the most useful one for making our way through life—this life and, perhaps, the one to come. Or would we get along better thinking in terms of *karma*, and *reincarnation*, and *avatars;* or perhaps we would do better instead with *classes*, and *masses*, and *economic forces*.

This pragmatic answer provides a way, perhaps, of making sense of many Christians' reasons for believing that their commitment is a rational one: the language of the Christian faith and its beliefs about the most basic realities provide a good road map for getting around in the world—the human world and the spiritual world. It is a system that works. However, this proposal suffers from two deficiencies: it is fairly vague and, in addition, most Christians have no experience to allow them to conclude that Christianity is *better* in this regard than its many competitors—which brings us back to where we started.

3.4. Ad Hoc Apologetics

William Werpehowski has a promising proposal in what he calls *ad hoc* apologetics.

[10]See George Lindbeck, *The Nature of Doctrine* (Philadelphia: Westminster, 1984), 65.

This approach to the reasonableness or rational justification of features of Christian faith avoids recourse to foundations of thought and experience abstracted from particular frameworks of thought and experience. Justification, rather, is a matter of inference to the most coherent explanatory account of how Christian and non-Christian are mutually implicated in an area of belief or practice. It moves from a set of shared commitments toward a deeper agreement that crucially reflects, on one side, coherence with background warrants in Christian belief and, on the other, coherence with non-Christian projects and purposes. Because theological apologetics proceeds from particular and perhaps partial areas of convergence toward justification, it cannot but be an ad hoc affair.[11]

Werpehowski is assuming that Christian apologists live within a Christian framework where a (relatively) consistent set of beliefs, along with the practices or forms of life in which Christians engage, provides both the stimulus for certain kinds of experiences and a framework for interpreting the experienced world. Non-Christian dialogue partners have their own interpretive frameworks. Insofar as each framework shapes the experience of its adherents, Christians and non-Christians live in somewhat different worlds. Part of apologetics is simply communicating to the outsider what it is like to be a Christian—to do the things Christians do and see the world as they see it. This involves showing how the framework hangs together—showing that it is coherent and consistent.

Now the difficult question: What if the non-Christian framework is equally appealing, equally coherent? Werpehowski's answer here depends on his belief that areas of shared experience or agreement on values can be found despite radical differences between networks of beliefs. One cannot predict where such areas will be found, and this is the reason for calling his approach "ad hoc"—one takes up the argument wherever a point of entry can be found. The apologist's goal is to show that Christianity gives a more intelligible account of what the other person values or experiences than his or her own belief system.

Werpehowski illustrates his claim with an example from the sphere of medical ethics. Christians and non-Christians may agree on three critiques of the medical profession: (1) it is often paternalistic in not allowing patients to be fully informed or to participate in decisions about treatment; (2) it is overly belligerent in the face of suffering and death, being willing to sacrifice all other values to prevent them; and (3) it is overly fascinated by technology, which leads to lack of involvement with the patients themselves. Ethicist William F. May has argued that these three characteristics stem from a view of death and suffering as overwhelming and unredeemed destructive power.[12]

One can see from this account the possibility for an apologetic exchange. If the Christian and non-Christian share these perceptions and concerns about the ethics of medicine, then the non-Christian may come to under-

---

[11]William Werpehowski, "Ad Hoc Apologetics," *Journal of Religion* 66 (July 1986): 287.
[12]In William F. May, *The Physician's Covenant: Images of the Healer in Medical Ethics* (Philadelphia: Westminster, 1983).

stand and appreciate how May's diagnosis *explains* that shared critique. But this diagnosis gains its intelligibility from its relations to Christian beliefs about the redemption accomplished in Jesus Christ: from a Christian perspective, suffering and death can be taken up into the power of reconciling love; the evils of suffering and death are not ultimate.

The non-Christian is then faced with a choice: Adopting May's very persuasive diagnosis calls for an acceptance as well of the theological presuppositions that make it intelligible. If those theological presuppositions are not accepted, then the non-Christian must find some way of reconciling May's diagnosis with his or her own belief system. May's assessment of contemporary secular attitudes toward death suggests that this will be especially difficult for an atheist.

Werpehowski does not expect any one such exchange to provide sufficient reason for adopting the entire Christian belief system. Apologetic arguments must be cumulative—showing bit by bit that this construal of the world fits better than others.

3.5. Historical Approaches

Two philosophers have contributed to what we shall call *historical* approaches to adjudicating between competing webs of belief: Imre Lakatos has proposed a criterion for choosing between competing scientific research programs; Alasdair MacIntyre has written about competing traditions in ethics.

3.5.1. Imre Lakatos

Lakatos's work in philosophy of science can be applied as well to religious belief systems.[13] His criterion for choosing one system over another is based on the recognition that when we discover an inconsistency between a theoretical belief and one based on experience (a fact) we can always find a way to restore consistency by adding more theory (a point made by W. V. O. Quine as well). But sometimes the additional theory only fixes the immediate problem without improving the network of beliefs in any other way. When a research program is generally repaired in this way, it is "degenerating" and ought to be rejected. However, if the new additions not only fix the inconsistency but also allow for the prediction and discovery of new facts, then the research program is "progressive," and ought to be accepted. A famous article in philosophy of religion nicely illustrates the kind of theorizing that Lakatos intends to *rule out* by means of these methodological prescriptions. Antony Flew writes the following parable:

---

[13]See Lakatos's article titled "Falsification and the Methodology of Scientific Research Programmes," in *The Methodology of Scientific Research Programmes: Philosophical Papers, Volume 1,* ed. John Worrall and Gregory Currie (Cambridge: Cambridge University Press, 1978), 8–101. See my *Theology in the Age of Scientific Reasoning* (Ithaca, N.Y.: Cornell University Press, 1990) for an account of how Lakatos's methodology can be applied to theology.

Once upon a time two explorers came upon a clearing in the jungle. In the clearing were growing many flowers and many weeds. One explorer says, "Some gardener must tend this plot." The other disagrees, "There is no gardener." So they pitch their tents and set a watch. No gardener is ever seen. "But perhaps he is an invisible gardener." So they set up a barbed-wire fence. They electrify it. They patrol with bloodhounds. (For they remember how H. G. Wells's *The Invisible Man* could be both smelt and touched though he could not be seen.) But no shrieks ever suggest that some intruder has received a shock. No movements of the wire ever betray an invisible climber. The bloodhounds never give cry. Yet still the Believer is not convinced. "But there is a gardener, invisible, intangible, insensible to electric shocks, a gardener who has no scent and makes no sound, a gardener who comes secretly to look after the garden which he loves." At last the Sceptic despairs, "But what remains of your original assertion? Just how does what you call an invisible, intangible, eternally elusive gardener differ from an imaginary gardener or even from no gardener at all?"[14]

Flew's parable serves as a warning to Christians not to add so many qualifications to their theological claims that they end up with no real claims at all. Similarly, Lakatos's methodology was designed to rule out scientific theorizing that responds to disconfirming evidence by making exceptions and verbal changes that protect the theory from falsification and in so doing to weaken its empirical claims.

We can apply his work to the apologetic task by allowing it to raise questions about how religious traditions change over time. Does the theoretical network become increasingly complex and at the same time more and more detached from experience, or do theoretical refinements lead instead to greater adequacy for explaining and interpreting new experiences? Lakatos's work leads us to look at traditions in terms of progress and degeneration, growth and decline.

3.5.2. Alasdair MacIntyre

Another historical approach is MacIntyre's.[15] We mentioned MacIntyre in chapter 12, when it became necessary to think of the Christian belief system not merely as a web of beliefs held in the present, but as a tradition— a 'three-dimensional' web with a series of past formulations. For MacIntyre (as for Lakatos), the criterion for acceptability of a tradition has to do with how it changes over time.

A tradition is, according to MacIntyre, an argument extended in time about how to interpret and apply its formative texts. Traditions go through stages. In the earliest stage the authorities (the classic texts) have not yet been called into question. In the second stage, inadequacies are identified—inconsistencies, inability of the tradition to account for some experience, challenges from outside. In a third stage, the tradition is reformulated to meet these inadequacies. It is important to specify that in the

[14]Antony Flew, "Theology and Falsification," in *New Essays in Philosophical Theology*, ed. Flew and Alasdair MacIntyre (London: SCM Press, 1955), 96.

[15]See Alasdair MacIntyre, *Whose Justice? Which Rationality?* (Notre Dame: University of Notre Dame Press, 1988).

third stage some core of shared beliefs survives the reformulation (recall the continuity criterion from chapter 12). If not, it is unclear what one would mean by saying that one was reformulating an old tradition rather than starting a new one.

In the absence of a strong competitor, adherents of a tradition are entitled to claim that their tradition is true if it has been tested by raising as many questions and objections as possible, and has been shown to withstand those challenges. That is, it has been shown capable of reformulation, in ways faithful to its origins, to answer new objections, account for new experiences, and so forth.

If there is a competing tradition, the first step in judging between the competitors is to describe and criticize each tradition in the terms of the other. When we have done so, one of four things may happen.

1. We may be able to show that the rival has problems it cannot answer, while ours does not. In this case, we are vindicated in our commitment to our tradition.

2. Even better, we may be able to show that our tradition has resources for solving the other tradition's problems, and its adherents may be converted to our tradition.

3. Either of these situations may be reversed, showing the superiority of the rival.

4. Neither of the two traditions may be able to show its superiority. In some cases the lack of resolution itself may defeat a tradition without providing an alternative. Or there may be long periods of time in which two or more traditions are unable to discredit their rivals.

We cannot summarize MacIntyre's historical grounds for these claims, but it may be helpful to give one example of what he means by a problem that a tradition cannot solve, since relativist arguments often depend on the assumption that a tradition will always seem to its adherents to be able to solve all of its problems. The tradition of Greek philosophical ethics involved a conception of human nature such that whenever a person understands what is required morally, and sees that he or she is in the proper circumstances to act accordingly, the person will so act. In other words, the tradition provides no concepts to account for the observed fact that even strong-willed and well-trained people sometimes know what ought to be done, and know that this is the appropriate time and place to do it, yet fail to act accordingly. The Judeo-Christian tradition, on the other hand, is well equipped to account for this phenomenon.

MacIntyre's views have interesting consequences for apologetics, including the problem of religious pluralism. In contrast to relativists and pluralists, he maintains that it is at least sometimes possible to provide a rational justification for accepting one tradition and rejecting its immediate competitors. Part of the argument will be based on Werpehowskian ad hoc apologetics: finding a concern shared by adherents of rival traditions and showing that one's own tradition is better equipped to explain the shared experiences or solve the commonly recognized problem. The overall justification will consist in taking a long-term historical look (Lakatos) at how well the conceptual resources of one's tradition have compared with others in meeting life's problems (the pragmatists) and accounting for new experiences.

It would be valuable to know how often it has been the case that defenders of one tradition have been able to show that their tradition is superior in this way to its most pressing competitors and have been able to win over the latter's adherents. MacIntyre has shown that this *sometimes* happens. But are we more often left with the fourth possibility listed above, where no tradition can defeat its rivals? As we have seen, philosophers differ in their judgments here. There is a spectrum of possibilities ranging from complete relativism at one end (no way to judge between competing traditions), to absolutism at the other (one tradition shown conclusively, once and for all, to be better than all others). No one working with a holist account of knowledge is likely to argue for absolutism. So the interesting positions from the point of view of apologetics are those like MacIntyre's and Lakatos's that move some distance up the scale from relativism—even if they cannot answer the question how often the criteria they propose will actually work.

A clear consequence of MacIntyre's work is that it calls for the redefinition of the scope of apologetics. Apologetics absorbs into itself the work of theologians, historians, and biblical scholars. Theologians are doing apologetics insofar as they are working to display the coherence and consistency of the tradition, relating current theory to past formulations—especially to the biblical texts—and applying it to current problems. Historians are doing apologetics insofar as they are recounting the narrative of the problems that the tradition has encountered and overcome.

MacIntyre's account of what it takes to justify a tradition suggests, in fact, that apologetics can never be accomplished by a single author in a single volume. And it cannot be accomplished without thorough and sympathetic knowledge of the competing traditions, both religious and secular. This is too daunting a task ever to expect to finish, but to participate in the task, to contribute in some small way to the cumulative argument *is* to have a share in the tradition. For the Christian it is to participate in the ongoing argument about how best to interpret and apply our formative texts.

4. Truth

The topic of truth is complicated enough outside of religion. Theological claims present added perplexities. For Christians the issue is further complicated by the fact that Jesus said *he* was the truth; Christians thereafter have taken to speaking of *the* Truth, with a capital T. In this section let us sort out a few of these issues—beginning with philosophers' accounts of the truth of ordinary language, and examining along the way the added complexities that arise when we speak of truth in religion.

There are at least four kinds of theories of truth: correspondence theories, coherence theories, pragmatic theories, and the theory that there is no single adequate theory—rather, we have to look at the various and assorted uses of the word 'true.'

The correspondence theory is probably closest to our ordinary sense of what we mean in claiming that a statement is true: it is true if it corresponds with the facts. This view of the matter seems perfectly adequate for many statements. Accordingly, 'There is an oak tree in my yard' is true just in case there is an oak tree in my yard, and false if there is not. Critics of the correspondence theory, however, claim that the closer we look at the supposed correspondence between statement and reality the more elusive it becomes.

First, there is the problem that many sorts of statements do not bear so close a relation to observable reality. This criticism often leads philosophers to consider instead the coherence theory. On this view a statement is true just in case it coheres with the rest of a body of beliefs. So, for example, $f = ma$ is true because it is logically tied to other parts of a system of scientific laws and theories and descriptions of observations.

A second criticism of the correspondence theory arises from a more careful scrutiny of sentences that *do* relate to observable states of affairs. Some philosophers note that we often make the mistake of assuming that language somehow pictures or mirrors reality. But the fact is that it does not; there is no resemblance whatsoever between the sentence 'There is an oak in my yard' and the visual characteristics of my yard. Some have attempted to give more precise accounts of what the correspondence really amounts to. For example, J. L. Austin says:

> 'Corresponds' also gives trouble, because it is commonly given too colourful a meaning, or one which in this context it cannot bear. The only essential point is this: that the correlation between the words . . . and the . . . situation, event, etc. . . . is *absolutely* and *purely* conventional. We are absolutely free to appoint *any* symbol to describe *any* type of situation, so far as merely being true goes. . . . There is no need whatsoever for the words used in making a true statement to 'mirror' in any way, however indirect, any feature whatsoever of the situation or event; a statement no more needs, in order to be true, to reproduce the 'multiplicity,' say, or the 'structure' or 'form' of the reality, than a word needs to be echoic or writing pictographic. To suppose that it does, is to fall once again into the error of reading back into the world the features of language.[16]

This last sentence gives us one clue to the persistence of the correspondence theory. In order to describe the relation between language and world, between the statement and the fact to which it 'corresponds,' we have first to describe the fact linguistically. Then there appears to be a close resemblance (identity, in fact!) between the sentence 'There is an oak in my yard' and the fact that there is an oak in my yard.

A second source of the illusion that language pictures reality may be the fact that our imaginations go to work when we hear or read a sentence—in this case, picturing my yard and the trees in it. When we compare the sentence to the reality, it is not the sentence but the associated mental image that either does or does not match what is there.

---

[16]J. L. Austin, "Truth," in *Philosophical Papers,* ed. J. O. Urmson and G. J. Warnock (Oxford: Clarendon Press, 1961), 92–93.

This and other criticisms of the correspondence theory of truth have led some to propose still other accounts. The pragmatic theory recognizes that we can, by convention, associate whatever sentence we like with a fact or situation, *but* (and this is a very important 'but') some patterns of association will prove easy to live with and some not. For example, the human race (or at least the English-speaking part of it) might have decided to say 'this is green' when confronted with grass, but 'this is blue' when confronted with leaves, and 'this is red' when confronted with frogs and cats' eyes, and. . . . But this would be a terribly unhandy system. The pragmatic theory of truth recognizes this necessary relation between 'truth' and getting along in the world.

Because of the difficulties of imagining a pictorial relation between religious language and divine realities, philosophers of religion and philosophical theologians have been more apt than other philosophers to resort to pragmatic theories of truth. Lindbeck's and Hick's accounts of the truth of religious language are two such instances. George Tyrrell, too, thinks of truth in terms of getting along in the (spiritual) world.

The greater difficulties in imagining a correspondence between religious language and divine realities have also led to theories about differences between religious and ordinary language. In the medieval period much stress was placed on the claim that language about God is analogical. We can predicate 'love' of God, for instance, only if we recognize that 'love' is used differently of God than of creatures, but not entirely—there must be similarities, analogies.

These days there is much emphasis on the metaphorical character of theological language. 'God our Father' is a metaphor, since God is not (literally) our male parent. But if all theological language is metaphorical, can we speak at all of truth? 'God as father' might be enlightening, provocative. But is it *true* that God is our father? How to decide if it is any more or less true that God is our mother?

It may be the case that we need neither a special pragmatic theory of truth nor a special theory of language for religious claims if we but realize the limits of the correspondence between language and reality in the ordinary cases. If language never pictures reality, then we need not resort to special pleading when we realize that religious language does not provide a picture of God. The real difference between religious language and language about visible objects is that our associated mental images of material objects are more likely to turn out to be adequate pictures than our associated images of the divine. The description of religious language as metaphorical may well serve to remind us of this fact, but should not prevent us from applying the concept of truth in the religious domain.

Holist thinkers (both within and without religion) would like to use elements of all three theories of truth. The beliefs around the edge of the web or net are true primarily in virtue of some sort of relation or connection with items of experience; beliefs in the interior are true primarily in virtue of their coherence with the rest of the web. The qualifier 'primarily' is important, of course, because the constraint of coherence *transmits* the constraint of correspondence-to-experience throughout the web. And while we are *in a sense* free to arrange the beliefs within the web in any number of ways, in practice we must choose the simplest arrangement for pragmatic reasons.

The reference to holist theories of knowledge provides a good point of entry for discussing the theory that one ought not look for a single theory of truth, but rather to examine the assorted *uses* of the word 'true.' When we are working within a web of beliefs and have no reason to call the whole into question, use of the word 'true' is relatively unproblematic. We use it to certify some beliefs as belonging to the whole, and we use 'false' to label the ones that must be excluded. When we raise the further question about the 'truth' of one web versus another, however, it is a different matter. This is perhaps not a problem for secular philosophers. If we think of the current web of belief as the sum total of our civilization's shared knowledge, it is impossible to imagine replacing it by another entirely different system, and so the question of the truth of the whole never arises. But when considering the web of Christian belief, it is all too easy (for some) to imagine replacing it (with another religion, perhaps) or doing away with it altogether. So the question of the truth of Christianity as a whole, or the question of what is *the* Truth, arises (legitimately) from awareness of this possibility.

Before proceeding further with the question at hand, we need to make a slight digression. When I say "It is true that there is an oak in my yard," I am actually *doing* two things at once: I am providing an *evaluation* (a commendation) of the statement 'There is an oak in my yard,' and I am *committing* myself to, standing behind, endorsing, the statement. Now, in addition to 'true' and 'false,' we have a rich variety of terms for evaluating statements, such as 'accurate,' 'precise,' 'exaggerated,' 'overly general,' and many others. The difference between the evaluative and self-commissive functions of 'true' can be shown by the following: "Well, it is, of course, *true* that there is an oak in your yard, but it would be more *accurate* to say that there are three oaks." Here the speaker is willing, if pressed, to *commit* to the statement, and in that regard assents to its truth, but points out at the same time that 'true' is not the most apt *evaluation* of the statement.

Similarly, when presented with the trinitarian formula, "God is three persons in one substance," one might want to assent to (commit oneself to) the doctrine of the trinity, but at the same time have reservations about the *adequacy* of the philosophical terms 'person' and 'substance' to do justice to the trinitarian nature of God. In some settings, such as worship, the appropriate response is to confess one's trinitarian faith; in others, such as the classroom, it may be more appropriate to provide a more nuanced evaluation of the formulation.

The foregoing makes it possible to distinguish two uses of the statement 'Christianity is true.' In the self-commissive mode, it is perfectly appropriate, and means that I hereby commit myself to the whole of the Christian faith. In this case, the more rhetorically impressive expression 'Christianity is the Truth' might also be appropriate. However, when the purpose of the remark is not to indicate where the speaker stands but rather to give an epistemological assessment of the Christian web of beliefs, it is more accurate to use different terms. For example, Lindbeck speaks of the categorial *adequacy* of a religion, meaning that it provides an apt and effective language for speaking about and relating one's life to the Ultimate Reality. Philosophers of science, when speaking about entire theoretical networks (paradigms, research programs), speak of levels of acceptability rather than of truth or falsehood.

The *criteria* for acceptability of an entire religious tradition are those we discussed in section 3 above. If the results of our inquiry in that section are correct, then the strongest epistemological evaluation that anyone could make of Christianity (or any other major tradition) is that it has been shown (on the basis of such and such criteria—e.g., MacIntyre's) to be more acceptable, at present, than certain specified rival traditions. This will sound to some like a much too guarded statement for anything so important as religion. True. Religions by their very nature are such that they require 100 percent commitment. But recall the distinction we have just made between commitment and evaluation. We can be, should be, wholly committed to our own religious tradition, even though our limited knowledge (and limited ability to describe and communicate our grounds and arguments to others) means that we cannot make correspondingly unqualified evaluations of its epistemic standing. So level of commitment *of ourselves* to a religious tradition is one thing (and this may be one of the appropriate uses of the term 'faith'); philosophical evaluation of the tradition's standing vis-à-vis current standards of rationality is another. It is only *irrational* to give total commitment to a tradition when epistemic considerations point in a *different* direction from one's faith.

The criteria for appropriate self-commissive use of 'Christianity is true,' then, are: (1) that criteria of rationality provide a good measure of support for the tradition, and (2) not less than can be provided for one or more of Christianity's rival traditions. But, in addition, (3) professed commitment must be borne out in the living of one's life. One cannot rightly (reasonably) give assent in words that are not borne out in deeds.

For those of us who find ourselves at institutions of theological learning, one important aspect of our commitment *in deed* is to participate in the ongoing *critical* discussion about the meaning, applicability, and adequacy of our tradition.

EXERCISE FOURTEEN

1. The following four passages are summaries by Gordon R. Lewis of the apologetic methods of four mid-twentieth-century theologians.

> J. Oliver Buswell, Jr. finds Christianity's claims true by examination of observable evidence. On this approach inquirers do not start the investigation with any particular principles of reasoning, faith, presuppositions, or hypotheses. The mind as a blank tablet receives impressions from the observed data, traces their implications, and draws the most probable conclusions. The inductive method and principles of inference are themselves derived from experience. A conclusion is held to be true

when it corresponds to or integrates with, the relevant facts. No claim can be shown to be true beyond a high degree of probability. In view of the evidence he presents from the existence and order of the world, Buswell concludes that it is overwhelmingly probable that God exists.[17]

    a. What claim does Buswell's apologetic system seek to defend?
    b. What qualifier is included in his argument?
    c. In what do the grounds consist?
    d. What questionable assumption is Buswell making about a suitable form of reasoning for an apologetic approach such as this?
    e. What questionable assumption is he making about experience?
    f. Provide a rebuttal for his argument.

2.   Stuart C. Hackett thinks that Christianity's truth can be conclusively proved since the human mind brings with it to the investigation of evidence some "built-in" principles which make valid conclusions certain. Inherent in the minds of all men are the principles of logic (e.g., contradictories cannot both be true), and of causality (i.e., every effect must have an adequate cause). With the help of principles like these the mind systematizes its experience and draws necessary conclusions. A true conclusion coheres with the mind's categories and the facts of experience. From objective evidence similar to Buswell's (the existence and order of the world) Hackett "demonstrates" that God exists (36–37).

    a. Which of Hackett's inherent principles looks like a promising warrant for an *a posteriori* argument for the existence of God?
    b. What is Hackett's backing for this warrant?
    c. If this is the warrant (from question *a*), and the existence and order of the world are the grounds, what additional grounds does Hackett need to support his claim that God *necessarily* exists?
    d. Is Hackett a foundationalist or a holist?
    e. Why do you think Lewis put "demonstrates" in quotation marks in his summary of Hackett's apologetics?

3.   Edward John Carnell treats Christianity's truth-claims as scientific hypotheses to be verified by man's total experience. The hypothesis that can consistently account for both internal and external data with the fewest difficulties is true. The starting point is not the mind as a blank tablet, general principles of reasoning, or unsupported Christian presuppositions, but a hypothesis to be tested. The proposed explanation of the world is the existence of the triune God of the Bible. An inquirer is asked simply to consider whether this hypothesis, among many others, may be true. The test of verification is two-fold, involving logical consistency and factual adequacy. Carnell finds the biblical revelation of Deity to be consistent and to fit the facts. It fits the facts of the external world: the data of history, science, fulfilled prophecy, and miracles. It also fits the facts of the internal world: the data of conversion experience, values, ethics, and psychology. With overwhelming intellectual probability Christianity is thus shown to be true and so Christianity may be embraced with moral certainty (38).

[17]Gordon R. Lewis, *Testing Christianity's Truth Claims* (Lanham, Md.: University Press of America, 1990), 36.

    a. What form of reasoning does Carnell employ?

    b. Which form of reasoning, Carnell's or Buswell's is more promising for warranting an argument for the existence of God?

    c. What are Carnell's grounds?

    d. What is Carnell's warrant (in Lewis's words)?

    e. Is Carnell's qualifier 'overwhelming intellectual probability' appropriate given the form of reasoning he espouses?

4.   Gordon H. Clark agrees with Hackett that the human mind has principles of reasoning "programmed in." But he does not agree that the starting point of thought is objective experience. Any attempt to discover objective facts without an interpretive principle is pressed to the logical extreme of skepticism. . . . If evidence cannot tell us whether Christianity is true or not, what can? He answers, the interpretative principle that gives the most consistent system. Since everyone comes to evidence with presuppositions, Christians should admit that they do. Frankly Clark starts his thinking by assuming the existence of God and the truth of the Bible. He considers these to be fundamental axioms (analogous to mathematical reasoning) necessary to all thought about Christianity. Starting with the God of the Bible he deduces a consistent system of philosophy with the certainty of logical syllogisms. Christian truth-claims are accepted, then, because they enable him to devise the most consistent system of thought with the fewest difficulties (37).

    a. What is Clark's claim?

    b. What are the most immediate grounds for this argument?

    c. What is Clark's warrant?

    d. What questionable assumption is Clark making about the sort of reasoning that connects the Christian system of beliefs?

    e. Is Clark's view of the Christian system holist or foundationalist? Explain *why* you have so classified him.

5. The following passage is by Max Stackhouse, a contemporary theologian. His book is primarily about theological education; this passage is from a chapter on apologetics.

    Most of the views we have examined do not argue overtly that religion makes a fundamental, objective difference in the real world, or that we can reliably know anything about the relative truth and justice of any religious claim. That somewhat flat way of stating several complex matters points to a very common feature of contemporary thought that has in some ways invaded our consciousness and pervades academic literature about religion and theology: Religion is understood to be a derivative or epiphenomenal expression of something else—something more fundamental, more objective—that is thought to make all the difference in the world, and that can be used to assess the relative truth and justice of religion.

    That "something else" may be identified with psychodynamic or sociodynamic forces, with interests determined by race, sex, class, culture, or power, with the structural ways the human mind works, or with the functional needs of community survival. . . .

Others seem to hold that religion is important and interesting because its symbols, codes, and organizations can be "unpacked" to get at the "truly" significant or "more" interesting factors that they express, or because its coalesced symbols, codes, and organizational resources can be mobilized to help accomplish some "real" purpose in life—therapeutic wholeness, social integration, cultural cohesion, or a political-economic program. In any case, these understandings reinforce the view that the content and truth claims of a religion are not, in themselves, matters of the first order.

The problem can be stated this way: Religion is based on a fundamental presupposition that there is a metaphysical-moral realm that is real, transcendent to the empirical world, and simultaneously sufficiently present to human reflection and experience that it can be taken as the decisive point of reference for the understanding and guidance of empirical life and historical existence. Further, religion (all religions) presuppose that this metaphysical-moral reality has been sufficiently unveiled (that is, either revealed or discovered) so that humans can know something about it with enough clarity and security to take it as the foundation for belief and action. . . . Thus, religion presumes a first-order reality of a metaphysical-moral sort, epistemologically accessible, that can be used to interpret and guide all second-order matters—such as therapeutic wholeness, social integration, cultural cohesion, and political-economic programs.

. . . Today, however, there are pervasive doubts that religion is of first-order import, or that, if it is, we could know or make the case for its import in view of the great variety of religions that we can find in the world. These doubts . . . raise questions about the character of any teaching or learning that deals with religion.

. . . If theologians are to carry on their tasks with a good conscience . . . then a self-conscious *apologia* will have to be developed.

It is possible that three approaches would be fruitful in laying the groundwork for an *apologia*. One would be to adopt the critical methods that have been developed on nonreligious or anti-religious grounds, and to see how far they can go in explaining and interpreting civilizational and cultural history, reported human experiences of transcendental reality or ethical demand, and cosmological perspectives on the meaning of the cosmos. . . .

If, in fact, these disciplines can account for religious phenomena rather exhaustively, then those of us who have given our lives to theological commitments, institutions, and scholarship should be quite frank about it and give up what we do. . . . If, however, these critical methods cannot give an adequate account of such things, if religion is decisive for an understanding of civilizations, anthropology, and the cosmos, then it is incumbent upon us to make the case for what we do by turning the critical methods to their own presuppositions and showing that what they consider to be of first-order import is in fact of second-order import.[18]

a. For Stackhouse, a major apologetic problem is the fact that a number of competing hypotheses have been advanced to explain religious phenomena, and these nontheistic interpretations have dis-

[18]Max Stackhouse, *Apologia: Contextualization, Globalization, and Mission in Theological Education* (Grand Rapids: Eerdmans, 1988), 141–42, 144–46.

placed the traditional view of religion. He alludes to a number of such hypotheses. See how many you can identify.

b. What two claims need to be established to defend a religious interpretation of religion?

c. With what aspect of Hick's work would Stackhouse be in closest agreement?

d. Where do Stackhouse and Hick differ most radically?

INDEX

SCRIPTURE INDEX